CALL OF THE SEA

Varcy Saunders.

CALL OF THE SEA

by

FRANCE AND CHRISTIAN GUILLAIN

translated by
Caroline Hillier

LONDON
VICTOR GOLLANCZ LTD
1976

Acknowledgment is made to Kahlil Gibran and to William Heinemann Ltd for permission to quote three lines from *The Prophet*.

PRINTED IN GREAT BRITAIN
BY EBENEZER BAYLIS AND SON LTD
THE TRINITY PRESS, WORCESTER, AND LONDON

Contents

List of Illustrations

CALL OF THE SEA

I

A Small Baby—A Small Boat

IT IS THREE o'clock in the afternoon. Laurence is asleep, and for a while I can do as I like, think my own thoughts. Sailing free, under mainsail alone, the *Alpha* slips gently along at three or four knots towards the south-east, towards the Canaries. We left Casablanca a week ago. The weather is what my aunt would call 'ladylike': bright sun, a gentle wind and a pleasantly calm sea. The perfect weather for getting a golden tan if it were hotter, but it is only the beginning of December. A ray of winter sunlight slants obliquely across the cabin, is reflected brilliantly from the metal of stove and sink.

A gentle torpor lulls us to sleep. A vague somnolence weighs us down, slows our reflexes. My mind floats effortlessly from my body, as if the rest of myself were dead. The weight of my body no longer inhibits me; I can focus my thoughts on whatever I like—our first seven days at sea—everything else——

I feel as if I have at last emerged from a long nightmare of numbness and exhaustion. I have adapted to my new situation: I am here on a small boat, at sea, with a baby a few weeks old.

And God knows we had to put up with enough criticism before setting out on this trial voyage——

'A baby on a boat! Madness!'

'It's absurd, leave her with us.'

'Such a small boat, it's irresponsible of you . . . '

And so on, and so on.

These reactions were understandable, of course. It would probably have been more 'responsible' to have set ourselves up with our baby in Paris, in a small flat. We could both work. Laurence would have a 'real' bottle, in a 'real' cot. She would go along real streets, into the real underground, have a generous share of dirt, breathe in her proper ration of exhaust fumes. She would have all the excitements of city life, and on Sundays we would take her to the park. A good doctor would see that she got rid of her colds and 'flu, and that she got enough vitamins. In fact we would do our duty like everyone else.

On the *Alpha*, Laurence would only be breast fed, and her cradle would be perpetually rocked, so that she would have to adjust her balance even when she was asleep. Her body and clothes would only be washed in salt water: 'Salt water, oh *really*!' She would be in a violent, continual draught, night and day. Take care she doesn't get otitis, bronchitis, all the other 'itises. She would only inhale iodine and salt.

'And what about storms! What will you do if there's a storm?'

'Don't worry, we shan't make a point of putting her up on deck.'

We had thought about our plan for three years. We weren't setting out to sail round the world for the fun of it, or as an athletic feat. We were starting our family life on a boat. Before Laurence was born we had sailed on other people's boats. It was to live with Laurence that we built our 'nest', in steel, a solid and perfectly watertight nest, our *Alpha*.

We already hoped that one day, we would have a large enough sailing-boat to hold a lot of children. We would live close to nature, and teach them to read, and write, and do sums, to play music, to sing, to laugh, to love life.

To love life. Since Christian and I met in Tahiti in April 1965, it is this which has guided us, and given us strength. It is now 7 December 1967, and the *Alpha* is carrying us towards the Canaries; before this there were days and weeks and months of vicissitudes, during which we have both known much happiness and much unhappiness. We had to fight hard to build our family nest, our little home which is so tiny compared with the vast Atlantic, but so important to us. Because, as I know well, have learnt to my cost, nothing is given away free in life, or gratuitously. My childhood, my youth, Christian's childhood and youth; very different paths which might never have met, and yet . . . If one sets down everything which has made us, in black and white, it is as if one were writing a novel expressly devised to show how two people meet at twenty—and work through their neuroses together, and fight doggedly to define and shape the kind of life they want.

I am a child of the islands. My great-grandmother was a

member of a colonial family in Reunion, in the golden age of slavery. I can't remember if it was her father or her mother who was Madagascan or Indian, but there was a mingling of races, which showed very clearly in my mother's features and those of my sister. My great-grandmother was a very grand, elegant lady, gently brought up in the expectation of being served and cosseted. It is from her, no doubt, that the knowledge of plants that the women of my family have, stems: everything that grew was used to keep oneself healthy and beautiful. It was the great colonial era of voluminous dresses, hats and parasols. But when she was eighteen, slavery was abolished. My ancestors couldn't take it: how were they to work their land without slaves? They sold everything, and crossed the Indian Ocean in six months to go and live in New Caledonia.

There, their life was very different. They were given some land. They were pioneers. Every day they rode through their plantations, the fruit of their own hard work. Their daughter, my grandmother, was given a tough planter's upbringing. But she benefited from her mother's culture, her past refinement. All her life she was a great reader: when she died, years later, in Tahiti, they found boxes of books and magazines such as the *Nouvelle Revue Française*, which were sent over to her by boat—it only called every six months, then.

She grew up in New Caledonia. It was there that she met my grandfather, who came from France. His father was a Russian émigré, one of the left-wing intellectuals opposed to the tsar, who had been forced to flee to France with his two children. My grandfather, who grew more and more unstable as he grew older, dreamed of seeing the world. To do this he would need his share of his inheritance: he was pining away at the Lycée Saint-Louis, where he was a maths teacher. His father wouldn't hear of it until one day when, to force his hand, his son became involved in a scandal in Le Havre, where they had a country house. He then gave in.

My grandfather bought a large sailing ship, to be used for his voyages and for trading. He enlisted a crew and sailed for Reunion, and from there to New Caledonia, where he met my grandmother.

They had seventeen children. He was 68 when my mother was born. He died when she was ten. His children were born all over the world, wherever the ship happened to be: New Caledonia, Australia, Tahiti, Christmas Island. He was their teacher and taught them, after his own fashion, to read, write, add up, that was about all. I shall often think of him when I give Laurence her lessons based on the most advanced modern educational methods.

Four years after my mother was born, my grandmother, who had meanwhile had another son, decided to settle in Tahiti. She had had enough of travelling, she still had daughters to marry off and she found that her little world was now very scattered: my mother had sisters who, before she was born, had married when the ship was in one port or another; and who have now died without her ever having met them because she never visited those countries. From the age of eight she lived in Tahiti. She went to a convent school at a time when, contrary to what one might think, it was not permissible to show an inch of one's body in Tahiti. It was the era of gloves and silk stockings. Everything was concealed. She was sixteen when my father arrived on the scene.

My father was descended from poor Spaniards who had gone to live in France for political reasons. They had come from the roughest, most deprived part of Spain, the province of Soria. Which probably explains my father's exceptional strictness and integrity. His own father chose a French bride in the following way. When he was twenty-one, he needed a valid reason to stay in France. 'Marry a French girl,' he was told. He was taken to an orphanage. 'There are girls there whom they want to marry off,' he was told. It was there that he found my paternal grandmother. She had had no choice in the matter either. She was told at the orphanage: 'You're eighteen. You must get married.' It was all arranged. They were married in Bédarieux, near Montpellier, a sinister little village.

The least one can say is that it was not a rapturous love match. At the orphanage she had only been taught to sew and read. She never learnt how to write. My grandfather worked in a quarry, then on the railways. My father, François, was born, then a little girl, who died. In despair, my grandfather threw himself under a train. Thus my father became a semi-orphan at the age of nine. He was doing brilliantly at school, but had to go out to work: his mother took in as much sewing as she could, but she couldn't earn enough to feed them both. Until he was thirteen he was a notary's clerk. He earned almost nothing. He had to scavenge in dustbins—to see if anyone had left a little meat on a chicken carcase. Once, he followed some soldiers who were on manœuvres, didn't come back for eight days. He wasn't scolded : his mother cried with joy because she knew that during that time at any rate he had eaten his fill.

Afterwards he left the notary's office, where he was suffocating, to work in a vineyard. Every morning at four o'clock he had to set off at a run to do ten kilometres. But he still managed to educate himself. This man who had left school at nine became the most cultured man I have ever met. Later when I went to university, I still didn't meet anyone to equal him. When I discovered Teilhard de Chardin, he had read him twenty years before.

He went into the army at eighteen, was sent to the colonies, found my mother in Tahiti, and married her. She followed him, wherever he was garrisoned. In 1939 he left the army because the colonial troops were going to be sent to the Sahara, leaving their wives behind in France. He became one of the leaders of the Resistance in the Cévennes, and I was born in Montpellier on 21 January 1942. I can remember that before we went back to Tahiti five years later we lived in the utmost poverty, in a basement, a semi-cellar, in a village called Boujan. You had to go down steps to get to it. And of course it was damp, and bug ridden. We put the bed legs in jam tins filled with paraffin, but the wretched creatures had discovered that if they climbed up to the ceiling, they only had to drop on to the blankets. They devoured us. In winter there was no water. We melted snow to make soup. It is amazing how much snow one needs to make a litre of water.

Near to us lived a rag-and-bone man, and my brother and I used to collect chipped plates and saucepans without handles from him. Today, my parents wouldn't allow their grandchildren even to go into a rag-and-bone man's house: they would be afraid they'd catch something. And yet we used to drink out of the chipped glasses he gave us. My father wore himself out looking for work. It was hard, during the war, in the Midi. Even my mother, who was expecting me, went miles on her bicycle to try to find a little butter, a few eggs, in the mountains of the Massif Central. She often ate only flour and water. And she was also terrified for my father who had been 'ratted' on twice and then badly wounded. One day the Gestapo pulled out his nails.

After the war he didn't want to work as a labourer. He said to my mother: 'Let's go to Tahiti. It will be better there.' My mother was naturally delighted to go back to her island. He bought tickets for us all: my brother (sixteen years old), myself (five) and my sister (two). What a drama. Forty-eight days on an ancient troopship converted into a steamer—our exodus.

In Tahiti my uncle lent us a *faré*—a house. We immediately began planting vegetables. But they had to grow first, and we had no money to buy anything else with. My uncle gave us a meal at midday. The rest of the time, morning and evening, it was tea with a drop of American tinned milk with bread dipped in it. I wore some sandals which my father mended over and over again. It was November 1947. The convent school was the only one to which Europeans went. There were 120 of us in a room, and an old nun taught us—nothing. But I wanted to learn, and was furious. So I was sent to the elementary school, where the Tahitian and Chinese girls went. This delighted my father, whose religious upbringing had left him with a grudge against priests, except for his best friend, my godfather, an ex-army padre, whom I later met in France.

I exchanged the books of the convent school for those of the secular school. I was a little lost. History wasn't the same, Louis IX being more saintly to one lot than the other. My sister and I were the only Europeans. By talking to the others we learnt Tahitian and a few basic words of Chinese. In the same class there would be girls of six and eighteen—the island girls who were sent to school very late. They were rather like mothers to the others. We were the only two to have sandals. All the others went barefoot, wore thin dresses, no pants or bra. We were sometimes considered as Tahitians, sometimes as 'demis', sometimes as Europeans: all my mother's family had married Tahitians. All my first cousins were 'demis'. There is no race problem in Tahiti, but it caused psychological problems.

I wanted everyone to like me: this was the only way I could be happy. At home the atmosphere was fraught. I was a long way then from setting out on the path to happiness which today is the guide-line for Christian's and my life.

I now think that my mother wasn't to blame for her harshness. My grandmother, who in many ways resembled Queen Ranavalona, was a refined, severe, very authoritarian, vindictive woman. She was no longer young when she brought up my mother, and her husband had deserted her. My mother therefore had a very unhappy childhood in spite of her long dresses and lace petticoats, silk stockings and gloves, convent education. When she met my father, at sixteen, she was a very pretty girl, as instinctive and spontaneous as a Polynesian, but also well-read, full of the ideas of the novels of the Belle Epoque. My father, who loved sports, was delicate, a poet and a puritan.

No one talked about love in those days. Children were conceived in the dark. And, very soon, love was reduced to conceiving children. And my mother felt all the more deserted and aggrieved because my father seemed to her to be only interested in his children. As with millions of other couples, the gulf between them widened, and led to an ever growing imbalance. And as always in such cases, it is the children who pay the price. Their parents quarrel over them, don't get divorced because of them, and it is on them that they relieve their tensions.

It was also the time when one started 'training' children as soon as they were born. Rigorous timetables, strict educational theories, parental authoritarianism, submissiveness on the part of the children, respect—methods which, if applied by unhappy parents, very soon deteriorated into a systematic depersonalization of the child. It could lead to a kind of terror. One lived in fear. Fear of doing something silly, fear of being told off and punished, fear of making a noise, of getting dirty. To help me over this adolescent crisis, during which I was completely obsessed by the desire to kill myself, I studied psychology in depth, which helped me to understand more and suffer less.

Like many children, we had two lives. The real one in which Daddy and Mummy quarrel, shout, insist, command, punish, make you cry from morning onwards; and the other, the fiction one puts on for other people and oneself: the happy couple, the good children whom they love so much—children who are spoilt, petted and happy. I wouldn't want to live any part of my childhood over again. We had no friends, no special corner where we could hide our secrets. Parents had the right to know everything then, even our thoughts, for our own good.

Twenty years ago in Tahiti, visitors were received like gods, because the island people were so cut off from the outside world. But for the people who lived there life was hard, because during the five years of war Tahiti had had to be self-supporting. Ships no longer called. And for 50 years nothing had been planted there, everything came from France or America. A bad habit which had tragic consequences. When we arrived on the island, there was nothing: a few cows and a few wild pigs which my uncle hunted on Sundays. Virtually nothing. The first butter we had came from the United States after goodness knows how many ups and downs. It had melted and been refrigerated about twenty times. Cheese, from the same source, tasted like soap. Paraffin was very scarce, very expensive. Cooking was done over a wood fire in the *faré himaa*: a small hut put up a little way from the house, so that if it caught fire, it wouldn't matter too much. Every day we had to go to find wood for the fire, to make the tea. To prevent the saucepans getting too black, they were rubbed with a very harsh soap made from coconuts. Every detail had to be thought out. Which explains why, later on, I was able to adapt so quickly to life on a boat.

We sowed seeds, kept hens and rabbits. The netting had to be very strong so that the rats couldn't get at the babies and eat them. The only two dangerous members of Tahitian wildlife are the rat and the mosquito—the latter has almost disappeared today. Vegetables grow very quickly in that climate, without much attention, luckily, because our timetable was very full. It grew dark between six-thirty and seven o'clock depending on whether it was the dry or rainy season. Almost as soon as we were out of school we had to see to the hens and rabbits. We soon found ourselves with 70 rabbits, and rabbits eat.

There are no fences in Tahiti: the plots lead into one another and houses are never locked. When your neighbour's tree is covered with fruit, you take what you need, and offer the same in return. Everything grows the whole year round. To supplement our crops we went out foraging in the island: young as we were, my sister and I followed our parents across the valleys in search of fruit. The island of Tahiti is divided like a cake:

the plots of land are triangular with their tips converging at the mountain in the middle of the island. By tradition, the area where they meet is common ground. Anyone can pick the oranges, bananas, lemons, yams; hunt pigeons, pigs and wild fowl there. Little boards indicate that 'from here on, it is all yours'.

They were tough, those expeditions. We cried with tiredness on the way home.

On other occasions, our parents took us to a more distant valley. They had brought their bicycles from France—the famous bicycles of their foraging sorties to the Massif Central. Pedalling valiantly, with us on the carriers, they climbed to the highest part of the island where racing cyclists went to do their training. The latter had to get off here, and push their bikes. We sailed past them: the Massif Central training.

Gradually, our situation improved. My mother sewed. My father got a job with the customs. To begin with he earned very little because he had signed on as a local; as if he had been born in Tahiti. At that time their pay was very different to that of employees who came from France. My father, who never belonged to any political party—so disgusted was he by all the dishonest goings on he had seen—fought successfully, on his own initiative, for local employees, with equal qualifications and doing the same work, to be paid the same as the others. 'Yes, well, keep quiet about it,' they said to him. 'We'll give you the maximum salary, but no one will know.' He published this proposition in a local newspaper. Next he demanded that Tahitians should have the right, as did Europeans, to go to France every three years, to get to know France, the mother country for which they had fought during the war. 'We can allow you to make these trips,' they said again, 'but we can't do it for everyone.' He refused. And four or five years later, Tahitians were given the right as well.

I would like my children to have this absolute integrity. I shall endeavour to bring them up with this idea of honesty— with no cheating, no making concessions.

Laurence is asleep, cradled by the *Alpha*. My past brings me back to her, to this being to whom I give myself completely—to her and to Christian. Christian. We share together the warmth of the islands, the white sand, the palm trees which lean over the transparent waters of a lagoon teeming with fish. We love hunting, gathering fruit, the water, the pure air. We are friends, utterly and completely. I am forgetting for the moment all the misunderstandings and unhappiness, the painful stations of the cross on the way which leads to happiness. The love between our bodies is our love of life, of our naked bodies in the sun, in the water or on the sand, the love of all that is good together, of everything unique, of all that is productive: it was because of this that Laurence was born. We don't yet have the perfect father-husband, mother-wife relationship which we strive towards each day. Each is responsible for himself. Christian takes care of the boat; I take care of Laurence.

I had been so poorly nourished, in France during the war, and afterwards in Tahiti, that I was a thin, fragile child, rachitic even. But I was consumed by a desire to learn. I got through all my primary school studies in two years. In the evening I begged people to make me read and write. I was always on the book of the class above. I was moved up a class. The teachers used methods suitable for pupils who were at different levels, and who couldn't all speak French. Methods used everywhere today: with pairings, groups and so on. So I find modern mathematics perfectly easy to understand.

At ten I was moved to the sixth form of the secondary school, which was called the École Centrale. The masters were primary-school teachers from France promoted to secondary-school masters and thrilled to be so. They ruled over a black mob, over classes of 50 pupils who were bent only on creating chaos and whom they were quite incapable of controlling. I couldn't rest until I was taken away, and I found myself at the convent again, which was very good in the higher grades. And I learnt history the other way about all over again.

Four difficult years. I was well aware of what was happening at home. I shut myself up in my ivory tower. My brother and sister tried to resist my mother's influence. There were fights. I had a horror of opposing anyone, especially anyone stronger than myself: what would have been the point. So I did everything I was told to do as well as I could, down to the smallest detail. Which didn't help to brighten the atmosphere.

At school I worked hard so that my teachers would like me. To get away from home I would have to study. But there were no scholarships then. And you took the baccalauréat in New Caledonia. I wondered how I could get there one day. When I was in the fifth form, I explained the problem to a young nun whom I liked very much. 'They are going to start giving scholarships,' she said. 'The first will be given in two years' time, when you are in the third form. We'll try to get you one, but your parents will have to give their approval.'

I knew my parents wouldn't hear of my going away by myself. My father's puritanism was matched by my mother's inhibitions and they had a morbid fear that their daughters would go to the bad. If we saw a pretty girl in the street and I had the misfortune to make some admiring comment, I was reprimanded. If a woman had a child without being married we weren't allowed to speak to her. A pretty girl was, by definition, a fallen woman. One day, looking at a photo of class five, a friend's mother said pointing to me, 'She's sweet.' I cried with emotion. My father never paid my sister or myself a compliment for fear it should lead us astray. And we were in Tahiti, the island of pleasure.

I was still in the fifth form when, thanks to an extended loan, my parents bought some land six kilometres from our house. Every evening after school we had to go there on our bicycles. And as there was no electricity except in the town of Papeete, we gardened at night by the light of pressure oil lamps. No running water: it took two of us to lift the heavy zinc watering cans from the river to the plot. The chickens, and rabbits, were there too, still ravenous. We built a wooden hut where we could sleep on Sundays. The beds were made of wood, and the mattresses from the small amount of kapok we had been able to find.

Then, still with a long-term loan, my parents were able to build a house with parpen walls, roofed with corrugated iron, with a cement terrace round it and a little pond. There was more planting. My mother grew magnificent flowers there, every kind of hibiscus and bougainvillea. And there was always a plant to cure our ailments. Luckily, for doctors were rare in the islands. If you had an operation there was a good chance of not recovering because of the lack of air-conditioning and anti-biotics.

I did seven kilometres by bicycle four times a day. I was very thin, I couldn't go on. I had to ask my parents if I could be a semi-boarder at school. As finances were a little better at that particular moment—my father sold eggs, and rabbits, to bolster his salary—they agreed. Semi-boarders had to come half an hour earlier than the day-pupils in the morning, and leave two hours later in the evening, after prep. It was marvellous.

It was by spending the whole day at school that I came to realize I was both European and Tahitian. I liked to change my dress at midday, like the Tahitian girls, and wash my hair every day, always be very clean; whereas the European girls, in the tropical heat, always smelt of sweat, seemed very dirty to us. We liked to have our dresses washed with *eau de Javel*, very fresh: the others cleaned theirs with spirit.

My whole life was centred on my studies, with one aim in view: to be top of my class and win a scholarship. And I got one: I was given one of the three awarded in the island. I was the youngest. However, my father was torn by the fear of my going off alone and the desire to have me continue my studies. At fourteen, I would be in the second form. He said that in Tahiti the BEPC was quite good enough. I could work for the civil service; and if I learnt to type I could get a good job, 'especially for a woman'. But even he couldn't refuse one of the three scholarships in the island; so he decided a nun must accompany me to France. Many dreadful things could happen to a young girl alone on a boat for a month! The ruling was categorical: 'She must take such and such a boat to be in France for the beginning of term.'

There were other young people on the boat. When I got to France I was to go to Dole, where my godfather, my father's best friend, was the curé, and go to the Ursuline convent. I remember that at Panama, one of my travelling companions wanted to kiss me. I told him I didn't want to—because of my studies. He wouldn't believe me, and yet it was true. I was convinced I had to make a radical choice between sexuality—or at least what I knew of it—and my studies. I had noticed that my friends who began to flirt no longer did anything else. So I chose the path of studiousness. I had to succeed in my studies, there was no other way. And I was also convinced that I must keep myself for someone whom I would be in love with one day. It was all rather vague in my mind, not very concrete: I thought about babies without thinking about a husband.

I quietly savour this reawakening consciousness of myself, as if I were learning to walk again after a long illness. Then I realize that, close to me, 50 centimetres from my bunk, Christian exists. I have been living egoistically for myself alone, and for my daughter who is a part of me. I feel almost guilty. But it is an exquisite pleasure.

The skipper is stretched out on his bunk. He is reading, but glances regularly at the compass fixed at the head of his berth, to check our course. Round him, the sextant, direction-finder, the charts and books on navigation, in impressive heaps, remind one of his important mission: he is responsible for the survival of the boat, of his wife and child.

II

A Nice Girl

IN TAHITI, HOLIDAYS were ruled by the crops. There were holidays for pollinating the vanilla, for the coffee harvest, because labour was short. Apart from that, holidays were spent at home. When I arrived at the Ursuline convent at Dole, the subject of my first essay was: 'You have been on holiday. Write about what happened on one of the days.' I was completely at a loss.

Unlike my father, my godfather the curé was very liberal. He thought it was ridiculous not to allow me to travel alone. As soon as he arrived in Dole, he had revolutionized everything. He got rid of the pretentious gilt in the collegiate church, had the plaques taken from the pews which marked the places of the rich. He had asked the Ursulines to let their girls out between five and seven to do their shopping. We had more freedom at Saint Ursula's than at the Lycée. My letters were sent to the rectory, and no one opened them. Thanks to my godfather, instead of being cloistered, girls participated in the life of the parish. I helped with the old people, and with the religious education of the small children. Not by making them learn their catechism, but by taking them out, making them aware of the world around them. We showed them an apple tree, bought them three apples, let them eat one, taught them to love nature, which God created. That is true religious education. When my godfather left Dole the whole town turned out: his intelligent and warm personality irradiated the whole of that part of the Jura. One day, I remember, I found four small children living in one room, a miserable place which their mother nevertheless managed to keep spotless. The poor woman was ashamed, didn't want to let me in. Then she told me she had been waiting three years for a small flat. My godfather fought to get her one straight away.

The Ursuline nuns were very young. And it was thanks to their generosity of spirit that I spent the three best years of my youth at Dole. But I was often ill: I had had none of the childhood illnesses in Tahiti, where one is safe from infections. In Dole I had one after another. In the sanatorium, I worried: would my studies suffer? Yet I wasn't behind: at fifteen I was able to indulge in the luxury of taking a psychology course meant for teachers. It was there that I learnt to accept my family by learning to understand them.

At first I was regarded rather like an exotic animal: the magical word Tahiti. Film crews had brought back photographs of crowd scenes from the island, with half-naked girls under the coconut palms, and I had difficulty in explaining that at that time girls in Tahiti swam in shirts and shorts, the bikini being unknown in the islands, and the influence of the missionaries still strong.

I spent the holidays at school, alone, since my friends had all gone home. I enjoyed the solitude. I had my own room, I never slept in a dormitory. The grounds were large and full of flowers and fruit. I played music, wrote poems. I ate alone at a big table; sometimes an old lady whose duties were a bit vague came to share my meal, which was passed through a hatch from the kitchen. And I read and read: all the books which I had been forbidden to read and which were in the convent library, especially philosophers, even Sartre and Camus. And books on psychology, my great passion.

We have been at sea a week and Christian is already on his fourth novel: I have never seen him absorb so much literature. It's a pleasant way to keep one's mind alert. His only relaxation. Because except for the navigation he does everything single handed.

It isn't that I dislike the seaman's life. But a baby takes up more time at sea than elsewhere. From six in the morning till six at night, I feed, change and wash with scarcely a break, only stopping to prepare our meals; and so on till evening. At sea, movements are slower, more tiring; the boat makes you use your muscles all the time. I feel perpetually overwhelmed by all that there is to do.

Also, the *Alpha* was designed to be sailed by one person. I have to be absolutely free for Laurence, whatever happens. And Christian didn't want to force the hard work of a seaman on me, since being a mother at sea is difficult enough in itself. However, it doesn't stop me from time to time heaving on ropes so that my hands are rubbed raw, helping to hoist two anchors without a windlass, or diving to fish something out of the water.

Christian wanted a very strong hull, and rigging which would stand up to anything. At twenty one doesn't have much money, and the *Alpha* cost us a lot of elbow grease, imagination, and economizing—exhausting when one is expecting, and then feeding, a baby. Christian went from harbour to harbour in search of second-hand gear, finding a twenty-year-old sextant here, an aeroplane compass there, and blocks and shackles. Winches which were too expensive were replaced by blocks and tackle, which allowed us, for instance, to hoist the jib. And the *Alpha*, with her very simple, but very solid, rigging and masts, now carries her precious cargo, our little family, towards Las Palmas in the Canaries.

Yes, I was happy at Dole, in spite of adolescent problems which I struggled to resolve. However if I think of the poems I wrote then, I am struck by the despair in them, the loathing for life so common at that age. One theme continually recurred : life is like an ocean of glue in which it is difficult to keep afloat.

Another contradiction : I was top of my class, and yet I failed the baccalauréat two years running. And I had to go back to Tahiti, where I arrived in the middle of the school year, in December, because the authorities had booked my plane flight then.

I was lucky enough to have an intelligent headmaster. 'You've got a failure neurosis,' he told me. 'I forbid you to attend lessons before next term. And you may only hand in work during the term after.' The neurosis was the result of my education, as for so many other children. Reassured, under control again, I did very well in both baccalauréats in spite of having meningitis and typhoid. It was still just as bad at home. Yet my mother was irreproachable, did everything a mother should. She looked after me at home when I had typhoid, as the doctor had strongly advised against hospital. My father was still working extremely hard, growing grey on our behalf. Did

anyone realize quite how sad our family was? Or was it I who
saw everything lopsidedly? Or was it just that life was like that?
My brother had married, gone away. I had no room of my own.
I slept in a sort of passage which my father used as a library and
office. Everyone went in and out of the three doors. I wasn't
allowed to put anything on the table or on a wall, not a single
print of my own. The system was beyond reproach. The
depersonalization was total. I can still feel its effects today. I
realize that I have problems of this kind with Christian, which
many couples would probably recognize: for example I only
buy clothes which Christian likes. I often think that I would like
to spend three years of my life choosing what I like or don't like
myself. But I could never do it. I don't want to hit myself. I like
being left in peace. The pattern is set. I have moved on from
my parents to Christian.

After my second baccalauréat I went to do advanced maths
at Lyon. I wanted to do an engineering course, but arrived too
late to enrol. So I began studying for a physics degree, and
continued this at Clermont-Ferrand. I also continued to get all
the childhood illnesses which I hadn't yet had. At Lyon I threw
myself heart and soul into choral singing. I persisted in repres-
sing any kind of a sex life. I still think that it's necessary to have
one period of one's life, between sixteen and eighteen, when one
sublimates one's sexual emotions. It's an amazing age, when one
wants to do everything, learn everything. Sublimation gives one
a great burst of energy for one's studies, for creative activities.
Of course it's only a stage which one must later leave behind to
become truly adult, to blossom out physically. In short, when I
got back to Tahiti, with my degree certificates, I was the perfect
old maid. They were setting up a Post Office bank system. No
one knew if it would work or not. I was Tahitian, had diplomas;
they took me on for a trial period as an inspector. And having
come back to the island for a few months only, I stayed there.
I was a real electronic brain. If one of the 6,000 account holders
telephoned me during the day, I knew at once if he had a
credit or a debit, and how much.

I still needed some physics certificates, for which I was taking
a correspondence course, and I would have taken the exams
later in France, if fate hadn't stepped in. When I wasn't
working, I listened to Bach, whose mathematical purity I loved.

I liked the unaccompanied music, with its superimposed melodies. I also listened to Monteverdi, the first classical composer to herald jazz, who included dissonances in his scores. And Francis Poulenc. I read very few novels. I liked true-life accounts, and philosophical studies, or factional novels such as Kazantzakis's *Christ Recrucified*; *War and Peace* for its historical perspective, and Saint-Exupéry's *Citadelle* because it was romantic, in search of an ideal. And also Teilhard de Chardin, and Freud and—the list is endless, because I had more than enough time to read. In spite of working and earning my living I was still forced to live with my parents, otherwise there would have been a scandal, and in Tahiti, that is unthinkable. 'An island is a prison and the sea its bars,' Christian said one day. At home I was treated as if I were seven years old : I was 21, but I was given ten minutes in which to get home from work. If I stopped to gossip with a friend, I was interrogated.

I had lived in France for several years however, and my behaviour was clearly exemplary. I couldn't go to the cinema if my parents didn't come too. And as they were getting on, they didn't often want to go out. My mother still reacted oddly. One day I bought a little electrophone. I wanted to keep the polystyrene packing, as I thought I'd soon be going to France. I asked my mother where I could keep it.

'Put it on top of the wardrobe,' she said. 'There's plenty of room there, it won't be in my way.'

Next day, at five in the morning, I heard her say to my father : 'Look! France is taking advantage of us. She thinks she can do anything now. Yesterday she bought an electrophone, and do you know where she put the packing? In my wardrobe, if you please.'

She had clearly achieved what she wanted.

'Why did you put it there?' my father asked me angrily.

She must have been very unhappy.

The incident, unimportant in itself, is symbolic of our whole childhood, our youth. Why did my mother twist things? Why didn't my father realize this? And was she conscious of what she was doing? Why were we all prisoners of each other? Was it because of the war? Because of our grandparents? Or was it the penalty of the whole system, a society with its strict moral codes, its frustrations which destroy the individual?

One day we all got together, parents and children. With my brother and sister we described, analysed, explained everything we had felt all these years. Our despair, our secret tears, our desire to do well, our dreams of a happy family. We couldn't go on. It was horrible. Everyone cried, even my brother who had got married long ago. We didn't resent their love for us, as they believed. There was a climate of mutual mistrust between parents and children.

Did this trial by jury help us at all? Perhaps it helped each of us to take stock. Our parents were exiles, terribly lonely. No one had ever helped them to resolve their problems. And to cap it all we had now thrown in their face their failure in bringing us up. Had we any right to do so? Weren't all parents the same? And ours better than most? And I told myself with even more fervour, just as I had done when I was unjustly chastised at six years old : 'I must remember, I mustn't forget; I must never do that to my children.'

My children? At that time I was afraid of having any, afraid of not being able to make them happy myself.

Your children are not your children.
You can give them your love, but not your thoughts.
Because their souls live within the house of the future, which you cannot visit, even in your dreams.

I think back to our first day on the *Alpha* with Laurence, a week ago.

Sailing peacefully along, taking our time, with our whole lives in front of us. Outside, the sun shining softly, and Laurence's pink bath thermometer registering sixteen degrees. A light following wind driving us forward : 70 miles a day. We are sailing down to the Tropics, to the heat. Each day we gain one or two degrees. We are still wearing woollen clothes. Soon we'll be naked. Marvellous.

We're alone—Christian, Laurence and myself. But we have an excellent helmsman, the ideal crewman, who doesn't talk or eat, drink or smoke, who never complains and never sleeps : our automatic pilot, our *girouette*. As it has a wind-vane—*girouette*— on top, we've christened it Gigi, a girl's name. Gigi was born in a workshop in Casablanca, where Christian cleverly knocked

her together from a few bits of wood and metal, to a very
precise plan. She keeps us on course, better than any person
could, at any speed. With a little flick of her tail, she rights the
boat in a masterful manner whenever a wave threatens to bring
her round. She has complete control of the *Alpha*. We only have
to take the tiller in very bad weather. She's fragile and we
frequently say a prayer for her. If only she lasts as far as Las
Palmas. Because if Gigi fails us—as I am completely monopolized by Laurence—Christian is the only man left at the helm.
But we trust her. Happy to be on our *Alpha*, our new boat, we
sail with a fair wind till evening.

I was 22, and my friends pitied me for being kept a prisoner by
my family. I needed to talk to boys and girls of my own age. I
still had no wish to flirt, but I was at the age when one wants to
be part of a group, to share their warmth, their problems and
hopes. My friends' parents became my allies: they were responsible for gaining a little freedom for me, by various subterfuges,
so that I could go out. I began to go dancing—modern dancing,
at a distance from one's partner. I felt all legs and arms, but
managed somehow.

Adolescent and spinsterish, I loved to talk for hours about the
origins of the world or paleontology. And as I was the only girl
to prefer such weighty topics to dancing or flirting, the boys
listened to me amazed. One of them was called François. He
was the son of a civil servant. His parents were very fond of me
and helped me as much as they could to escape from the
depressing family atmosphere. Was it because I thought I was
ugly, or because he was shy, that our relationship remained so
pure, and platonic—that we didn't even hold hands? For him,
more than the others, I offset the very physical life of Tahiti. So
at parties, and in nightclubs, we sat side by side, and talked.
About everything, for hours, from mathematics to history, with
philosophy thrown in and other more or less nebulous sciences.
Thanks to him, thanks to his family, I was able to escape.

François was unusually intelligent and well-educated. He
idealized me, saw me as a character from *Gone With the Wind*.
He was aware of all that was going on in the world, and far less
wrapped up in his books than I was. We discussed Hinduism. It
was he who dragged me away from Bach long enough to get to

know the Beatles, Joan Baez, Bob Dylan. We were, of course, in love with each other, but we pushed this fact to the back of our consciousness. Perhaps we would have achieved a more mature love—but Christian intervened.

The sea is very attentive. Is this a good omen? It's certainly how I like it best. Just lively enough to bear the *Alpha* along in its dance, and giving us the long swell typical of these coasts. This fills me with energy, and I can wash the napkins as quickly as Laurence dirties them. Our skipper Christian looks very askance at the guardrails with their decoration of white squares. 'It really looks terrible.' But his argument is weak, because we're alone and no one can see us. 'If I go about', he adds, 'the jibsheet and mainsheet will tear down everything on the port side.' One mustn't get in the way. He's right. So the disputed articles will be confined to the sternrail, only 2.50 metres long. In view of the daily consumption of a small baby, it's not very big. I shall be forever fetching and carrying.

And suddenly I feel frustrated in my capacity as a woman. Nothing on board has been planned or thought out with me in mind. All too often on boats there is room only for men. However much yachting has developed, few women sailors go round the world. During the voyage they usually lead a man's life, and are very proud of being just as good sailors. In the West Indies I met a very solid German girl who was sailing alone from Hamburg to the Antilles and back. She was an irresistible force: she could easily do without windlass and winches on her eleven-metre sloop.

But I have never seen a book which relates the experiences of a wife and mother aboard a small sailing boat with a baby a few weeks old. Yet I have met more than one family at sea. In fact a woman armed with a baby, a make-up box and women's magazines coming on board is like an ugly duckling appearing in the nest. She must make haste to become a swan. And time seems to drag when one is trying to get rid of the hateful grey down, when one feels ill at ease, disorientated. One hears oneself saying that the place of a 'real' woman is not on a boat. I love sailing, the sea, the wind, the solitude, the sun, the natural and healthy life. A boat gives me all that. Yet although it seems completely logical to me that the captain should be the only master on board, apart from God, for the sake of our safety and happiness, I still rebel against the permanent supervision of everything I do. It reminds me too much of my family. I am depersonalized once more. I lose all initiative, all imagination, spontaneity.

There is something there I can't quite understand. I must try to regain my equilibrium. Am I losing the ability to adapt which has been so valuable to me up till now, because of Laurence?

As it is clear that without the *Alpha* we would be dead, the skipper decides the place for each object according to its importance for the proper functioning of the boat. For example, it has been decided that the most practical place for the tools so that they are easily accessible is the cutlery drawer. When I want a knife, I have to move several kilos of metal. The oil left on a spanner often drips on to the spoons. Ugh! Sometimes it makes me wild.

I had gone to a nightclub secretly with François. We were sitting there and talking as usual. A boy came up and asked me to dance. In his arms I felt like a child in the arms of a grown-up. Safe. He told me I had lovely eyes, a banal phrase which I found moving. I had always been told I was ugly. And François didn't appear to be interested in such things. When I looked in the mirror I considered myself ugly, and it was true, because I was unhappy and full of complexes. If a boy told me I was beautiful, I despised him, told myself: 'He's making fun of me.' If anyone held me close, dancing, I felt assaulted. They tried to get close to me through my body. But Christian won me by looking into my eyes.

When we look back on our first meeting, Christian remembers a violent and immediate physical attraction. I don't. I don't remember having been swept off my feet, or a violent desire to make love. But can I trust my memory, confused as I was by the presence of François and all my inhibitions?

François, Christian and I were almost inseparable. We were three friends. But we were all so different. Christian struck me as a tanned playboy who roared around in a red sportscar, and made a lot of money taking instant photographs down by the harbour, at parties, and on holidays. He acted like a catalyst on

Above: France and Christian Guillain with their three daughters, Laurence, Mareva and Aïmata

Above: Florent Guillain, the orphan son of a carpenter, who built the harbour at Dunkirk, and became Minister for the Colonies

Left: His son, who was absorbed by the adventures of France and Christian until his death at the age of ninety-two

The port of Papeete in Tahiti, thirty years ago

Passing through the Panama Canal

François, made him aware that he could love me properly, physically. And as François grew more and more fond of me I fell in love with Christian without being aware of it. I was bemused, at the mercy of events.

We had met in April. Until July we didn't make love. My saner self told me that he was not the boy for me, that he was far too young—two years younger than I was—that he had no job, and changed girls as the fancy took him. But he was a drug I couldn't do without. It was at the time when I was convinced that I couldn't love more than one person in my life. I didn't know what to do. It was Christian I loved. Since he wanted to take me and carry me off, I would go with him, no matter where, no matter how. I would obey his instincts.

After our meal of rice and corned beef, comes the washing up. Armed with a ten-litre bucket, securely fixed to a rope, I draw up some sea water. If properly thrown, the receptacle fills up immediately, giving the arm which wields it a hefty jolt which jerks you forward. I hold on tight to the rigging.

'I think we'll get a good night,' says Christian. 'It's a shame I haven't got a boom to hold the jib. With the wind taken out of it by the mainsail it's flapping and getting very worn. I'm going to lower it. There are also Gigi's bolts to check, but I feel lazy tonight.'

At last everything is in order. The skipper has made his first night round on deck, the baby is sleeping well wrapped up. I stretch out and repeat 'a good night'.

Our first night on board with Laurence. It's completely dark in the cabin. Outside, the faint light of the stars barely mottles the sail. There's a new moon. Gradually the wind dies down, then dies away completely. But the feebler it gets the more the *Alpha* rolls. The famous long swell is getting up. A long nightmare is beginning.

Without wind the boat goes mad. She rolls like a poor wretch who has lost his sense of balance. Her 'wings' flap, quivering, useless. The boom swings stupidly from one side to the other, making the shackle on the main sheet crack loudly each time on the steel hull. There is no breathing rhythm to adopt to feel more comfortable, because there's no rhythm. We're tossed in

2

all directions, furiously and rudely buffeted, with the added misery of knowing that we're making no progress. The ceaseless, irregular movement finally exhausts us. We go to sleep, but it's a vicious circle. We fall asleep, but at the same moment the sea jolts us and wakes us up. She'll make us pay for our dreams. You pay for everything, even a sunset.

Christian goes up on deck at least ten times, but there's nothing he can do, except start the engine and take the tiller. Which would only add to our misfortunes. Better to reconcile oneself to the situation, save one's pains and wait. As I'm breast feeding Laurence I can't risk being seasick. I take some Marzine, which knocks me out even more. Then, miraculously, fall asleep.

The sun shines down on the minute *Alpha* bravely breasting the waves. The cabin is now a nauseous gaping hole where one has to make every effort not to be sick. But Laurence wakes up very bright and refreshed.

I move like a sleepwalker. Wonder what state the skipper is in.

'All right?'

'Better. I'm over the worst.'

He's lucky. In my semi-conscious state I have to see to Laurence, the washing, cooking. The round of daily tasks begins all over again, remorselessly, inescapably.

Our one dish is stewing in the SEB, our precious pressure cooker, securely fixed to the stove which Camping Gaz have given us. We have no gimbals, a system which would allow the Domino—the little stove—to keep in a horizontal position whatever the angle of the boat. Only a hermetically sealed pan can cope with the endless, sudden lists. For the same reason, for water, we have a whistling kettle which is completely sealed. I guard the kettle and pan jealously, because they can't be replaced before the next port: no shops at sea. So each object becomes immensely precious. You don't waste anything, throw anything away. If the boat is disabled, a crossing planned for ten days can easily last a month, or more. So you have to provide for this and economize on water and food with it in mind.

Disaster: just now when I was emptying the washing-up water, I threw out a teaspoon. We've only got two left. That's

why I hate the half numbed state I'm in. I have no strength,
my reflexes are slow and I'm very clumsy. I grow more and
more afraid of falling overboard each time I have to go on
deck.

From the very first day Laurence was quite at home. For a
start she sleeps for seven hours at a stretch. This suits me, but
I'm frequently tempted to wake her up to feed her. I wait
patiently, and at last she opens one eye. Her little mouth
works energetically at her wrists: soon there'll be the urgent
cries of a hungry baby. I struggle against the sleep which is
drugging me. Lie her down by my side. I mustn't go to sleep;
I might smother her by rolling on her. Wedged against the
bunk board, my back arced against the wood, I brace myself
each time the boat rolls, to protect my offspring.

Laurence continues at this slower pace for the first two days
at sea, but she takes in a double amount at each meal. Then she
returns to her usual four-hourly rhythm, but still has a ravenous
appetite. After the first feed I'm a bit worried. I tell myself
a baby that age can't be seasick, but I can't prevent myself
watching over her anxiously for the next couple of hours: a
baby only takes an hour and a half to digest its mother's milk—
three hours for cow's milk. But it's all right. Her stomach is in
better shape than ours.

Then I have to change and wash her. I sit on my bunk and
hold Laurence between my feet, in her basket, so that she can't
roll either way. I give her a quick clean-up with cotton wool
and baby oil, under a blanket because it's still cold. From time
to time I warm her up with my breath.

Finally—the nappies have to be washed, the dear little
squares and triangles which one would gladly throw in a
washing machine—or overboard. When you're broke and want
a boat at twenty, disposable nappies are out of the question: we
live on 100 francs a month, which would just about cover their
cost.

I rapidly discovered that sea water is the best detergent. No
need for soap, even for special 'salt-water' soap. I lean over the
side, plunge the things straight into the sea, and the sun takes
care of disinfecting and bleaching them. Drying is another
matter. With the wind behind us—our usual mode of sailing—a
boat rolls a lot, and I have to hang on all the time. Because of

the *Alpha*'s small size a washing-line is out of the question. I can only hang four napkins at a time on the sternrail. And one's always at the mercy of a clumsy wave which can break on the hull and wet the washing. And you have to take everything in at midday, when the sun is at its height. Otherwise it'll never be dry. Whatever you do, the salt stays in and gradually grows damp. After using one nappy, Laurence's skin was covered with little red spots. I cursed my fate for being there. Burst into tears. But that was no help.

'Christian. Look. It's terrible.'

We couldn't possibly carry enough fresh water for the washing. What could I do? I found some thick white cream in the medicine box, which stuck obstinately to clothes and smelt strongly of cod-liver oil. I spread it on thickly. A few hours later her skin was as good as new, quite healed. I continued to apply a thin layer until she got used to the salt. After four days I only needed to use talc. We'd won.

Years before Laurence was born, I had pored over books on child-care and child psychology. But life at sea upsets everything: it's the opposite of 'normal'. A regular life? One's always at the mercy of the weather or a technical hitch: a ripped sail, a parted rope. Then too, as we're sailing westwards, we're continually changing time. So from the start I never imposed a timetable on Laurence. She regulated herself of her own accord to the rhythm of a feed every four hours. From the age of three weeks she never woke me at night. Otherwise I'd never have lasted as far as Tahiti—the goal of this first voyage—with all the privations our financial situation imposed on me.

Laurence is never isolated. She shares our three square metres in a state of perpetual upheaval and flux. As we go from port to port only occasionally seeing the same faces, I have to take care that she feels secure. But a yacht is a privileged mode of transport: you sleep in your own home every night, wherever you are.

To feed her—in spite of the reserve of Guigoz milk, dented tins given to us at a reduced price—I have none of the alternatives found on land. But nature always finds a way. In the old days in Tahiti, when a woman had no milk, as there were no mammals to milk, babies were given the pulp and milk of very young coconuts, the juice of raw fish, crushed bananas and papayas. They got everything they needed for healthy growth, thrived and grew strong.

The beneficial action of salt water against dehydration, for healing burns, is well known. So is the rich nutritional value of plankton. I'm convinced that a human organism, even that of a breast-fed baby, has great powers of resistance: when I was a child an island passenger schooner got into difficulties at sea, without a radio transmitter to send out a distress signal, or an adequate supply of food and water. After a few days search parties were sent out. But fifteen to twenty passengers, among them children and young babies, existed for a fortnight without even getting ill. Of course this was in warm seas, as we usually are. But clearly these people didn't panic, and knew they should bathe in salt water. But even serious studies on the subject haven't tempted us to risk the experiment. We didn't set sail lightly. Christian is an excellent sailor. This will be clear from the way he crossed the South Pacific to New Zealand on the *Walborg*, a Swedish nineteenth-century schooner. Very heavy, seventeen metres long, with square sails and practically no motor, this historical monument was sailed by only five men. And Christian perfected his knowledge of navigation, taking astronomical bearings every day.

But the best sailor can't prevent his boat rolling in a heavy swell without any wind. I took Marzine four times in 48 hours in reduced doses. My head grew a little clearer. Clear enough to tell myself calmly that hell can't be any worse than this: being sleepy and yet unable to sleep. Worse still: to be forced, in spite of the heaviness of your head and limbs, in spite of feeling sick, to cook, and wash—and wash up. To be responsible for the life of a baby, to be obliged not to make the slightest error which might prove fatal. Not to fall with all your weight on her cot—and it's so easy to fall to begin with. To take care when carrying boiling liquids, which an unexpected jolt might send flying. It's terrible, the feeling of not being quite in control of oneself, at the precise moment when one needs to be so more than ever.

I do everything like an automaton, as if I were drugged. I have a ghastly feeling it will never end. My book for young mothers says one sometimes feels very depressed four weeks after the birth, in moments of tiredness. And yet I don't regret Laurence's existence for a single moment.

But we're making no headway; we've even stopped praying for Gigi.

'What on earth are we doing in this tub?'

Christian smiles. We love our tub, our nest, our *Alpha*. It's just a pity there isn't any wind, that's all.

III

A Presentable Young Man

CHRISTIAN SPENT HIS childhood being shunted from one boarding school to another.

Born in Paris, where his father was a doctor, he was separated from his mother when very young, lived in Morocco, then with a godmother in Germany, and was then sent back to Paris to experience the joys of private schools, from Sainte-Marie de Monceau to Notre-Dame de Boulogne; so he doesn't remember his schooldays in the same rosy light that I do. Far from it. He was the eldest of five brothers, who were always separated because of their various schools. Instead of being integrated into a family, each of them learnt to act as a separate individual. It is for this reason, I feel sure, that he remembers with such emotion the holidays he spent with his grandfather, his father and uncles, his brothers and cousins in the house they had at Equihen near Boulogne. He remembers loving the stormy seas, fishing, long walks on the deserted beach. They were the only times when he felt he belonged to a clan he was proud of. He admired his grandfather, a legendary patriarchal figure, who loved his wife tenderly all her life. And his uncles—doctors, engineers, artists, musicians. Robert Guillain the great Chinese scholar. When later, Laurence asked Christian about death, Christian told her: 'We go into the earth and our bodies are changed into one of the statues which your uncle Pierre makes, into grass, into that flower which smells so sweetly. Your great-grandfather died one fine spring day. He's still there in us, proud of what we are.'

Christian's great-grandfather, Florent Guillain, was Minister for the Colonies. The son of a humble Paris carpenter, he was a self-made man, and Christian has a great admiration for anyone who has started from scratch and achieved what they set out to do: the carpenter's son went to the *École Polytechnique*, became a marine engineer, and was then responsible for light-houses and beacons, before becoming a minister. Lighthouses and beacons. It seems like fate. So also does the fact that another ancestor of Christian's commanded the frigate *Le Tonnant*, at the battle of Aboukir, at which the French fleet was defeated by Nelson. His legs blown off by a cannon ball, he ordered that he should be put in a barrel of straw so that he could continue to give orders, before dying of his wounds. *Le Tonnant* was to be the name of our third boat.

Christian and I got our first boat, the *Alpha*, by working hard for it. And he is proud of having lived up to the standards of the Guillains.

After doing his military service, Christian found himself in New Caledonia—good-looking, fit, but without qualifications or money. Our destinies were drawing closer, because he had dreamed of going to Tahiti since he was a boy. Three months work in Nouméa enabled him to buy the famous red Fiat sportscar in which he later rushed around as a playboy in Papeete, and he also met the head of the Central Treasury—somewhat like the Chancellor of the Exchequer for overseas territories.

'They're going to open a catering school in Tahiti,' the latter told him. 'There's a future there for a boy like you. There'll be a chain of top hotels and you could be manager of one of them.'

Hearing the name Tahiti Christian didn't hesitate. He had nothing to lose and everything to gain. He was delighted to get his fare paid to do a catering course in Papeete. On arrival—an administrative slip-up—he couldn't find the school: it hadn't yet been opened.

He asked himself what a boy of twenty who has just done his military service can do at the other end of the world, without friends, relations, or money. With nothing except a car, which needed petrol. How was he to earn his living?

He had no particular goal in mind, but he was in Tahiti. It was the realization of a dream. An old dream. So he made a list of everything he could possibly do. Window-cleaner? Which would mean, for him, setting up a window-cleaning business, because he knew himself well enough to know that he couldn't stand not being his own boss. He went round the

shops, and gave them a quotation for doing their windows—
and saw he was on to a good thing.

For a time he was a hack for a Papeete newspaper. The local
press is very important in the islands. He asked a journalist to
bring him a polaroid camera and some colour films from the
States. He was then able to try one of the other numbers in his
list of 'possibilities for a young man of twenty in Tahiti': taking
instant photographs, in an island where such a thing was
unknown, the only mobile photographer being unambitious.

Being 'new' in Tahiti he attracted a lot of attention. In his
red car, which was his trade-mark, he was counting on taking at
least ten photographs a day. At ten francs a photo he would have
100 francs a day; a princely sum for a boy who had never had a
sou, whose father never gave him pocket-money, and who
made his own way into the army after leaving school. And the
first evening, he took 150 photos. It was a revelation. Especially
as he was thoroughly enjoying himself, my handsome, tanned
Christian, with his pink shirt and smiling face. I remember
having seen him two or three times roaring about like a mad
thing in his red sportscar. Everything I disliked.

He went from nightclub to nightclub; everyone wanted
photographs. He counted his money each night, put it in the
bank the next day. He told himself that life wasn't so difficult
after all. He spent two months in France, living it up, impres-
sing his friends and relations. Then he came back. And before
meeting me, he met a boat. A Hollywood sound engineer and
his wife had called in at Papeete harbour in their yacht. They
were sailing round the world. He got to know them, and they
talked. He went on board their boat, the *Carmellia*. For one who
had never been at sea, except on a passenger steamer, it was a
great discovery. To live on a boat. The *Carmellia* had a marvellous smell of wood. To sail away, discover an island. A way
of breaking free from everything, from memories of childhood
schools, from social restrictions. A way of using all one's
abilities, stretching oneself to the full. The shipmates of Tom—
the skipper of the *Carmellia*—had just left. He found himself
alone with his wife Nelly. He suggested to Christian that he
should continue the voyage with them, sharing expenses and
crewing. Christian accepted enthusiastically: a new life of
adventure stretched before him, endlessly. While they waited

2*

to go, he would live on the yacht. It was then that, as I sat in a
nightclub one evening talking about Teilhard de Chardin, he
asked me to dance.

December 2: Laurence's third day on board the *Alpha*. It's
dead calm. The long swell has slowly died down. It's over, and
we gradually forget we ever felt sick. Anything we throw overboard keeps pace with us, travelling at a speed of one or two
knots in the current. The rigging has stopped clanking. Silence.
Schools of dorados, who have come to look at us, play all
around us. Laurence is telling us lots of interesting things. Her
eyes and head move constantly, punctuated with serious 'aa e,
aa e, aa e' sounds.

However, we can hardly make the crossing using the motor,
and we begin to wonder if the wind will ever get up. But the
enforced delay does us good. I take advantage of it to dry
everything quickly. It's a real pleasure to collect ten dry
nappies in one go.

A dead calm is a holiday at sea. The rhythm is broken; the
boat is still. The sun enfolds you in its warmth, penetrating
everywhere, even below. I get the bedding and clothes out on
deck to air in the sun. Sometimes a long swell makes us imagine
things, fills our minds with the idea of fantastic underwater
monsters which—in our dreams—could alone explain the slow
motion of this inert mass of water. Christian seizes the opportunity of having his one bathe of the crossing. I am more
prudent. I remember Cindy, a young American girl, who went
swimming with her husband in mid-Pacific miles from anywhere. They left their three-year-old son on board, without
securing him to anything. When they got back on board the
Sea-Wife Cindy threw down a bucket for some sea water. The
receptacle had barely touched the water when two sharks
appeared, and one of them carried it off. Cindy hugged her son
to her and was cured for ever of bathing in mid-ocean.

At last, on the fourth day, there's a light breeze. It's good to
feel the water moving past the hull again, only separated from
us by three millimetres of steel. No one dares say anything, for
fear of frightening the zephyr away. The rigging moves gaily
into action. The *Alpha* glides gracefully along like a large white
bird. The wind's behind us again. A gentle breath just strong

enough to blow us along and give us hope. At last I begin to
look beyond the stove, my baby and her nappies. I reproach
myself for having limited my horizon in this way.

The sky is clear, cloudless. From time to time an adventurous
wave breaks on the stem and scatters in a shower of rainbow-
coloured spray. The sea is a huge living creature, volcanic or
lazy. She goes from caresses to a hurricane, from charm to
anger. One hardly has time to get an impression of her before
she's transformed, replaced by another equally fugitive image.
Only a giant camera could capture her moods.

I hope the fine weather will last. According to the Casablanca
fishermen there's a gale here once a fortnight. We left just after
a stormy spell, and should reach Las Palmas before the weather
breaks again.

From ahead, the *Alpha* looks slender. The wake she leaves in
the water adds to the impression of length. At the moment she's
only nibbling at the kilometres, at a speed of four knots—the
speed of a fast walker. A luxury in this jet age. We are doing
thousands of kilometres under our own steam. We're dependent
on no one. We can go wherever we like, wherever the wind takes us.

Phosphorescent green dorados appear silhouetted in our
wake. They look flat, cut through the water like thrown knives.
Suddenly one of them leaps out of the sea, showing its sulphur
yellow belly.

'Christian! A fish!'

The line is stretched taut. The creature fights desperately
with great blows of its tail. The rest of the school hurries up and
surrounds it curiously, appearing not to understand what's
going on. The sight always makes me feel a bit sick, but one has
to kill to eat. The captain cautiously draws in the line. The
other dorados are still circling round the poor prisoner, and it
would be easy to harpoon another.

Only two more metres of nylon to reel in. The dorado looks
as though it's tired of fighting. One sharp blow—and hup.

'Blast, it's got off the hook.'

Farewell, raw fish *à la Tahitienne*, grilled fish, fish soup. I
mentally put away my frying pan, the oil, the large knife, and
it's that damned corned beef again.

Christian sees my disappointment, and says very tenderly:
'Look at all the others. We'll catch plenty more.'

Day five. We're stricken with 'flu. We ache all over, with sore heads, throats and noses, and a temperature. Bed. I share mine with Laurence, don't attempt to isolate her. Not a cough. She's growing visibly, full of smiles which are still uncontrolled. She doesn't even notice the germs we've succumbed to. However, I check my prescriptions and the big chest of baby medicines regularly. We avoid using medicine whenever possible, but are prepared to take any steps to save our daughter. In port, I wouldn't let anyone go near or touch Laurence. I would sometimes have to be very diplomatic: 'There's nothing I'd like better than to give her to you. But I can't take the risk of her picking up a germ. Out at sea, you know, without a doctor.'

People are kind enough to understand. And it suits me, because I am as jealous as a cat showing her claws if anyone goes near her young.

'Careful! Don't hold her like that! She'll be sick.'

And it usually ends by my saying 'Give her to me!'; a bit hard on her proud father.

On the sixth day, at midday, the skipper announces that in spite of the small amount of wind during the first few days our daily average is 70 miles, although we're sailing with mainsail alone for lack of a jib boom.

Encouraged by this good news, I wrap up my little parcel warmly and take her up into the cockpit to feed her in the open air. She's snugly installed when a wave breaks violently on the after-deck, drenching us both. I roar with laughter and cover her little face with kisses as she opens, wide, astonished eyes and grimaces at the taste of the salt water. It's a christening of a sort. We stay in the cockpit.

For Laurence, the world, life, is something which moves all the time. The wind which blows up her nostrils, almost suffocating her. A bright storm lantern swinging above her head. A perpetual effort, even when she's asleep, to tense her muscles and keep her balance so that she doesn't roll about in her cot. And Daddy and Mummy always there.

I'm beginning to feel like a mother. A woman who has a husband and a child. A few years ago I thought that was enough in itself to make one adult. And now I feel as though I'm ten years old and playing with my dolls. With Christian, I blossomed in the sun, in spite of all our difficulties. And then Laurence arrived—a shining, perfect symbol of our happiness. This seventh day is a gift from heaven. Our 'flu has gone, and seabirds indicate that land is near. On deck I can savour the mixture of water, sky and light. The sun warms me through my sweater. My body shivers expectantly.

On the foredeck, which serves as my look-out point, I can feel the boat come alive like an animal breathing, as I sit there. The stem plunges into the water and rises regularly, like an animal swimming with its head half submerged, lifting its muzzle now and then to breathe. In this light wind, one can feel the sail about to quiver at the slightest variation in the pressure. And so it could go on for hours, days, months.

Life on a small boat subjugates you completely. All your movements are slow-motion, rather as if you were swimming under water. Your centre of gravity shifts and you have continually to keep your balance, which makes you aware of the weight of your body all the time. One moment you're hanging by your left arm, the next resting all your weight on your right buttock—taking care what you're leaning against. It can be very painful.

Everything one does takes a certain time to carry out, which makes you consider it and think it out carefully, and appreciate it at its proper value. For instance, if I'm thirsty, I ask myself first if I really need a drink. I wait until my throat's dry. Then I grip the partition which separates me from the stove, heave myself out of my bunk. After a few acrobatic feats, I've got a glass in my hand. My feet firmly planted against the lockers, I lean on the sink and pump up some of the precious fresh water which we use only for drinking. I rinse the glass in salt water and put it away immediately. Everything must be in its proper place. The idea of a glass of water has taken on a particular significance, and the same amount of effort goes into each action made throughout the day.

And yet we're drunk with freedom, without quite knowing why we use this word in our cell-like prison. Because it's what we've chosen? 'Freedom is the possibility of making one's own decisions,' my philosophy professor said. But how many have the courage to choose?

I should add that for us this voyage isn't comparable to the month's holiday you spend on a yacht on the Côte d'Azur. It's not a question of minor discomforts which the holiday weather will soon make you forget. It's our first experience of the life which we intend to lead for as long as possible, for ever perhaps. So each possibility for improvement is carefully noted. Christian is already sketching plans for a new boat. We would like a more comfortable arrangement inside, using the small volume of habitable space to best possible advantage. Each of us dreams quietly, in his own corner, and from time to time a phrase, a word, reveals our common preoccupation: an after-cabin with a real double bed; a flush-deck or a very flat deck.

Having thought up all these new ideas, I immediately think 'why'? I'm not pining to go ashore. I'd be very happy to spend another week under these conditions.

Each day, after taking our bearings, Christian marks our position on a chart with a little cross. I admire the accuracy of our course: since we left Casablanca the crosses have followed each other in a perfectly straight line in the direction of the Canaries. I'm full of admiration for my skipper, who watches day and night over the boat. He never sleeps deeply. He keeps an eye on the sail, the self-steering gear, and compass, from his bunk. He's always alert, aware of each part of the boat. He suffers with the mast when it creaks, feels a straining stay like an artery of his own body. He listens to Gigi and tells himself he must check her bolts. But it's so difficult to get up, so good to lie there a little longer in the last rays of the sun, reading one more page.

There's constant noise all round us. The water slides past the hull with a sharp hiss. From time to time a wave breaks loudly on the stem or stern. The whole boat labours. The efforts of the mast, the rigging, the sheets, the self-steering gear, join in a cacophany of sound to which the ear quickly grows accustomed. The captain's on deck immediately there's any unusual noise or unexpected movement, to find out what's causing it.

But it's I who raise the alarm this time: 'Christian! Gigi's bolts have worked loose.'

He's on deck immediately, on the after-deck, clinging with all his might to our precious Gigi who's already leaning at an angle of 45 degrees over the abyss.

'France, the spanner and some wire.'

Laurence has woken up and is crying and I yell at the top of my voice: 'You be quiet, it's not the moment.' Stunned, she shuts up.

We just manage to save the essential part of our automatic steering gear. The bolts had slowly loosened one by one, and a joint had worked loose on the deck.

I go back to the cabin. There's a strange noise of trickling water.

'Christian. Quick! Water's coming into the boat. Hurry!'

'Find some corks, tallow, rags. It's the holes in the hull we made to fix the self-steering gear. Because there are no bolts there now.'

Luckily everything's in the kitchen drawer.

Christian doesn't panic at all. I'm almost in tears. Endless reproaches spring to my lips and I'm just about to yell that he should have. . . . The water's coming in and I imagine Laurence drowning. I must hurry, keep calm.

Suspended in a bosun's chair, his body in the icy water, Christian stops the holes one by one, while I take the tiller. The big blue-and-white towel is ready on the cockpit bench to dry him. But I have the awful habit, at such moments, of thinking about those great fish.

At last it's all over. We've forgiven each other and the skipper makes fast the tiller. It's growing dark. We just have time to see what we imagine is the Canary Island of Lanzarote, just visible in the mist to the south-west. While I prepare some split peas with corned beef, Christian hurriedly tries to mend our helmsman. He looks at the land, the horizon: 'If all goes well, it should be hot showers and steak tomorrow.'

We smile. The skipper somewhat bitterly: he feels responsible for the accident with Gigi. He should have checked before. It was slack of him.

Slackness—is it really the right name for this difficulty in passing from the idea to its realization? This feebleness that seems to attack everyone at sea? Is it the energy needed to make the slightest movement which reduces life at sea to essentials, to survival? On a yacht, in mid-ocean, one tries to save one's strength as much as possible, because a lot of energy is used up involuntarily, just by the motion of the boat. But is anything beyond that a lack of will power? One can't really answer this question, or escape the vague feeling of guilt which gnaws at one, uneasily.

The sun goes down and I ask timidly: 'Shall we take watches? I'll help if you like.'

'No, I'll secure the tiller and stream the log to know how much distance we've made. We're bound to drift a bit.'

The wind has dropped. We go to sleep. In the night, the wind frequently changes direction, and we end up sailing close-hauled. Christian keeps getting up. There's no light on the horizon, which is odd. Each time the wind changes, we half wake and remember that land isn't far off and that we no longer have a functioning Gigi to take us there. Will it take one day? Two days? The hours slowly pass, punctuated only by the rocking of the *Alpha*.

Every day at dawn I feed Laurence on deck, while the sun comes up behind us like a great ball of fire on the horizon.

Christian puts on the kettle for breakfast and looks at the log: 'Only fourteen miles. And we've drifted a lot.'

There is a following wind again. It has freshened and makes us want to make up the lost ground. Christian puts on his yellow oilskin: 'I'll take the tiller for a while.'

I bring him some breakfast—a rusk and butter and some tea. Lanzarote is no longer in sight. We set course for Las Palmas. We're still sailing under mainsail alone. It's eighteen degrees—spring heat. From her cot in the bottom of the cockpit Laurence gazes out. . . . She's so fat she looks almost swollen. She's growing so fast.

I love seeing Christian's smile on her lips.

IV

A Difficult Course

THE MORE CHRISTIAN felt he owned me, when I had decided to link my destiny to his, the more he made me suffer. He said I was strong, with the energy of an adolescent and a virgin. He, who was diffused and flippant, could draw strength from me. For years I had to suffer, sink lower and lower, give him everything I had, to the last drop. Our happiness would only be possible when we could climb this slope again together, a difficult achievement, during the course of which we became a true and strongly-bound couple.

In giving myself to him, in Tahiti, I left one kind of slavery—with my family—for another. I didn't realize that I was conditioned to bondage, but it was in fact the case. True, Christian said he felt I had great strength; but I could never influence him in any way. I could never make him do anything. My strength in fact lay in powers of resistance: I was used to reasoning, studying, struggling. And one inescapable fact had been brought clearly home to me: that I must devote myself to my studies, get a scholarship, go to France, refuse to be a secretary and so on. I had forged myself a will.

When I met him, Christian was a lost soul whose parents took no interest in him and who had never had enough affection. By an unconscious twist of sadism, he needed to hurt people to be happy; and he was getting his revenge for all he had had to suffer. He treated me badly. And I, who had always been punished for trifles, who had undergone real mental torture, didn't realize this. I didn't know that it wasn't normal for a boy who said he loved me to make me suffer.

I would arrive at the harbour on my moped. He would be sitting, bronzed and mocking, on the deck of the *Carmellia*. He said I was wet, and often hit me. I didn't object. He only needed to give me the smallest part of himself, and I was ready to swallow all his insults. And at home the situation was deteriorating. If I got back half an hour late there were terrible scenes. One day my father greeted me by slapping me and shouting that I was a tart. He had never before used such a word. I couldn't understand it.

'You can do what you like,' he said, 'as long as no one knows about it. Our reputation.'

It was a shattering blow : it was unfair and hypocritical.

'If he speaks to me like that,' I told myself, 'he doesn't love me either.' So I made up my mind to leave. But as he had sworn to kill me if I left home, I had to leave secretly.

My 'escape' was like a detective story. As everyone knows everything in Tahiti, I had to use cunning. I wrote to a friend on another island to ask her to telephone my Postmaster General and ask if I could have a fortnight's leave to go and stay with her. Of course, the postmaster telephoned my parents. This ruse was vital, because if I had told the truth my father would have done everything he could to stop me.

Every morning I took a little parcel of things with me, and gradually emptied my wardrobe. On the last day, when I was supposed to be taking a boat to go to my friend's island, I knew I would never be coming home again. I had been unhappy, it was true, and yet I felt sad. I looked for a moment at all my father's records and books, and could only remember the few happy times. My childhood and youth had been filled with music. It woke us up in the morning, and soared round us all day. It was hard to tell where silence ended and music began; each was as exquisite, as dense as the other. And the books. There were more than 3,000 in the house; I slept in their midst. We were all great readers, but my mother held the record for quantity. Outside was our wilderness, great trees fifteen or twenty metres high which I had climbed to study or meditate there for hours. The sky, the coconut palms. At other times I lay in the soft green grass, gazed at the sky through the palm fronds, by day or night, by moonlight or in the dark. All Tahiti rose up before me, and my throat was tight with tears, on the threshold of this house I was leaving, and which I had hated so much.

I hid in the hold of the *Carmellia*. Until the last moment I was terrified that my father would get wind of something and arrive at the harbour to stop us leaving. Christian waited until we were out at sea before letting me out of my hiding-place. We were sailing westwards, towards New Zealand, continuing Tom and Nelly's world cruise; they were amused at my plight. Later, I wrote to my parents saying that I was staying on at my friend's for another fortnight. After a month, they realized what had happened: they had discovered I had taken all my things. My father went to ask the police to get me back. But as I was well over adult age all he could do was rage. It was over.

We spent seven months in the Society Islands, cruising from one bay to another. Seven hard months for me, who as a 'crew member sharing expenses' spent most of the time cooking and cleaning. Luckily there were the beaches, the marvellously clear water where Christian could indulge in his passion for under-water fishing. I didn't fish but I swam alongside him. Tom and Nelly ate and drank a lot, read kilos of thrillers, smoked canna-bis, and rarely went ashore.

We gradually realized that the *Carmellia* could hardly have been a worse boat. The hull was rotten, patched up with cement. It had managed to get from Los Angeles to Tahiti, but we understood why Tom's crew had left. There was every reason to be scared. On the night of my flight we had nearly sunk. Tom had had his boat repainted black in Papeete harbour, and had not sailed for six months. As the sun was very hot, and black a much hotter colour than white, when the planks dried they cracked and parted; you could see daylight through them on the waterline. When we heeled over the boat began to fill. We had to bail all night. Because, naturally, neither the electric pump nor the hand pump worked. We paddled about in the dark—there was no electricity—stumbling and being sick, and wishing that we could die. It was hell. Finally, at dawn, we saw an island. If we hadn't succeeded in reaching it we would have died, because the boat was still filling in spite of our exhausted efforts. After that Tom had his boat caulked after a fashion. I was shattered. I didn't want to abandon Christian, but it was hardly an auspicious start to my sailing career.

The holes in the *Carmellia* had been filled with cement and painted. The rotten wood continued to come away bit by bit. Give me a steel hull any day.

I was frightened in the water. It was Christian who taught me to know the sea. When he swam he was completely happy and relaxed, and I gradually learnt to feel the same, to forget the childish fear and inhibitions which made the water appear dangerous, treacherous. I learnt to let myself go like a foetus in the dark blue depths of the bays, to forge straight ahead without thinking of possible dangers, to communicate with the watery element. To swim like that is sheer delight. When you are afraid you project your fears. Thanks to Christian, I gradually got over this.

Sometimes my fears return in these mysterious bays: you're not wearing a mask and you open your eyes and see cloudy water. That great fish could be a tunny-fish, or a barracuda, or a shark. The spell is broken; you swim away at a fast crawl, as quickly as you can.

Christian knows sharks. He respects them. They respect him. He's no more afraid of them than he is of dogs. And they don't attack without cause: the only accidents I've seen in Polynesia have been when a fisherman was cleaning a fish which bled into the water, while he had a leg in the sea. The shark comes to get the fish and bites off the leg with it. Or an underwater fisherman attaches his fish to his belt, as they do in France. Or a ship-wrecked swimmer becomes exhausted, and the shark smells that he's in a weak state. Like all Polynesian fishermen, Christian trails his fish at the end of a long line. If the shark wants the fish, he can take it without going near the man. If you're fit, and not afraid, sharks won't attack you—as a rule.

I ought to have been happy on the *Carmellia*. Enjoying the physical life, the swimming, fishing, running along the beaches. And I would have been if Christian had been less unkind to me. While Tom and Nelly looked on—which didn't help—he acted as though he despised me, tried to hurt me. It seems un-thinkable now, to us both, but it happened. I had to undergo every humiliation, every insult, blows. He was working off all his complexes, repressions on me. And as that kind of scene appears amusing to people without much character themselves, who have no very clear idea of their own make-up, we provided an entertaining spectacle for our travelling companions.

So I swallowed a bottle of barbiturates. And instead of leaving me to die in peace, they made me sick. I spent two days in a comatose state, more wretched than ever, in body and spirit. For me life was over and there was no such thing as happiness.

I don't know if it was because of his highly alcoholic diet, but at the end of his seven months cruise to the Society Islands, Tom fell sick. Kidney trouble, I think. We had to go back to Papeete. We spent Christmas on board. We had hardly any money left. I started working in a travel agency; taking tourists round the island.

Christian, who had learnt a lot about the sea on the *Carmellia*, looked around at the harbour, on the off chance. And he saw the *Walborg*, a gigantic fore-and-aft schooner, which had been a Baltic cargo-ship for eighty years. A young Swede, Böse, had bought it for a song, and refitted it. He remade all the sails himself, by hand, hundreds and hundreds of square yards of them, made of cotton. Nothing on the boat was modern: no bottle screws but dead-eyes from the time of Christopher Columbus. A huge square sail which you no longer see, but which is very effective in following winds.

The boys were looking for a crewman, but didn't want a girl: it was hard enough sailing this great boat anyway. Christian went alone. I was to join him later, in New Zealand.

However I felt very lost when the *Walborg* sailed majestically out of the harbour. I was alone in Tahiti. I couldn't see my family, I was still on leave without pay from the Post Office, and only had my travel agency work. And I thought I would never see Christian again, although I hadn't told him so.

Christian learnt a lot on the *Walborg*, from these four lads who had already been everywhere: Sweden, France, the Mediterranean, the Atlantic, the Caribbean Islands, Jamaica, Panama, etc. They were great blond creatures, real Vikings. They had very poor food on the boat and not a moment's rest. At least half the day was taken up with deck work: emptying the bilges, sluicing the deck to keep it damp enough, mending sails, scraping the bowsprit, the masts, fighting the constant wear and tear.

The engine never worked. In principle, to start it, you had to pre-heat one cylinder with a blow-lamp. But it never worked. It was a huge diesel which weighed tons: the fly-wheel was gigantic. You had to get it going with bottles of compressed air which were always empty. So they never used it. Luckily the skipper, Böse, was an incomparable sailor. Christian later told me admiringly about their arrival in Raiatea. The island is surrounded by coral: you go into a bottleneck and then find yourself in the lagoon, which is only 200 metres wide. But the boat was speeding on. How do you turn, in a following wind, without an engine, when you know the manœuvring space needed by the *Walborg*? They were sailing at full speed. They had to gybe, that is, turn from sailing with the wind dead astern, into the wind, because the coral reef was directly in front of them. The tiller was no use alone. Böse, very cool and calm, took in the mainsheet—the mainsail on schooners is at the back —hauling on it determinedly. The wind caught the back of the boat, Böse let out the foresails, and the *Walborg* literally turned on the spot. 'It was incredible,' Christian told me. 'That great bulk, and going so fast. We were saved.'

The Viking crew made quite an impression arriving at the Cook Islands, with every sail set. These islands, which belong to New Zealand, have kept puritan rules from the oppressive era of English colonization, which the inhabitants find hard to take. Alcohol is prohibited, so they make 'bush beer', which they ferment in great iron vats. The Vikings had a good supply of alcohol on the *Walborg*, being heavy drinkers. There was a rave up, streams of girls on board. Neither the Swedes nor Christian wanted to go any farther. They indulged in a riot of drink and girls, who spent the day in their bunks. They never saw daylight.

They finally reached New Zealand. It was Christian's first long ocean crossing. It was then that he learnt to navigate by the stars. He was never idle: as he was the most agile it was always he who had to climb up the mast, when necessary. One day the tail of a cyclone hit the *Walborg* when Christian was on the squaresail yard. He still doesn't quite know how he managed not to fall off. The voyage lasted three months.

When Christian found himself on land once more, he felt an unaccustomed buoyancy and strength. He felt as though the world belonged to him. It is like an extraordinary drug, that you have within yourself and which the sea releases. Nothing is impossible when you reach this point of control over your body.

In Auckland the crew split up. Each went his own way.

Christian had already written to me from their ports of call; letters full of love and enthusiasm. He wrote from Auckland telling me to join him. And so in Tahiti I too began taking instant photos, to pay for my fare to New Zealand.

During this time Christian was also taking photographs, but on a rather different footing, with the two leading fashion photographers in Auckland who worked for Australian *Vogue*. These two Scotsmen introduced him to their models as the 'top French fashion photographer'. He passed his time surrounded by screens, projectors and gorgeous girls.

When I arrived in Auckland, the two associate photographers had split up, and Christian was no longer working. Neither of us had a sou. But Christian told me firmly: 'I know how to sail. I've learnt enough now to know that I want my own boat.'

From that day on, we lived with the idea of getting a boat. To make a bit of money we started to work in a big store. I sold cosmetics and Christian was in stock control.

'If you go to evening classes,' we were told, 'you'll get on.'

Well, yes. But an employee's life wasn't much fun. Christian with his packing-cases, and I standing behind my counter all day. At the end of the week we got our pay: according to the law of the land, mine was half that of Christian, because I was a woman. I wouldn't stand for it, and Christian backed me up. So we took our £30 (£20 + £10) and stalked out of the shop by the main door as if we were clients. It was marvellous to be in the street again. We strolled along completely happy and carefree, feeling as if we had just come out of prison.

And we found ourselves in a Pan-American plane on our way back to Tahiti. We decided it was the only place we knew where we could gather the funds to buy our first boat—our *Alpha*.

We arrived in Tahiti at ten in the morning in brilliant sunshine. Once more, Christian was arriving as he had done before, without family or relations—there was no question of seeing my family—and with no money. But he had inspired me with his faith and we both had one aim, one idea only: to get the money to buy a yacht.

We got a room at the cheapest hotel in Papeete. Put our rucksack in the corner of the room. We hired a scooter, bought two Polaroid cameras and a box of film, all on credit.

We told ourselves: 'Now all Tahiti belongs to us. In a few weeks, or months, we'll buy our boat.'

It was June. We worked day and night for six months without a break. We had to win. To get our first boat, achieve the first most difficult step, starting from scratch to get the 50,000 new francs we would need.

We did what Christian had had such success with on his arrival in Tahiti, but on a grand scale; we exploited the instant-photo field methodically, relentlessly. It was in fact a goldmine. Arrivals and departures at the airport. Filmstars mingling with the crowds, the new arrivals being rapturously greeted. A holiday mood, with flowers everywhere. At each arrival or departure of a plane the whole island is there, with music playing, and the whole scene is charged with emotion. Everyone wants a photograph. In this relaxed, friendly, happy and carefree atmosphere, where life is one long holiday, with dancing and singing, we worked to the rhythm of our cameras—click—click—click.

And the money poured in. To keep up this frenetic pace, we had rented a comfortable house. We bought a car, an extra camera each, electronic flashes: in view of the money which came in it was sensible to invest. So as not to run out of film, we bought it by the crate-load. We ate a lot of raw fish and fruit to make up for our lack of sleep, because we were at all the celebrations, every night.

Tahiti was no longer poor as it had been when I was a child, after the war. Tahitians, who can count on never being cold or hungry—because the island is one large vegetable garden—spend everything they earn, feel no need to look ahead, save, stock-up. So money flowed freely, and some of it came our way, as we sped everywhere taking our photographs.

In the harbour we saw the great navigators, Moitessier, Deshumeurs, Paul Smet, and others, on board their sea birds, their steel-hulled boats of 9.50 metres—and our boat took shape: it would be a steel-hulled sloop of 9.50 metres. Christian wrote to all the shipyards.

Our nerves were getting ragged with all the work. To relax, we went swimming. And there, stretched on the sand, we didn't talk about getting married, or children, but only about boats.

And one day Christian said, almost solemnly: 'We've got just enough to buy the boat. I've had a reply from a Dutch boat-yard, at Dokkum. I'm going to go there to order it.'

I would have to spend four months alone in Tahiti again.

A few days after Christian left, I realized I was pregnant.

Having put down the first instalment in Dokkum, Christian went to the Côte d'Azur. He was looking for second-hand gear for his first boat: charts, a sextant, anchors. He met an American on a fourteen-metre schooner which he had had built, all in teak, in Hong Kong. He needed a crewman to go to Hawaii. Christian couldn't go that far: he wanted to oversee the building of the boat, he had further instalments to pay, and he had to hunt around like a scrap dealer for all the second-hand gear. When the boat had been paid for, there would be very little money left over for sailing it, and a new sextant costs 2,000 francs, a chart ten francs—and you need hundreds of them—an anchor 1,000 francs, and so on.

'That doesn't matter,' said the American. 'I've got a fast boat. We'll go as far as Gibraltar. I'll drop you off there and you can take the train to Amsterdam to go and see your boat, pay the second instalment, etc. You can then join me by plane—I'll pay for everything—we'll cross the Atlantic, and you can come back by plane.'

Which was what they did. Christian recruited his brother Didier as crew, and while the boat was being built, he had the pleasure of crossing the Atlantic, picking up the gear he wanted on the way.

Meanwhile, in Paris, he had received the letter telling him I was pregnant. I was sure he would be quite indifferent, as it didn't enter into our scheme of things at all. Even I didn't dare let myself be happy at the idea of having a baby. We'd only thought about a boat.

I cried when I read Christian's enthusiastic letter: he was wild with joy and told me to join him in France immediately. I was numb with surprise. I did what he told me: sold all the equipment and got on the first passenger steamer.

'I've never been more in love with you', he told me, 'than when I saw you walking down the gangplank in your white mini-dress with your little stomach.'

The arrival of the steamer from Tahiti in Marseille is a

moving sight. Tahitian families living in France, so far from their homeland in the sun, come to meet their friends and relations, whose brown skins remind them of the sea and the palm trees.

We arrived in Dokkum with our rucksack, two bowls, two plates, and the money to pay the final instalment on the boat. At the north of the canal, we saw our *Alpha*—gleaming white. We held hands like children. We couldn't believe it.

A solemn moment. Christian took the tiller of his first boat, the first boat of his own. Until then he had sailed as a crew, had obeyed orders. And now he was the skipper, and a father-to-be, but for the moment, naturally, he couldn't be expected to think of anything but this white bird, already skimming towards the sea.

In three months we had crossed Europe along the canals. We were eager to hoist the sails, but had to wait until the Mediterranean. Holland, Belgium, France. On the Seine we stupidly nearly lost the *Alpha*. In a lock, our propeller got caught in some ropes. We couldn't move. An enormous barge was descending on us. This mass, with its engines stopped, was still making way and couldn't stop. The lock loudspeakers were going mad telling us to clear the way. The siren howled. Christian dived into the pea-soup of dead rats which is what the Seine is on the outskirts of Paris, and succeeded in extricating the propeller at the last moment. I was already in tears of despair: our brand new *Alpha*. Christian managed to slam her against the side, and the barge passed with a few millimetres to spare.

We were towed to immediately opposite the Île Saint-Louis. We stayed there a month. Christian had to go down into the filthy water again to mend the propeller. And we set off once more, longing to be on the open sea.

The canal de Bourgogne was very calm, but going down the Rhône was quite another matter. It's a very turbulent river, strewn with gravel beds, rocks and whirlpools. We should have taken on a pilot at Lyon, but it was too expensive. We had entered on our period of frantic economizing.

'We've got to get as far as Tahiti,' Christian said.

Rationing was strict.

When we got to the Camargue—a foretaste of the Amazon—

there were no more buoys. With the combined speed of the current and the engine Christian hardly had time to read the references on the charts, instructions such as 'keep within fifteen metres of the bank', or 'head for the right bank at an angle of 45 degrees', or 'keep at a distance of ten metres from the right bank', 'steer over to port again', and so on. It is imperative to follow these instructions if you are to avoid the shoals. If you don't follow them metre by metre the boat is lost.

At Port-Saint-Louis we experienced the amazing sight of the turbulent Rhône flowing into the sea, the shore covered with wreckage and deadwood. Twisted branches, old packing-cases, toys lost by children on a nearby beach, no doubt packed with bodies now in August. But we sailed out to sea. We raised the masts, hoisted the sails. The second solemn moment since Christian took the tiller of the *Alpha* in Dokkum: our white bird spread her wings.

We were heading for Saint-Tropez, because Christian's godmother has a small vineyard near there, at Luc-en-Provence, and we had to start thinking about somewhere to be while I had the baby: time was running short.

I was eight months pregnant when we got married at Pégomas, near Cannes, where Christian's father is a doctor. An elderly American couple whom we met at the last minute acted as witnesses. They gave us our only wedding presents. We were on our own and it was completely informal: I wore a mini skirt and one of Christian's shirts.

Until October, we 'tried out' the *Alpha* in the Mediterranean, then there was the wine harvest at the vineyard. I cooked and washed up for the men, tried to forget how tired I was. Christian helped with the grape-gathering—we needed the money. And my baby was born in Brignoles, on 18 October of the year of grace 1967.

Three days after Laurence was born, Christian decided to go as far as Casablanca with his brother Didier, so that the *Alpha* could cross the Mediterranean before the winter. The Mediterranean is the most dangerous of all seas, particularly in winter. They would steer a direct course towards Casablanca, via the Balearic Islands, Almeria and Gibraltar. It felt very strange being left on my own with such a small baby—my first. I was anxious to rejoin them at Casablanca, especially as a letter from

Christian, posted in the Balearics, was most enthusiastic about all the *Alpha*'s good points. I used the 400 francs Christian had left me sparingly, so that I would be able to pay my fare on the steamer *Ancerville*—which would be 280 francs. I had to live for a fortnight in Luc on the remaining 120 francs, and then take a train to Marseille. And what would I do on arrival in Casablanca? Christian had only been able to give me a rough idea of when he would get there.

However, tired as I was after the birth, I didn't want to wait any longer. In Marseille Christian's family didn't want me to set out with Laurence. I was amazed to hear his nearest and dearest call him an irresponsible wretch, and tell me that I shouldn't join him but stay in France, where they would help me. But in spite of my tiredness, and all the difficulties, I felt that something precious bound me to Christian, and that it was not the moment to give in. I arrived in Casablanca with twenty francs in my pocket. I was keeping them to buy a present for Christian.

The yacht club where the *Alpha* was supposed to have arrived, was a good way off. Four kilometres. I didn't know what taxis cost, and didn't want to risk taking one in case I couldn't pay. So I walked. Seeing me walking along in the dust and heat, with my baby on my arm, taxi-drivers drew up beside me. I shook my head. Finally one of them said : 'I'll take you—you needn't pay.' So I got in. I shall never forget this kind gesture.

Christian was there. He hadn't come to meet me because he didn't know exactly what day the boat would arrive. I thought he could have at least tried to find out. But since I was there at last, it didn't seem the moment to begin complaining.

And our *Alpha* was rocking gently in front of the boat club. I was full of emotion at the thought that it would be our house, our home. We were often told that she seemed larger inside than out. She is 9.50 metres long and 2.75 metres wide. You can stand up inside, fore and aft. Drawing 1.65 metres of water, and with a steel hull, you have height below decks even in the forecastle where there is a double bunk. We only used this when in port. The door of the washroom can then be opened to separate us completely from the saloon. This has two large bunks which we use at sea, and a long box-bunk which goes under the cockpit, in the stern, on the starboard side. In

Casablanca Christian was collecting provisions for the crossing, and the bunk was covered with sacks of potatoes and onions. Laurence slept at my feet on the port side, on my bunk. At the head of the bunk were the stove and sink. We had three square metres to move around in, round the folding table. The cupboard was opposite the washroom. A good light was assured by extra large portholes, which could be protected by steel shutters if necessary.

I stared at the *Alpha* admiringly as if I had never seen her before. All white inside and out, except for the inner planking and a few panels of polished mahogany. I found her at Casablanca still beautifully white. Christian had taken advantage of the low tide to repaint the water-line. But she already bore the scars of a rough passage. The beautiful polished mast was pitted from the storm which Christian and Didier had met off Ibiza.

The skipper seemed happy to see me come aboard with our three-week-old Laurence. But the dust-ups he had experienced in the Mediterranean had made him a little worried: 'It's rather small after all.'

I replied, 'Oh she's grown a lot already, she weighs four kilos.' Not very much for a little deck-hand.

Christian looked at the mast, firmly held by the beautiful rigging of his dreams, and touched the shrouds. He said as if to reassure me: 'It would be good enough for a fifteen-metre schooner.'

My idea of Morocco was coloured by the rosy memories which Christian had of his ten years' life in the *bled*. I thought we would make pilgrimages to Sidi-Slimane, Rabat, Moulay-Bousslem. I longed to pack a rucksack and go to Marrakesh. So I found it hard to understand Christian's violent desire to leave as soon as possible for warmer seas, especially as we had spent more than two years in the Pacific. But it was the sailor not the man speaking. And the sailor is the slave of the sea.

The seasons impose a timetable on us. The passage to Tahiti is the same for all boats that want to take advantage of a warm tropical temperature and the trade winds, and to reduce the risk of cyclones and bad weather. You must leave the Mediterranean before the end of autumn and get beyond the Atlantic coast of Morocco. The best time to go from the Canaries to the

West Indies is between October and March. Then you must leave the West Indies before the northern summer, so as to avoid cyclones, which are frequent in those parts towards the middle of the year. And in the Pacific it is a good idea to get to French Polynesia before the hot season, which begins in November and may also lead to heavy storms.

It isn't a good idea to leave your boat in the harbour for a few days while you go inland. You never know what might happen. If a mooring-line or an anchor is stolen the boat will drift away. If the harbour is not well-sheltered, a gust of wind can slam her up against the quay. One of our friends, an Australian, recently lost a boat like this in Patagonia—a superb steel-hulled seventeen-metre yacht: the skipper had gone off for three days. The wind got up, a mooring-line parted, and the *Solo* sank. Yet the skipper was an experienced sailor.

The time of year, the dangers of a boat alone in port, were an ideal pretext to leave Casablanca as soon as possible. Or more precisely to reach the West Indies as soon as possible. Christian admitted later that he couldn't really believe that his dream had come true until he could drop anchor from his own boat in a turquoise lagoon, fringed with white sand and coconut palms.

We only stayed in Casablanca for three days, during which we explored the old Medina. Between two feeds we wandered through the Arab quarter like lovers. Surrounded by veils and trailing robes I felt naked in my mini skirt. Stalls of everything one could possibly eat overflowed on to pavements in little heaps or pyramid-like mounds. I tasted sweetmeats dripping with honey. There was a strong smell of spices, mixed with that of the sea and of *patchouli*. I noticed the way women carried their babies on their backs: these children were lucky not to spend their days alone in a 'nice clean room', or in a park 'out of harm's way'. But Laurence was asleep on the boat, because Christian had assured me *souks* were the breeding ground for every imaginable germ.

We got in the rest of our stores. Christian haggled everywhere. The stallholders seemed to expect it. One got the impression that to do otherwise would have disappointed them. But coming from an island where one doesn't bargain, where one doesn't remark on a price—although these are sometimes

ridiculously high—from sheer politeness, I couldn't help feeling
a little embarrassed. But I soon realized that it was almost a rite,
or obligation, a game in which neither side is the dupe. But a
game played by immensely poor people nevertheless.

One could live on almost nothing in Casablanca, which was
fortunate considering the state of our purse when we bought our
provisions. I have still got a careful list which the skipper made
in the log book:

12 large 1 kilogramme loaves	0.30 francs each
5 kilos of oranges	0.30 francs a kilo
3 dozen eggs	1.60 a dozen
1 kg fresh butter	3.00 francs

All vegetables, whether fresh or dried, were 20 or 30 centimes a
kilo. We have often thought about that list since.

When you see how primitive the working classes are, you
realize that the franc is worth its weight in gold here. The
abject poverty which surrounded us inspired a desire to get
'them' out of there and at the same time to take to our heels.
But not pity, because one felt they were very proud, and very
dignified. I admire these people who have managed to keep
their traditions intact in spite of modern European civilization
which is firmly installed on their doorstep. Because as soon as
you leave the market, Casablanca is an ultra-modern town, with
luxury flats and wide streets. The Arabs slip unobtrusively
along, adapt, and continue to live their dignified lives, remaining completely Moroccan. Moreover you feel that they enjoy
a new independence which at times borders on arrogance, and I
can understand this. From a very early age I was unable to see
why anyone should consider a country his because he discovered
it before his neighbours. Christopher Columbus arriving in
America and saying 'This is Spanish territory' seems illogical
to me. I have seen in France too, how even 100 kilometres can
make integration difficult: in les Rousses, a little village in the
Jura, a family which came from Besançon or Lons-le-Saunier
years ago are still labelled 'strangers'.

Casablanca is also the yacht club, with its visitors' book which
you leaf through eagerly looking for the names of those who

have set out before you. Each yacht which passes through is invited by the sailing club to leave its name, accompanied by a photograph if possible. We found several boats which we had seen in Tahiti there, in particular the *Vencia* belonging to Pierre and Catherine Deshumeurs and Bernard and Françoise Moitessier's *Joshua*. We were careful to note particulars of our own voyage, including our extra hand of four kilos. A solemn ritual, which made us feel we were joining the band of great sailors. And it's the last message which one leaves at any port, before setting out for the unknown, towards death perhaps: because the sea is merciless.

Casablanca is Loïck Fougeron, a good friend to all sailors. A little enigmatic, he is always there when you need a helping hand, or invaluable information for getting a repair done, or having automatic steering gear fitted.

Casablanca is the concrete sink at the foot of the yacht club steps I monopolized every morning, plunging my hands in the icy water. I had imagined all kinds of difficult situations before Laurence was born, but not washing nappies.

Casablanca was all the yachts which were leaving at the same time as us for the West Indies. They were all talking of voyaging round the world, a dream which sometimes comes to fruition, and which is satisfying in itself. Of twenty boats that year, we would be the only one to reach Tahiti. We had travelled round the world several times already, with the help of a plane or sea-plane here, a steamer or someone else's boat there. Now we were in our own cockleshell, going back to Tahiti in search of the sun, and desert islands; to work there for a while. I was well aware that we had not only chosen this life because of the call of the sea. It was also because we had no profession which would enable us to live in a town where we would have a house and garden, a swimming-pool or the sea nearby, skiing or riding, and a life-style which would give us time to see each other and our children.

It was to preserve our family life and to live in the natural surroundings we loved, and to satisfy our desire for travel, that we chose a solution within our reach; a small boat. It was our sea-borne mini-car, our gipsy caravan.

We met some friends by chance at the yacht club. On Jean-Claude Brouillet's *Erna*, a superb and beautifully painted

Laurence takes a bath

Laurence inspects the jib

Christian Guillain

seventeen-metre ketch, we found Eric Deschamps, who had lost the *Railleuse* on a reef in the Tuamotu Archipelago—the Danger Islands.

The *Erna* had just come into the harbour. The rattling of a chain being let out attracted our attention. A few minutes later a Zodiac put out, and I shouted: 'Eric!'

Christian dived and swam rapidly towards him.

'Good heavens,' Eric said, 'you here. Is that your boat? And baby? I've got one hour to get in some stores before we leave. Rendezvous at Las Palmas.'

Just like that. What more natural than to make a rendez-vous for a spot a few hundred miles away. In a good wind.

On the *Mamari*, an 8.50-metre sloop, we found Ken and Marie. On the *Ain-Taiba*, the Valin brothers: they had had it built as a modified version of the *Joshua*. They had constructed the interior themselves. While Henri explained the advantages of a vegetarian diet to me, I watched a child of six playing on the deck of the *Anahita*, the late Bernicot's boat. I couldn't repress a shudder when Henri said: 'Bernicot fell from that mast, to the deck: a fine end for a sailor.'

There was no time to get to know the other boats which, under flags of every colour, only stopped long enough to restock with provisions. But we would meet the *Solmar* with her varnished hull, and the *Rhâ* with her Swiss flag later on.

The meteorological office announced that the storm had died down at sea. The wind had moderated. The others had already set sail for the Canaries. It was vital to leave at once; and on 30 November we set sail at about ten o'clock. Loïck had given our automatic steering gear, our beloved Gigi, a final inspec-tion, and had shaken his head doubtfully. On the jetty, where several members of the yacht club had gathered, a 40-year-old paterfamilias had made a last attempt to convince us of the folly of our undertaking.

'You don't have to go. Spend the winter here and give her a chance to grow a bit.'

And they made the suggestion which was made at every port, without fail: 'Leave her with us: we'll send her on by plane as soon as you're safely across.'

Leave my daughter? She was part of the adventure, as we were. Loïck threw us the last mooring-line, and I took the tiller while the skipper hoisted the jib. We never use the engine if it can be avoided.

The wind filled the canvas. A furrow of white foam sprang up in our wake. I loved hearing the 'flip, flap' as the sail unfurled. The *Alpha* flew on, with her wings spread wide, irresistibly drawn towards the open sea, or *moana* as it is called in Tahitian.

Christian repeated his anti-seasickness prescription, as if I had never set foot on a boat before: 'Drink plenty of water, eat well, wrap up so you don't get cold, and rest as much as you can.' A marvellous programme.

Christian was at the helm. I hurriedly stretched myself out at his feet, on the cockpit seat, to feed Laurence.

V

Christmas At Sea

THE TENTH DAY. It is nightfall, and there is a light directly
ahead of us. Four flashes every thirty seconds—Las Palmas.
Land, wonderful land lies ahead. Our friends will have arrived
already and must be worrying about us.

While I sleep Christian steers us towards the shore. It takes all
night. At breakfast, at about six, I find him exhausted from
lack of sleep but smiling radiantly: 'Look.'

In front of us, under heavy rain clouds, lies Las Palmas.

We are very excited, and deliriously happy to have completed the first ten-day crossing alone with our baby. We
suddenly realize everything that might have happened: a
storm, and heavy seas with Laurence being sick. We're delighted that we're all three alive, and in good form. We begin
to understand that to be alive is not to be dead, not to be lost
overboard.

Another yacht, a little ahead of us, is also sailing towards Las
Palmas. As it's raining we can't make it out very clearly. It has
two masts and its rigging looks like that of Bernard Moitessier's
Joshua. Or is it the *Ain-Taiba*, with Didier on board? No, it
can't be. It should have arrived long ago. It's obviously using
its engine. It's the only thing to do with so little wind and the
endless rain.

At seven Christian starts the engine. A good little ten-hp
diesel which, with much putting from its one cylinder, brought
the *Alpha* 4,000 kilometres across Europe by river and canal.
For an hour and a half, in the rain which trickles under our
oilskins, we try to make some headway, make up for lost time.

At midday we're still at sea and the sun still isn't showing
itself. Christian starts the engine again and at about four
o'clock we reach Las Palmas harbour, where there is a heavy
swell. Laurence's nappies bedizen the guardrails.

The *Ain-Taiba* got in this morning, and it was her we saw earlier on. There's a piercing whistle—Didier signing to us to go alongside the *Ain-Taiba*. There's not very much room in the harbour, even for a small boat. You can't see the jetties. Cargo ships and Japanese fishing-boats, several metres tall, berth there permanently. The only corner we can see is a long way from the centre of the town, and with dust blowing over it in thick clouds. Finally, having fixed the fenders, I throw the mooring lines to Didier.

'I was very worried not to find you here when I arrived this morning,' he says. 'With Laurence. Then I thought perhaps it was you we saw early this morning. How is my god-daughter and niece?'

'Fine,' says Christian. 'We didn't have any wind the first few days. It was maddening. The day before yesterday Gigi worked loose. But we managed. We didn't take watches because there wasn't any rush. How did you get on? I thought you'd be here long ago.'

'We got off course. I don't think the sextant was properly adjusted. We hugged the coast as far as Agadir. We took exactly the same time as you did.'

Obviously a day or two either way doesn't matter to us. The main thing is not to tire ourselves out unnecessarily. There is no cosy house waiting for us at the other end where we can build up our strength. If you want to live face to face with nature like this for any length of time you must respect her laws. So we discipline ourselves to go to bed and get up with the sun all the year round: in the Tropics we have twelve hours sleep. We don't eat highly spiced or much cooked food. Vegetables are eaten raw or steamed in their skins in salt water. We don't drink coffee, or even tea, or any alcoholic drinks.

After ten days of healthy existence on the open sea, the polluted, foggy air that surrounds us here is getting us down. Las Palmas is abominably dirty. The water is covered with a disgusting layer of thick black oil, and anything dropped overboard is completely unusable.

From the quay the boats are moored as follows: three cargo ships docked alongside one another, a fishing smack, the beautiful *Erna*, the *Ain-Taiba* and the *Alpha*. It won't be easy going ashore with the baby. But we're delighted to find Ken,

Eric and all the crew of the *Ain-Taiba* with their guitars, singing to the frenzied beat of *'des sous, des sous, c'est ça qui nous rend fous'*.

They rush up to look at our little deck-hand, with her plump little dimpled face. Laurence smiles happily and gazes enquiringly at them. Ken shakes his head, thinking of Marie who will join him in Barbados, in the south of the Lesser Antilles.

'You're crazy,' says Jean-Claude Brouillet. 'But I don't know. They'll be the happiest years of your life.'

Eric, who is wondering behind his heavy horn-rimmed spectacles how one can find a mere 'digestive tract' interesting, suddenly sees the attraction, and photographs her from every angle.

When we've seen to the boat, Jean-Claude invites us to dinner. It's a welcome break after ten days at sea, after our day-long efforts to make our way in the rain into this dirty, wind-swept harbour.

On the *Erna*, where the décor, music and laughter remind us of Tahiti and the sun, we can forget for a while that it's only ten degrees in our cabin, and that we have no shower or washing machine, or running water. On this superb yacht where every-one has his own wash-basin, with running hot water, I gaze longingly at all these refinements and am amazed to think that it was all part of my life once—three years ago. I realize that I'll never again have all those little things which make a woman's life easier. But I'm happy.

Jean-Claude gives us ten rolls of reversal colour film and a strong safety belt. So we'll have a colour souvenir of our first long voyage together. And thanks to the safety harness, I shan't be afraid when Christian goes to set a storm sail up forward.

Our stop at Las Palmas is purely utilitarian. We need to take on stores for the Atlantic crossing and repair the automatic pilot. But the port has nothing to offer a small boat. We have to cross six other boats to reach the jetty.

The town of Las Palmas is very spread out, as we soon find from our long daily treks to get our post. Every day we go to the yacht club, two kilometres from the harbour. The main post office is even farther and there are letters waiting for us there, and in the harbour-master's office. Letters are very important to us at sea. They are the only means we have of keeping in touch with friends and relations—those one sends are as precious as those one receives. Three weeks without any news can sometimes cause one's family to be worried enough to send out search parties.

Las Palmas is a typical tourist resort, with its smiling, wheedling poverty; you never know if someone's going to do you a favour or swindle you. With its duty-free shops where you find cheap walkie-talkie sets, cameras and radios, together with every kind of souvenir in wood or plastic. Another—rather special—tourist item: boys and girls of sixteen to twenty-two from Scandinavia or the States, roaming the world and living haphazardly. On a beautiful beach fringed with palm trees, like an illustration in a travel agent's brochure, there is a notice saying: LEAVE YOUR LEFTOVER FOOD HERE. Parties of rich tourists descend on the beach to picnic. When the visitors have gone, a beautifully tanned, bearded youth or a blonde Swedish girl come and collect the food. 'It's quite simple,' a young American tells me. He has come to live there for a month in a hut he has built on the beach. 'When a steamer comes in, all the passengers get off armed with a little lunch basket supplied by the ship. There's always too much food. Why throw it away? They're embarrassed, and delighted to see the notice.'

When these youngsters grow tired of the place, they try to sail on elsewhere, aboard one of the many yachts that call in at Las Palmas.

The town is very Spanish. Beautiful smooth golden skins that never look skinny or naked. Shy faces which reveal a warm sensuality. Incessant chatter, and great dignity of manner.

For the last three days Christian has been mending the rudder of the self-steering gear himself, using the workshop of a local carpenter, who is kindly letting him borrow tools and wood. I've seen the rudder blade. It's thick, and heavier than the last one, which split. I hope Gigi will soon be mended. I feel as though we've lost a part of ourselves. Then she's back—with the sun. We slip the mooring lines. En route for Fuerteventura— Gigi's back and we must try her out. Didier, tempted by the thought of underwater fishing, jumps aboard with his kit which he throws into the forecastle.

Contrary to all logic, we are sailing with a head wind. It's fun. At nightfall the wind drops. There is almost a full moon and we sing on deck until about midnight to warm ourselves up. The *Alpha* drifts peacefully on till dawn. We laze about for two days and the boys fish. At Lobos, where we drop anchor in a stormy bay, there are some small cube-like bungalows surrounded by white rocks and sand for tourists who like the desert. The barrenness is alleviated by a solitary palm tree. One wonders how it got there.

A strong east wind takes us back to Las Palmas, where it is grey and raining again.

22 *December*. Where will we spend Christmas? No one dares ask, and the question hangs over us, oppressive as the lowering grey sky, and depressing as the endless drizzle which prevents the washing drying. I was hoping for a decorated tree for Laurence, and mountains of presents. She's just two months old. But it's not for me to decide.

I wash and wash, pumping up the fresh water. I've counted: it takes twelve strokes of the pump to get a kettleful, 24 for a bowlful, 47 to wash and twice 47, that is 94, to rinse. It's maddening. Especially when you've got to bend over the sink.

And it's nearly Christmas. I'm miserable. I haven't got any presents to give. When I got to Casablanca, Christian asked me if I had any money left. I had hidden away my remaining twenty francs in an envelope, under Laurence's mattress, so that I could get a present for Christian, and one for Laurence, and Didier—just small presents. But he asked me if I'd got any money because he hadn't any cash for the stores. I said: 'Yes, but . . . '

'Good. Give it to me then.'

And I handed it over miserably, without saying anything. He might have guessed—but how could he?

I was broken hearted. Christmas was spoilt: it wouldn't be Christmas for me. It's hard when you've got a baby two months old. Christmas is far more what you give than what you receive. Christmas is other people's happiness. Christmas. Where will we spend Christmas?

Christian bustles around. Boxes of provisions arrive and, to our amazement, disappear into the lockers. It's astonishing how much a boat will hold. It can't be true, that we're going to spend Christmas at sea. I'm so tired. What shall I do?

The boat is filling up, and settling lower in the water. Didier installs all his things: he's leaving the *Ain-Taiba*. No one tells me anything, but I hear them say we'll be filled up with oil and water tomorrow. Are we leaving then? And it's 22 December today. The problem of my Christmas presents goes round and round in my tired brain. Mouchka has given me some for Christian, his brother and Laurence. But I haven't got anything for them. If we could only stay here, we could go and sing carols, play the guitar with the others, be poor and lonely together, and it would be a proper Christmas.

I timidly suggest: 'Surely we aren't going to leave on Christmas Eve.'

'Why not? What do you want to stay in this awful, filthy, depressing harbour for? Our first Christmas at sea will be wonderful. It's a family occasion. Anyway, we've made all the arrangements. We leave tomorrow morning, as soon as we've been filled up with water.'

'My washing isn't dry.'

'Too bad. Anyway it never stops raining here.'

Too tired to answer, I see myself sinking in an endless mound of napkins which won't dry and which I can only hang up four by four, while the others remain in a soggy mess slowly rotting in a bucket tucked away out of sight. Will I have enough to keep my baby dry? The problem obsesses me, wears me out.

It's still drizzling at Las Palmas, and the harbour is still rough. The boats moored alongside each other rattle and bump at regular intervals with a gloomy clanking. Gigi's white shape is silhouetted against the dark, menacing sky. I'm wearing a grey jersey outfit. Everything's grey, tonight.

The wind blew all night, whistling in the rigging, and the clatter of metal and wood kept us awake. Christian got up three times to secure the halyards of the mainsail and jib which were beating against the mast. And this morning as if by magic, the sky is blue, and the sun is shining, making everything look brighter. Ideal sailing weather.

It's now ten o'clock. We go round the harbour to say goodbye to our friends: 'See you in Barbados! Merry Christmas. Happy New Year.'

Laurence is on deck, well wrapped up in her little nest.

The skipper notes in the log book: 'Left harbour 10.10. Good north-east wind, about force six. Gigi's working well.'

And he streams the log for the first few days.

Suddenly, there's a mass of birds right in front of us.

'France! Quick—the line!'

It's a school of tunny fish or bonitos: the tunny fish chase shoals of little fish which leap in the air in their fright and are caught by the sea birds. You only need a lure, which shines like a small fish, for the tunny fish to bite. In Polynesia they use a bit of gleaming mother-of-pearl, slightly curved, and crescent-shaped, without a hook; the bonito takes the lure, the fisherman draws in the line with a wide sweeping movement, and the fish lands on his legs which he's covered with a gunny bag. The fish unhooks itself of its own accord, and the fisherman casts his line again immediately. His basket is soon filled. Sharks usually join in this bloodthirsty sport; they are after the bonito. Sometimes the boat brings back a sword-fish.

We use an ordinary spoon armed with a hook. It's fixed to the few yards of wire attached to the end of the nylon line so that a large fish can't bite through it. As soon as the spoon touches the water there's a tug. Christian lands a fine six- or seven-kilo bonito. That's enough for us. We reel up the line, which could get tangled in the log.

I cut off some fillets straight away. We eat them raw, and I crush some to extract the juice, which Laurence thoroughly enjoys. I dice the rest into cubes to marinate in lemon juice, à la Tahitienne. The head—the best part—will make a delicious risotto for supper.

'Constant strong wind,' the log for the next day says. 'Impossible to run with the wind directly astern, because we veer too much to the west. On the quarter. Waves as high as the mast.'

Leaning against the engine, with my five-kilo baby in my arms, I admire the efficient way Gigi works. Every time a wave tries to bring us to, she firmly rights the seven- or eight-ton *Alpha* with a little movement of her 25 by 12 centimetre trimming tabs. To see the tops of the waves I have to raise my head as far as I can. They're like a wall in front of me. I can't bear to think what would happen if that great mass broke over us. But, being so low, we ought to sink like a barrel and re-emerge after the deluge—provided we hadn't shipped too much water. Being cautious and apprehensive by nature I'm amazed to feel

3*

safe. It's because I have faith in our skipper, and in the *Alpha*.
Metal casks aren't smashed by the sea.

It's a dramatic kind of Christmas Day. But nothing to what
Bernard Moitessier must have seen rounding Cape Horn. We're
all fighting against sea-sickness. Christian and Didier were sick
last night, but it wore off. I'm still feeling the effect of the
Marzine. But I can't take the smell of tobacco and Didier has
to smoke his Gauloises outside. It's a good idea anyway. There's
no question of opening the forehatch in this weather, and there's
not much ventilation. I don't want Laurence to breathe in
cigarette smoke.

Tonight the sunset is a wonderful blaze of red and mauve,
making the sea violet as the twilight deepens.

Nightfall, at sea, is a crucial moment. Before it's dark, you
must see that: the boat's perfectly in order; you've had a meal;
Laurence is in bed. The skipper has got to be able to find the
right sized spanner or the electric torch in the dark without a
moment's hesitation.

As it grows dark, Christian scans the horizon and casts an
expert eye over sea and sky. He estimates the strength of the
wind, and tries to foresee as best he can what kind of weather
there'll be during the next few hours.

At night there's no light and it's difficult to judge distances. If
the sky is overcast the darkness is complete. It's very difficult to
change a jib quickly. Even more difficult to see a seam which is
tearing. Although Gigi steers perfectly the skipper feels very
alone then and responsible for us all. He never sleeps deeply
but keeps a watch over the *Alpha*'s progress from his bunk.
Which is why we always leave the roof open and sleep under the
stars all the year round.

Underwater life becomes more alarming. Creatures become
phosphorescent. Plankton loom up in luminous green sheets.
Sometimes a bluish-green shape several metres long glides round
the boat like a ghost pursuing us. The silence, broken only by
the creaking of the *Alpha*, makes you shiver apprehensively. You
are in the middle of a black desert.

But tonight our skipper doesn't look as preoccupied as usual
at this time of day. He's happy. He hasn't even asked if supper
is ready. It isn't, because we'll dine late tonight, at about half
past eight. It's Christmas Eve.

Thanks to the *Erna*, our fare will be festive: a Cassegrain cassoulet instead of turkey. A Mont-Blanc praline mousse instead of a yule-log. And as a finishing touch, a small bottle of real Champagne. Unfortunately our stomachs aren't quite ready for such a rich meal. But . . .

'Christ the Saviour is born. Sing Choirs . . . ' Christian has just switched on the radio receiver. It's a surprise, because it's usually kept strictly for time checks; we have to save the batteries. And now, just by turning a switch, he has linked us to the rest of the world: 'Ring bells . . . Silent night, holy night . . . '

We only left the Canaries two days ago, but we're already a long way off. If we wanted to go back it would take at least ten days in this weather. And a month separates us from Barbados the other way. Lost in the middle of these huge waves we're safe in the *Alpha* as we keep our first Christmas at sea. And we are filled with wonder as the tiny cabin resounds with the voices of thousands of men and women like ourselves who are singing the same carols in every language: 'While shepherds watched . . . Adeste fideles . . . Oh Christmas Tree . . . Christians awake . . . Hark! The Herald Angels sing . . . ' We've never experienced anything like it. If only all the people who are singing tonight could know how it warms us on the *Alpha* this Christmas Eve, although we're each wearing two or three sweaters, and it's only fifteen degrees outside—and if we meet a submerged object in the dark our hull could split open, landing us in water four or five kilometres deep.

Our Christmas is very frugal. Christian is the only one who gives any presents: Didier a box of cigars, Laurence a little rubber lamb which makes a cheerful 'squeak, squeak' noise, and myself a beautiful stamp album. I'm miserable at not having anything to give. And yet filled with the marvellous joy of Christmas, because of this little 27 by 18 centimetre radio receiver.

We go to bed utterly exhausted, feeling more deprived than ever. No Christmas tree, no snow. No illuminated streets, or splendid dinner or piles of presents. Tonight Christmas is only these voices which belong to human beings like ourselves. 'I bring you good tidings . . . ' We're so happy we can't speak. We're not listening, we're *there*, part of Christmas. We're singing with the choirs and our own voices, our whole life, rings out from the little set. Each one recalls his childhood Christmasses. We relive them afresh, vividly, like old men savouring for the last time the joys and disappointments of a lifetime, as if we were about to die. Tonight we are there in the stable, and Laurence is our divine child. She's asleep, but I'm sure that she can feel our happiness as she lies there, that it enfolds her.

The rattling of her counting-frame wakes me from a deep sleep. The emotions of the previous evening have tired me out. When I sit up I see a little face smiling at the lamb hanging above her basket.

'Happy Christmas, Laurence! Your first Christmas.'

Didier's still asleep. I envy him. We can make a diabolical din all round him and he still doesn't wake up. If there's an emergency we have to shake him.

It's a lovely day and Laurence feeds hungrily. When she's full she goes on sucking for the fun of it, and plays with my dark hair. I'm touched by the utter confidence she has in me, and sometimes feel afraid of disappointing her. In her mother's arms, nothing untoward can happen.

'Ouch!'

I screamed so loudly that Laurence was scared. She screamed too, starting to cry. I'd spilt the boiling hot chocolate Christian made all over myself. Luckily none went on Laurence. Christian scrapes a large potato to make a cold poultice. Later I'll put on some grease. If it was more serious I'd give my leg a good soaking in salt water. When on land the best thing is to cover the burn immediately with the sap of a young banana tree.

After drowning, fire is the worst danger on a boat. We take every possible precaution. We have no petrol on board—our engine uses oil—and gas is in small cylinders. In fact, since these were filled in Las Palmas there's been a strong smell of leaking gas. The difficulty is that gas sinks to the bottom of the boat. To get rid of it you've got to extract it. If it is allowed to accumulate it will explode at the smallest spark. We ought to throw the cylinders overboard and use the Primus, which burns on paraffin. On checking we can't find a leak. But the smell? I open the locker under my bunk: the smell is so strong it knocks me back. Then I see a green streak, and am greatly relieved to discover what has happened: when we had the cylinders refilled we disconnected the pipe which joins the cylinder to the stove. The pipe is covered with a thick green liquid which makes the gas smell strongly if it is escaping. While the pipe was on the sink the liquid ran over the draining board and dripped into my locker. So there's no leak. I'd been imagining the *Alpha* exploding like the *Romance*. Her skipper was stranded in his bathing trunks on a minute dinghy all night after an explosion caused by a bottle of methylated spirits. He was almost frozen when luckily he was spotted by a cargo ship. After this scare we seriously consider getting a good Primus with two burners. But they're expensive.

I've got used to the large waves, but I limit my excursions on deck as much as possible, only going out when it's essential, to put the washing out for instance.

'Christian! the line's taut!'

But he's already there. The system he's set up in the cabin, which originally consisted of a line to the big toe of his left foot, has dislodged his pillow. He likes to know at once if a fish bites so that a bigger one won't come and snap it up—with the spoon. We've already lost at least three in this way. Didier and he haul in the line, winding it round a bit of board as they go along so that it won't get tangled.

A fine dorado weighing eight or ten kilos struggles on the deck, beating its great tail, while Laurence watches with a mixture of fear and delight. Its colours fade quickly: its blue and gold back changes to a luminous green and then to a dull grey. Its sulphur yellow belly rapidly becomes a dirty white. Its skin was perfectly smooth only a minute ago, and now it's rough, showing each scale.

'Look, Christian! It's got some eggs!'

We sprinkle the fish with lemon juice and it makes a fine feast. I make an incision by the head and round the gills, and the skin comes away easily. We fall on the deliciously fresh raw flesh like savages.

I've got a pain.

It's very localized, up by my appendix. A burning sensation, which comes and goes. It must be a slight inflammation of the ovary, which the doctor said I had when I was expecting

Laurence. But it gets worse and worse. Then stops. It must be my ovary. But it's hurting again.

My right side hurts, still in the same place. It's not getting any worse. It must be my ovary. I hope it is. I hope—but supposing it isn't? If it's . . . Remember that American who left Panama for Polynesia with his wife. They were alone on a lovely eleven-metre sloop with a white plastic hull. A fortnight later the American came back alone : his wife had had a burst appendix.

No. It can't be possible. Anyway we've got antibiotics and syringes ; three syringes and four needles. Christian's never done an injection but he can learn. You can do anything if you have to. I can last out for ten days or so. But we're at least three weeks from the nearest hospital. If I can only last a fortnight.

Laurence will be motherless. Christian couldn't go on alone with her. Who would he get to look after her? She'd be put 'in care'. In a home. No, it's too awful. My darling little daughter put in a home. 'After all we've done for you,' they'd say when she was fifteen. How would she be brought up, and where? No, it's not possible. I can't have appendicitis. The pain's still there, coming and going.

No. It must be my ovary. It must be, otherwise the pain would get worse. I'd be in agony and couldn't bend my leg up to my stomach. It *must* be my ovary. I haven't done anything to deserve that. Besides, the pain's wearing off, not getting worse. I'm terribly hot.

I creep into Christian's bed and he smiles.

'Christian, do you think it would be possible to go back to Las Palmas?'

'It would take at least a fortnight. It's out of the question in this weather. It wouldn't be any quicker than going to Barbados. But what's up?'

'Nothing. It's silly. I had a bit of a pain.'

'Where?'

'You know, my ovary, I think. I thought it might be appendicitis.'

'Don't be silly. You know how it is at sea—the instinct to survive. Divine providence perhaps. People are never really ill. It's impossible. Besides, you've never known that happen?'

'Maybe.'

To live with the thought of death, feel as if each moment were your last. Perhaps it would help us to waste less time in trivialities, to live up to our aspirations, devote ourselves to them more fully.

VI

Flying-Fish In The Atlantic

IT'S VERY FASHIONABLE to cross the Atlantic, but it remains a major undertaking. On a boat the size of the *Alpha* it takes at least 28 days to get from the Canaries to the West Indies. And you must have an extra month's supply of food and water in case the voyage should take longer. Menus have to be worked out carefully, bearing in mind that people have very large appetites at sea. You must have fresh foodstuffs which will last well, a reserve supply of vitamin pills, and enough water.

We bought ten kilos of green bananas at Las Palmas. We've been at sea six days and there's only one each left. Bananas take up a lot of room and are deceptively bulky. As they all ripen at the same time even if each 'hand' is carefully wrapped in newspaper, one is forced to eat them quickly. It's very difficult to find bunches of bananas in the markets which are green enough. We'll try to do better in the Antilles, so that they last longer.

The bread is beginning to go mouldy today. Here, too, in spite of 'baker's' packs, with treated paper and plastic bags, all the bread begins to go mouldy at the same time. Possibly because there are four of us living in a very small space so that the atmosphere is hot and damp. Cabbages, lemons, onions and potatoes last well, the cabbages say a fortnight, and the rest at least a month, provided you inspect them regularly and take out any which are going bad. If we had a freezer, or even a refrigerator, we could of course store tomatoes, pimentoes and cucumbers. Luckily we catch at least one dorado a day. We'll have plenty of fresh fish all the way to Tahiti.

We carry 600 litres of water: three litres a day per person for two months. Laurence has her own special allocation—160 litres provided by Evian. I give her some between each feed, so that she doesn't get dehydrated. She also has a two months' supply of Guigoz milk, in case I can't feed her.

You must also ensure you have enough fuel to cook with. A German, who was sailing alone from Los Angeles to Tahiti, had carefully installed two cylinders of gas on deck. He didn't notice or smell the gas escaping and found himself with a few tins of food, 50 kilos of uncooked rice, an equivalent amount of flour, and no gas. After a few spectacular attempts to obtain heat by burning diesel oil, he had to eat rice soaked in cold water for 25 days.

Our lack of funds means that we have to ration ourselves strictly anyway. We can't buy milk, or butter or cheese : they're too expensive. I'm feeding Laurence, and had no time to rest after she was born. One uses up an immense amount of energy on a boat, so I often feel very weak, which will probably lead to a more serious depression later, and spoils much of the pleasure of the voyage for me. I feel that the two men are enjoying the sea despite me, that I'm only there on sufferance, a mother with a baby. I'm getting thin and I've got wrinkles, and Christian notices but doesn't seem to understand that it's simply because I'm not getting enough to eat. What can I do? We know that we've got precisely 110 francs a month until we get to Tahiti.

A lucky break. The wind has died down, the weather continues fine and this respite gives me renewed energy. I sing as I work, from morning till night. I've watched Laurence playing for an hour : she does all sorts of things with three rings on a chain. It makes me laugh when her little hand, still not able to judge distances properly, goes out towards something and falls on thin air. Even when she's alone she babbles away, smiling to herself, which makes me feel she must be happy.

'Hell, what a bore,' Christian says under his breath.

It's dark.

He shuts the roof. The rain is beating down on the deck and the skipper's sleeping-bag is soaked. Laurence and I are lucky to be on the other side of the boat. Whenever a wave breaks on deck or there's a gust of wind it's always Christian who bears the brunt. He was on deck to give a few turns to the boom to reduce the sail and was caught by a sudden squall.

He comes back drenched, puts the electric torch on its hook, dries himself and plants a kiss on my forehead.

'Is it bad?'

'Oh just a little squall. Luckily I'd lowered the jib before it got dark; I only had to reef the mainsail. My bed's drenched.'

I can't offer him mine as Laurence already takes up half of it, and I can only sleep curled up on my side—which I hate, but one has to make sacrifices for those one loves.

Christian gets a large blanket out of a locker and rolls himself up in it.

It's a funny idea having an engine on a small boat, in mid-ocean. Or not so funny. I have spent over an hour cleaning up splashes of thick, inky-black oil from the sump. Christian ran the engine for an hour this morning: what a din. Laurence hated it. The hand starter wouldn't work, and the skipper spent two hours greasing it everywhere. And the sump of the crank-case is indescribable, with the rocking of the boat at sea. There is oil everywhere, on the varnished woodwork, the mattresses, a toy, in the galley. I'll go on finding spots of oil in various places for at least a week, and they spread and never wash out.

The automatic pilot has revolutionized pleasure cruising, utterly transforming life on board during a long voyage.

I remember the watches we used to take on the *Carmellia*. Tom navigated and did the cooking, Nelly, Christian and I divided up the 24 hours into watches, which meant two four-hour turns each, which was very reasonable. We had two eight-hour periods free, during which we had to wash up, wash the deck, mend sails, eat, and sleep as much as possible. I would be fast asleep in my warm bunk when someone came to drag me out at two in the morning to go and take a watch in the cold, dark and rain. Some people love spending four hours peering at a compass on a starless night, but I don't. I've never met a crewman who bounds out of bed with cries of joy when it's his turn to go on deck. You pull on your oilskin with difficulty, swallow some hot coffee if you're lucky enough to have a Thermos, and it is only the thought of your mate which gets you up there to relieve him on time. There is, of course, the fantastic beauty of starlit skies, of balmy nights, the sunrise—gorgeous storms too, but when they happen everyone is on deck and there's no time to think. But you can enjoy it all just as much with an automatic pilot. All you have to do is go up on deck at the right moment. On the *Alpha*, if there's exceptionally bad

weather, we are fresh and rested when we take the tiller, thanks
to Gigi. Without her, life on board with a baby would be far too
exhausting. Even with her, the days seem far too short to me. I
only get about half an hour a day for reading.

I don't know what was the matter with me this morning. My
teeth chattered, I had a temperature, a migraine, shivered and
cried uncontrollably and felt terribly thirsty. I looked a sight.
I swore at Christian, and he looked annoyed. A funny way to
start the New Year. Christian must be right, I'm dehydrated.
Laurence has an even bigger appetite when it's rough ; so all the
liquid in my body has dried up. I've fed her for three days and
have only drunk the equivalent of three glasses of water in all,
at breakfast. It's far too little. Christian makes me drink a litre
of water with a tin of concentrated milk. I feel a little better.
The ideal solution would be to have a bottle of water always at
hand.

The forecastle has become unbearable. Didier, who is fed up
with being hurled from side to side, has installed himself in the
middle of the cabin on the floor. He is reading the Bible, wedged
between two chests.

'You know the Bible is awfully sexy. I would never have
believed it had such immoral things in it. And have you read
the "Song of Songs"? It's tremendous.'

While the sea harries our little nutshell, I think about the
Flood, the Red Sea rolling back.

It's the first time I've seen Christian put on his safety harness
to go on deck. The swell is so heavy that it is like being underwater. Everything is lashed down securely and we are sand-
wiched between the waves above and the ocean below. We
think of the cosmonauts bravely flying in their capsules. Our
steel hull is very reassuring.

Navigation poses a problem. It's very difficult to take read-
ings from the sextant in this weather. You need two hands and
you can't keep your balance without holding on. Christian can
only estimate roughly, using the sun when it makes a brief
appearance—if the *Alpha* happens to be on the crest of a wave.
And is it because of the bad weather that we can't hear Lisbon
any longer? We'll have to find another station on our old
receiver.

Those who talk of the great empty, silent stretches of the

ocean should be on the *Alpha* tonight. What with the noise of the waves, the crash of the hull on the water, the grinding of the mast, the screeching of the wind in the rigging, and a tin which is rolling about and can't be found, there is enough noise to waken the dead.

Every day Christian notes that we have caught the largest dorado since we left—which is true. Today it's ten or twelve kilos. There's a simple explanation: the same school of dorados has been following us all the time and they're getting bigger and bigger. We can recognize one of them because we cut it on the back with a harpoon ten days ago. That one will never take a bite at the spoon. But the school will stay with us as far as Barbados. Sometimes we find a tin lid which we've thrown in the sea in one of their stomachs. Yesterday—New Year's Day— we had our fish with mayonnaise, a present from the *Erna*. We try to eat some raw vegetables every day, making a first course for three people with a grated carrot, two cabbage leaves, two onions, six rounds of cucumber. We keep the salads small so that we can have them for as long as possible. Towards the end of the crossing we'll be eating raw onion with salt and raw potato dressed with oil and vinegar. Everything tastes good at sea—but I never get enough, as I'm feeding Laurence. And the malnutrition I suffered as a child has left its mark, so that I easily become weak. I often cry for no reason.

'The water's much warmer,' announces the skipper, who has just had to go for a swim to re-bolt Gigi who is getting much too independent again. With the wind blowing this way and that, lurching and rocking, she has struggled on valiantly hour after hour, but since Las Palmas the sea and the wind have given her no rest. Rudely buffeted, she has gradually worked loose, rattling more and more, and the skipper felt more and more guilty about her. It's not much fun putting screws in in the water when the boat's moving. Thanks to the harness we needn't heave to. Which would be very unpleasant in this weather.

'Guess what I found on deck this morning? Some exocoetus.'

I had difficulty remembering what these flying-fish were called. They have highly developed fins which enable them to escape from the hungry dorados. They glide over the water for a distance of 300 or 400 metres. We timed one, which flew for over three minutes: each time it wanted to come down it saw a dorado. Fear really did lend it wings. Exocoetus can go at a speed of up to 50 kilometres an hour. They are delicious to eat, cooked or raw. Their flesh is as tender as a sardine's, but less oily.

The sail shines in the moonlight; they are attracted by it, and crash into the jib, falling on the deck. As we are low in the water most of them managed to get back into the sea. But there are five left so we can have raw fish with our porridge, for our first breadless breakfast. It's encouraging, because flying-fish are a sign that we are now in the trade-wind zone. In a day or two the sea will be much warmer and the sun burning hot. We'll be able to go naked. Washing will be much pleasanter too. We have a shower every day, which consists of scrubbing ourselves with a brush and throwing several buckets of water over ourselves, including our hair. It makes our skin glow and we feel very fit. Laurence has a salt-water bath too, with water warmed in the sun.

'A month in this little capsule in the middle of the ocean is a testing time,' the skipper writes; 'hard on the nerves and sometimes a trial of physical endurance. You can't undertake the venture lightly. The nervous strain is immense. Having to get on with people for weeks on end, in a small space with no means of getting away, even for a minute. People's faults become extraordinarily exaggerated.'

Conversations tend to revolve round the basic problems of life on board: eating, sleeping. It becomes obsessional, irritating.

'If you want a crew, marry it,' one navigator said.

But even for a married couple it's a trying time. It's an abnormal situation. You've soon exhausted your partner's possibilities, or feel as though you have. You think you know them absolutely. And it is then, when you think you've said everything, that it's vital to still have something to say to each other. Otherwise it is fatal.

A year at sea, cooped up with your husband for 24 hours out of 24 is the equivalent of twenty years of married life. The unfortunate thing is that at the end of the year you are not 40: you haven't the experience, or maturity, or forbearance to be able to cope with someone whom you know so completely. You are still vulnerable. So you get divorced, or realize that you do really love each other.

It is worse with three. Although Didier is our brother and a discreet and pleasant crewmate, he is still there all the time, sharing our marriage. If you swear at your husband in private it's unimportant. But in front of someone else it matters. One reacts more violently out of wounded pride, and quarrels become blown-up because subconsciously neither of you wants to lose face. In a habitable space of five square metres I can't fling myself into Christian's arms after a tiff. Even if I did, both the third person—who is supposed not to have noticed anything —and Christian, would be embarrassed. So feelings which could still be salvaged at the time of the explosion are slowly forgotten, freeze and die.

We have considerable difficulties to cope with in our marriage. The arrival of a first child upsets the balance of a relationship, and you have to form a new relationship, between three people. The time I have perforce to spend with Laurence would have been devoted to Christian only two months ago. Life at sea is much harder than on land, and I'm never alone with Christian. And I'm far less demonstrative. Christian is badly deprived of affection. And so am I.

We don't quite realize what is happening, and neither of us can understand the growing gulf between us. We no longer communicate, but go off at a tangent. What can we do about it?

We're both very fond of Didier. It was we who wanted him to see Polynesia, because he loves the sun, the sea, underwater fishing. We never quarrel with him. But we're drifting away from each other, each of us wrapped up in his own problems : Christian worrying about his boat, I about my baby. But it would be over a year before we realized this.

One wonders what one is doing here [notes the skipper]. We must be mad. It means putting up with each other. Not expecting help from anyone. You don't have as much energy as usual at sea, and every little thing that goes wrong is enlarged out of all proportion, because you don't feel up to tackling it. I'm plagued by Gigi working herself loose, and the water seeping into the boat. I keep telling myself I must

mend it, and put it off until the last minute: but no one will
do it for me.

I could say the same about the washing-up, the nappies,
bathing the baby. No one will get the heavy buckets of sea water
for me, or hang the washing out, or take away the feeling of
fatigue which I'm ashamed of because it seems like laziness
when I have the whole day free without having to take the
tiller. But happiness is there, it exists, if only we could find it.

The ocean is like a vast symphony, an orchestra made up of a
multitude of infinitely varied colours, of living shapes, of spray
on your face, of sunrises and sunsets, which all move to the
rhythm of the wind. This powerful music, which has been a
part of me from the moment I was born, which is my life itself,
throbs and roars in my head. The music of the sea fills me; I
drown in it. I feel that my body can no longer contain it, that I
will explode; a great feeling of power surges through me, and a
consciousness of this beauty in which I am plunged, which I
breathe in, which takes my breath away. This beauty which
catches at your throat, at your guts, which makes you want to
shout at the top of your voice. Which makes you want to cry.

What immense happiness: life eternally renewed before our
very eyes, in all the perfection of nature. A wave, a bird, a fish
are never ordinary, they always have that delicate beauty
which corresponds to the aspirations of the soul—the *anima*
aspiring to all which it is not. All the most powerful, all the
most subtle human characteristics, are there in profusion in
these calm or turbulent waters.

The sea is a school which teaches one integrity, and courage,
and patience. One learns to think things through; and to discover the true value of things, the real meaning of the word
life, which is the opposite of death. The ocean is a marvellous
teacher. You can't escape her laws, her demands. She never
forgives. After an experience of this sort, you understand how
many thousands of years of work and research have gone into
the discovery of electric light, radar, cars, the luxurious and
comfortable houses of our so-called consumer society. And you
then consume these things with pleasure, and great gratitude
for the millions of people who have made the path of progress
possible for us.

Happiness at sea. The sea brings us face to face with ourselves. There are no neighbours, no others to refer to, no one to imitate, or to criticize you. Everything you do is either vitally necessary or fulfils a profound wish. My behaviour is no longer conditioned by society. I become aware of my personality, discover the meaning of sincerity—being frank with oneself. Because life is reduced to essentials and it is impossible, or dangerous, to encumber oneself with false reasons, false motivations. Life is so short: one mustn't waste the time which is given one. At sea one must always do the right thing at the right moment. The life of a crewmate, or even of the whole boat could be at stake. You finish up having the same attitude towards all your actions, or if you don't, it is better not to go to sea.

We're now comfortably in the trade winds. The weather is perfect; the wind moderate, the sea even. It's 27 degrees in the saloon. The forecastle hatch is permanently open and the *Alpha* is beautifully airy. We all, including Laurence, wear swimsuits all day long.

It's night, but the brilliant moonlight is keeping me awake. I'm on the brink of sleep. Plop. Something has just fallen on the floor. It's round and it rolls. It zig-zags from one side of the saloon to the other. Plop, it goes down the step, and continues. It's irritating, but I haven't the energy to go and pick it up. It's too comfortable in bed. It's still rolling. It must be a lemon. A little green lemon from Las Palmas.

A little green lemon—Ah yes, the Paofai primary school in Papeete. Every morning on arrival we went to the row of concrete sinks. All 300 pupils, except my sister and myself, the only *popaa* (Europeans) at the school, brushed their teeth. They washed their feet under the taps and had a drink, and splashed their arms and faces with cold water. They smelt of soap, *eau de Javel* and *monoï*—coconut oil scented with *tiaré* or *Ylang-ylang*. I felt very proud on the first day of term in 1948. My sister and I had very short dresses with yokes. For satchels we had strong paper carriers with a string handle. We had got them in Panama.

The lemon's still rolling about—it's maddening.

At school we were given half a green lemon. You had to dig into the pulp with your nails until they were perfectly clean and white. We scraped away until the rind was smooth inside. Some of the girls said in their lovely, drawling voices with a great rolling of 'r's : 'Oh, it makes my teeth grate.'

It was the period when I told stories which my friends said were lies. I was too shy to mix with the others in the playground. I invented a fabulous world full of gold coins and happy children. I absolutely had to win at marbles, I had to be loved, respected. I pleaded with the teachers for the others, helped them with their essays, and was generally nice in fact. I pity myself now for being so nice, because it was a shell behind which I hid.

The little green lemon is still rolling. Hey—it's stopped. No it's going on again.

When it rained, the girls didn't wear macintoshes. They had a dress to change into in a basket on their head. They got a long banana leaf and protected their heads—and the basket—with it, and roared with laughter. They hardly ever wore bras, and their bodies looked naked under the thin, wet cotton. When they got to school they changed, and hung their dresses to dry on the verandah. It wasn't because they were poor that they didn't have umbrellas. For some reason, which it is difficult for a Westerner to understand, it would have been 'shaming'—the word containing every nuance from extreme delicacy to ridicule, but without any overtones of morality.

The little lemon is rolling, rolling.

I remember one girl who always carried an old bag with marbles which she had won from other people. She must have been three or four years older than I was. She was common, but beautiful, with striking features, the angular face of the Marquisienne, and huge grey-green eyes. People said : 'Really, that girl's a tomboy.' Their voices rose in a shrill crescendo on the word 'tomboy', which was full of meaning, judging by the amount of disapproving or envious looks they gave. I merely concluded that she liked playing with boys, which was in fact true. A few years later she was riding a heavy motor-bike. Every time I meet her we greet each other with a big smile and much winking—which is a typically Polynesian mode of address. But I can't even remember her first name.

All the girls knew our names, but I can remember very few of theirs. Sometimes in the street I meet a fine fat bosomy mother accompanied by seven or eight kids. She'll say: 'France! You haven't changed at all.'

Hypocritically I answer: 'Nor have you. How are you? They're all yours?'

'Yes,' she'll say smiling in a slightly embarrassed way, as if her sins had found her out. And I'll often learn that she's had two or three *tanés*, but that now she's respectable, no more playing around.

'You were always a good girl. Are you married?'

And, according to which period of my life it is, I say, 'not yet' as though it is something to be ashamed of. It seems incredible to them at 21. Or else, confidingly: 'No, but . . . '

'Ah . . . (much laughter). You're right.' And I have to step down from my pedestal.

Then finally: 'Yes, and I've got a daughter X years old.'

'Goodness! I didn't know. To a *popaa*?' (Very impressed.)

'Well, yes. But he's lived for a long time in Nouméa, and Tahiti.'

'Ah (reassured). He's almost "demi" then. That's good. I'm so glad.'

Vroum, crash, bang—it's the whole sack this time.

'Damn,' groans the skipper.

Scrabbling in the moonlight, we have to pick up ten kilos of little green lemons, one by one.

Since we reached the trade winds and the bad weather left us, the men's favourite pastime is fishing. Didier tells us about the fantastic catches he made in the West Indies last year, and Christian plays around making triple hooks. Didier fishes for the fun of it; he loves the sport, beating his own record. Christian loves it when he hasn't fished for some time, but getting our daily ration rapidly becomes a chore.

We don't like killing creatures which love life as much as we do. So, to compromise, the skipper decides that we'll dry any fish left over to eat on the days when we don't catch anything.

It's a good idea, but we don't know the right method. In Tahiti there is so much fish all the year round that no one bothers to keep it. For me, dried or salted fish or meat conjures up the tough existence of Arctic fishermen, or the poverty of underdeveloped countries. We haven't quite reached that point. Christian is thinking about the delicious smoked kippers you get in Equihen.

'You have to cut very thin fillets, like this.' And he hangs them in the rigging. The sun is our refrigerator, he notes. If a dorado is too big, we cut off some to eat and the fillets dry in the rigging, where they hang nicely.

The next day, longing to try them, he takes some down for me to grill. He eats a mouthful raw on the way. They crackle in the pan and smell delicious. We attack our plates.

'Delicious,' Christian says.

'Famous,' agrees Didier.

'They're a bit strong,' I say timidly.

'That doesn't matter,' replies Christian authoritatively. 'Bonitos get a bit strong when they're kept too, but they're still all right.'

Suddenly he goes very red.

'It's awfully hot!'

His chest, back and arms are covered with red marks, which turn yellow and then violet. Then the patches start swelling up.

At the same moment Didier gets up to get some air: 'It's so hot. Good heavens, Guillain, have you seen your back and chest and arms?'

And we all shriek together: 'The fish!'

'I told you it was high. Try and make yourself sick, quickly.'

It sounds easy, on a boat at sea, but it's not. We all three stand in the cockpit with a finger down our throats, but it's no good. I fill a mug with sea water and add two tablespoonfuls of salt. Drink it down, feeling sick—and nothing happens. Blast. If you're not feeling seasick, it's incredibly difficult to vomit. We have to laugh at our ridiculous plight. We retch and swallow mug after mugful, and at last, by sheer will power, achieve it. But it took me over half an hour.

Then we all stuff ourselves with charcoal, and anything in the medicine chest that can be used for food poisoning. Didier and Christian are all right, but I don't know if it will have affected my milk. I consult Dr Spock and Laurence Pernoud, who are not very helpful. To be on the safe side, I give Laurence Guigoz milk for 48 hours.

She takes the bottle well, but makes a funny face, as if she were mystified. She's lost her usual liveliness, and doesn't chatter to me any more. 'Avoid abrupt weaning', my book says. I can't bear it. For two long days I keep Laurence beside me in the bunk and let her feed as much as she can whenever she likes. I don't give her any milk in a bottle but only Evian water. If she wants to live she must suck. On the third day my milk slowly comes back, and we've won. We've succeeded so well in fact that she can breast feed until she's thirteen months old. Her sparkle returns; she smiles and babbles again. Everything's all right.

In Barbados we learn that one must cut the fillets very finely and salt them before drying them, keep them away from the spray and that it's particularly important not to leave them out at night. And they told us dorados keep very badly.

Meanwhile we're off fish for the rest of the trip. We were lucky to have a reaction at once, as soon as it reached our stomachs. We could all have died of food poisoning, and one day fishermen would have found the boat drifting, with four corpses inside.

So we go back to the tins. It isn't really enough for us while we're at sea. Meal times become even more traumatic. I find it a little difficult to write about this—people don't usually mention this kind of detail because it is not very nice. But why not? It's only something that happens at sea; it stops as soon as we sight land.

I hate the sharing out at mealtimes, but can't bear to miss it. From the way he rushes up, Didier obviously feels the same. Christian is the central figure in the drama: it's the skipper who divides up the rations. We don't share out everything: rice, haricot beans, chick-peas, of which we have an eight-litre pan two-thirds full, are no problem. But sardines are more difficult. There's seldom the right number to be divided by three, and when there is, they're not the same size. You have to assess them, cut them up carefully and fairly, mentally weighing them. Each of you knows at once, without saying a word or making a movement, which bit he wants. And as with small children, even if you do happen to get the share you've chosen, other people's plates look much more desirable. Naturally this all takes place in complete silence. No one dares mention it; everyone is secretly rather ashamed, but twice a day the same emotions can be seen all too clearly for a minute or two on each face. As it's the skipper who divides the portions, he is the target for our suspicions. We both feel that he's doing better than us. We're wrong of course, and he isn't.

At sea, eating is of course vitally necessary, but it's also an important distraction. You're very hungry, you think about food all the time, and imagine what you might be eating on land at that moment. One spends hours looking at beautiful colour photographs of roasts, chicken, cakes, crème Chantilly, pêches Melba. One reads recipes, and simple words such as butter or vanilla send one into a trance. Yet on land we don't ever think about food. We spend as little time as possible in the kitchen and aren't at all greedy. And then as soon as we're at sea we commit the sin of envy every day, coveting our neighbour's share. As one can't question the skipper's orders, even if they have nothing to do with the running of the boat, one represses one's feelings and hates the others for a fraction of a second, and feels ashamed, because it's so absurd. One is angry with oneself for feeling like that, feels one is mean and to make oneself feel better prefers to think that it's the others who are. It's very easy to offload one's own sins on to other people. For a few seconds, Christian becomes the scapegoat hunted in the desert.

Didier is splicing the mainsheet, getting a few last puffs from the fag-end of a damp cigarette, which he has clumsily rolled himself. On the automatic pilot, the *Alpha* is slipping along at four or five knots towards Barbados. It's marvellous weather. The swell is lively without being rough, the sky a tropical blue. This isn't the clear hot blue of Provence, but a subdued blue, veiled with streaks of white cloud from the mists which rise from the sea in the heat. The sails and deck are brilliantly, blindingly white.

Christian is stretched out on his bunk on the starboard side. He suddenly looks at his watch, at the compass, at Gigi, at the sail. He seizes the sextant, gives a pencil and paper to Didier, who drops his splice and takes his brother's watch to use as a chronometer.

'Wow,' says Christian, 'it's ten minutes to midday.'

Balancing on his legs, he squints behind the sextant to

estimate the height of the sun. Didier jots down at regular intervals: 317°24′ 4″ at 9h 0m 45s; 317°18′ 2″ at 9h 09m 35s. In the cockpit the bath thermometer is floating in a yellow bucket: 27 degrees centigrade.

The *Alpha* will reach the Antilles in a few days.

VII

Land

LAURENCE HAS JUST had her morning bath. I'm feeding her on the foredeck, leaning against the pulpit. The stem rises rhythmically; the hull is covered with a coat of green weed which slows us up. The hull and deck are steel, so there are streaks of yellow rust running across the paintwork, but we don't remove them: in a few days' time they will be the signs by which the *Alpha*, our seabird, can be distinguished from the swarm of Sunday yachts and glossy charter boats which crowd the little harbours in the Grenadines. With the wind astern, we're sailing under the mainsail and the jib on a small spar. The motion is smooth and not at all tiring. The sun is directly overhead and I shade Laurence with my body. We set out 30 days ago. I think Pierre and Catherine took 31 days in the *Vencia*, so we should arrive tomorrow. But with so little wind . . .

My baby is asleep and the pressure cooker is whistling. It's rather difficult crossing the deck with a baby in your arms. Christian is in the saloon, spreading one of the many charts given to us by the *Saint-Briac* on the table. The sextant has been carefully put back in its padded box. A book of HO 214 tables and the *Nautical Almanac* are on the seat. He is fixing our position.

While I'm putting Laurence gently back in her basket where she lies comfortably spread-eagled, Didier turns the stove off. He opens the eight-litre pan which is two-thirds full of rice and rounds of smoked sausage, and looks delighted as the steam hits him in the face.

Finally Christian looks up with a satisfied smile.

'How far?' we both ask together.

'Only 175 more miles.'

We have been saying 'only' ever since we reached the half-way mark between the Canaries and the Antilles. This has replaced the 'already' of the first few days, but will be followed by an exasperated 'more' if we don't get there tomorrow.

While I dish up, Christian puts away the chart with its beautifully drawn curve of the *Alpha*'s course. He hangs the dividers neatly on the bulkhead, with the pencil, parallel ruler and rubber.

'It's high time we were there,' Didier grumbles. 'This is the sixth day we've been on this diet—rice pudding for breakfast, rice for lunch, rice for supper. We'll be puff-eyed by the time we get there.'

Since midday each of us has been watching the dark line on the horizon which never seems to get any bigger, because there's so little wind. Christian is experiencing the pleasure of a skipper who has succeeded in steering his boat towards a minute speck in the ocean. You can cross the Atlantic on a raft and find land on the other side, but it's extremely satisfying when you're only 25 to decide a month in advance on the exact point where you will land, and steer your own yacht there.

He writes: 'What a marvellous feeling to be on the other side of the Atlantic on my own boat! I really feel that I've achieved what I set out to do. There's a lot to do on board, but the sun is shining, the sea is blue, and soon there'll be white sands and a peaceful lagoon, and all our life in front of us.'

Didier is inspecting his clothes for the hundredth time: 'France, do you think you can get that spot out?'

For the hundredth time he uses an English word, trying to learn the basic vocabulary by heart in case he should meet anyone nice in Barbados.

I get out a white shirt and navy shorts for the skipper and start ironing a white mini-skirt. It takes me at least an hour to iron half a square metre of material with a flat iron worthy of a museum.

We get out razors and make-up box and I cut my two pirates' hair. We have to change from the hirsute savages we've become into well-groomed, elegant creatures. We represent France, since the *Alpha* is legally a bit of our country which has travelled across the world. We must do our best to look good.

We can sense that land is near. There's a warm haze of mist

round us. It's 9 pm. We sit under the waning moon and wait—
we're not at all sleepy.

The old lantern swings gently on the backstay. We haven't
seen another boat for 30 days, but there's a greater risk here. A
faint light dances over the water. Then there's the sputter of an
engine. It's very difficult to judge distances in the dark. A boat
seems to be coming towards us. Possibly attracted by our
light? It suddenly appears less than a cable length away,
coming straight across our bows. It must have seen us. There is
only a light wind, and we're hove to, which makes it difficult to
manœuvre. Christian shines the electric torch on the sail, and
signals. The boat keeps its course. I am shaking with fear but
Christian is calm and ready to start up the engine if necessary.
We have a hand starter, because other people's experience has
shown us how many yachts have run aground on a reef because
the battery was run down. And also, the skipper gives our little
Diesel a trial run every week. At the end of a few minutes,
which seem like hours, the old tub passes within a few metres of
the stem, without going a centimetre off course to avoid us.
Christian whistles loudly as the *Alpha* rocks violently in the
wake of the fishing-boat. They probably didn't even see us. I
shudder to think that we could have been peacefully asleep,
counting on Gigi and our light to protect us. To be so close to
disaster only a few hours from land.

Large boats generally see our steel hull on their radar
screens. Eventually they will sweep the sea with their powerful
searchlights to locate us. This had happened to us in the
Mediterranean once or twice. But on the main Atlantic and
Pacific lines, the radar isn't permanently switched on. A yacht
is small in comparison with the height of the waves and the
cargo ships go very fast. It sometimes happens that one isn't
spotted in time, and it's almost impossible to survive if the boat
is cut in two. Christian and Didier will take watches tonight.
To cheer himself up at the beginning of his, Didier switches on
the radio receiver and puts on the earphones. He rocks to the
music and it looks very funny when you can't hear anything
yourself. I take a turn and begin moving to a jerky rhythm. It's
marvellous to be in touch with people again: we've been cut
off for 30 days.

When you've been knocking around in a steel capsule and

4

haven't seen land for a month, you've almost forgotten what it's like. We feel as though our life on shore was in another world, like a dream. But when a real island rises from the ocean in the brilliant dawn light of the Tropics, with real trees, real sand, real houses, we feel as if we could dance over the waves to reach it. It's miraculous. At last we're here.

The skipper stands proudly at the helm. He must make a smooth approach, with no mistakes. We execute a slalom between the boats in the bay, looking for yachts we know, or French yachts, or just to say we're here.

'Where do you come from?'

'From France.'

'Hi! Paris!'

Barbados used to be English.

A man comes up to us in a little dinghy with an outboard motor: 'You're French?'

'Yes, are you? From France?'

'Yes, I've been here a few days. Come and moor alongside the *Vap*. Do you need anything straight away?'

'A little sugar if you can spare it,' says Christian, who has hated having his tea without it.

'A cigarette,' Didier adds, his eyes lighting up.

Our quarantine flag is hoisted with the courtesy flag. The authorities arrive and are very pleasant, and the formalities are soon over. At last we can land.

We weigh anchor at once and go on to Bridgetown harbour, where huge schooners are moored, some of which, with no engines, trade from island to island. Everything in this old English colonial town is ochre, red, blue and black.

It feels strange to be on land. You don't roll but you feel weightless, as if you're going to take off and fly. I long to run, and stretch my legs. At sea your whole body is perpetually in motion, but making contracted movements not stretching. No comparison with a good walk on dry land.

The streets are full of bustle. The population is pure-bred African, with few half-castes. There is a mixture of puritanism and smiling, slightly submissive expansiveness which is touching.

It seems to be the cool season—luckily—as it's 35 degrees in the shade. Woollen suits, stockings and coats are *de rigueur*. Even the babies can hardly see out of their layers of pink wool.

'She'll catch cold,' they say, pointing at Laurence who's only wearing a thin cotton smock.

We spend three hours in the grilling sun buying provisions. It's marvellous to be able to get tomatoes, fresh meat, bananas, mangoes and a papaya. Didier and Christian carry the stores in loads of a dozen kilos.

Near the market, old women converge on us from all sides: 'Let me have your pretty baby, let me hold her.' And they smile broadly, showing white teeth. I have to ward off their caresses tactfully. But how kind they are. During the whole week I never once carry a heavy load back to the boat. One of them always comes up to take my bag of shopping as far as the quay, from sheer kindness of heart. I have never known this happen anywhere else.

Faint with hunger, we leave the harbour to go and drop anchor near the *Vap* in Carlisle Bay. We are 200 metres from the beach.

We eat on deck for a change, under an improvised awning, while Pierre, the skipper of the *Vap*, tells us about his voyage. His boat is a motor-sailer, to which he has devoted all his time for months. He treats her as if she were a jewel, but much more carefully than any woman would. She seems like a floating palace to us. An after cabin, with the large double berth of our dreams, partitioned off, a saloon with all the woodwork varnished—it is all quite perfect, roomy, electric, electronic, automatic. But what a constant worry it must be. It would be sheer slavery, especially with a wooden hull: one has to beware of worms in warm seas.

The turquoise lagoon is so clear that you can see a spoon seven or eight metres down. On the white sand palm trees bend their graceful fronds to the limpid water. The sky above is a meltingly soft blue.

One can't really describe it: words and photographs can't do it justice. Any more than you can describe the blue mists which spread over Paris at nightfall in the autumn. All this light, these colours are our private world today, while some people are spending their day getting underground tickets. All we need to do to go on the beach is slip into the water, which is

28 degrees. I must hitch a lift to the shore to take the two large sail bags bursting with dirty clothes, and my three-month-old baby who is beginning to try to crawl everywhere on all fours.

Dong. Dong. Dong! I haven't heard a clock strike for months. Sitting on our bunk I quietly lift up the forehatch and put my head out to hear better. Christian is fast asleep beside me.

Dong. Dong. Dong! Twelve strokes. It is midnight.

The moon bathes the sleeping coconut palms in its golden light. A scarcely perceptible swell rocks the hundred-odd boats gently. I can hear the distant suck of the surf on the shore, and the cheerful clanking of rigging.

In a few days all the boats from the Canaries will be here: the *Mamari*, the *Anahita*, the *Rhâ* and possibly the *Ain-Taiba*.

The golden moon.

When I was seven we lived at Auae, by the sea, two kilo-metres from Papeete. I loved my silent encounters with the moon and stars. I felt as if the moon was enveloping me, absorbing me. There were hardly any houses and very few cars. You could lie in the middle of the road under the great arch of the balsam trees. There was no sound except for the lapping of the sea, and my father and I would stand there side by side, spellbound. I held tightly to his hand for reassurance. I felt as though I was going to be sucked up into those myriad worlds which shone above us, all round us. Their reflections made white zebra stripes across the dark water. I felt so small, so small. 'Look, there's a shooting star, a star which has burst. It could be a meteor. A few years ago a meteor fell over there, between Mooréa and Tahiti, and it caused a tidal wave.'

'Hi! What are you doing?' the skipper suddenly grumbles. 'Shut the hatch, the light's waking me up.'

Six o'clock in the cockpit. Our first feed. The sun, just coming over the horizon, is burning hot. The rude awakening of the Tropics—not at all like the slow progression of cold mornings which prolong the sleepiness of the night. As soon as the cock crows, there is an explosion of warm life. Birds squawk. The first tenders streak across the bay, making a great din. The tide has turned, the sea is higher and the breakers thunder on the deserted beach. A light breeze ripples through the coconut

palms with a gentle rustling. In the Tropics it is as if everything was rushing madly onwards, determined to live intensely,
like those rose trees from Europe which flower incessantly for
two years and then die exhausted.

Smells mingle with the sounds. The spicy smell of the water,
the delicious aroma of toast and coffee, and bacon and eggs,
which are being prepared all round us, the heavy scent of
tropical flowers—they all flood over the *Alpha* with the torrid
heat which suddenly engulfs the closed saloon.

The water is limpid: a fairly strong current drains the bay
into the open sea. Here and there a blond bearded head or a
large pair of blue eyes under a tousled dark mop emerge from a
neighbouring hatch. A little farther off a slender dark-haired
girl is contemplating a morning swim. Friendly greetings are
exchanged in every language, the most common expression
being the casual American 'Hi!'

Everyone helps newcomers spontaneously. In each port
this helps you avoid unnecessary trouble: thanks to one's
predecessor one will know the mood of the inhabitants and of
the authorities. He will know where one can do one's washing
and what it will cost; where one can get sails mended or an
engine repaired. He can tell you that European vegetables are
in short supply here, but that meat is extremely cheap, whether
it is fillet steak or shin of beef or stewing steak. They hack off
hunks of frozen meat with a saw. Whoever he may be, one's
'neighbour' knows everything one will in turn hand on to the
next arrivals. Sometimes he has news of yachts we know, and if
he has met any French people, he tells us their movements. The
world of the ocean-going sailor is very small.

Three masks, three tubes, three pairs of flippers, two weighted
belts, a wet suit and two Tahitian harpoon-guns lie in a heap on
the deck. The two guns are made of *purau* wood and float
beautifully. They are equipped with very long, fine arrows.
Christian de-rusts the points, checks them, mends a barb or a
slide. He changes the worn nylon which attaches the arrow to
the gun. I prepare the *tui*: lengths of rope to string the fish on.
One end has a float, so that it won't get caught on the coral
reefs. The other end has a metal bar ten centimetres long, to fix
to the fisherman's belt. As I have already explained, you make a
tui several metres long so that your catch will follow you at an

appropriate distance. If a shark is attracted by the blood, and attacks this easy prey, he has very little chance of carrying off one of my dear skipper's legs by mistake. Christian covers himself with coconut oil from head to foot, as a protection against the cold if they fish for a long time. Didier, who is never roused from his bunk however much din we make, leaps up at the familiar grating of the guns on the deck. The skipper is in the water. Without losing an instant the fishing fiend gulps down a bowl of porridge, pulls on his wet suit and dives in. I follow.

I glide voluptuously in the clear, warm water, in a state of weightlessness. It's as if my almost naked body were back in my mother's womb. Perfectly relaxed and happy. From the smiles we exchange, enlarged and exaggerated by our masks, I can tell that the others feel the same. The noise from on land no longer reaches us. I can hear a dull diffused hum, composed of high-pitched vibrations: intense under-water life or the sound of one's own body? It is all the same. Here and there silver scad swim past in pairs. There are not many clumps of coral. We are making for a wreck we spotted yesterday.

The slowness and fluidity of our movements in the water, the soft-focus effect all around us, makes our bodies seem smooth and regular, almost perfectly shaped. It's a strange world, where one's idea of distance is confused and objects look bigger, and yet insubstantial.

The mossy hulk of a boat is silhouetted darkly against the white sand. Little blue, red, black or bright yellow fish fix us with their round, shining eyes. They approach in waves, and in beautiful broken formations. The underwater pursuit begins. The dry sound of a loosed arrow rouses me from my dreamy state. I suddenly feel terribly guilty: Laurence is alone on board and she's awake. I sign to Christian, who makes an exasperated face as if to say: 'No more fishing expeditions then.' There's no risk of Laurence falling overboard, or burning or electrocuting herself. She can't suffocate or cut herself. But an atavistic 'you never know' relegates me to the ranks of home-bound mothers.

I'm on board the *Alpha* in two minutes flat. My little deck-hand is babbling on the saloon floor. I stand in the cockpit, ready to hitch a lift ashore with my two heavy sailbags of dirty clothes. The colours are very vivid in the brilliant sunlight. As vivid as beautiful black skin dressed in red, green or yellow—

the colours of the island vegetation. The lagoon, the coconut palms, the tropical sun, remind me of what Tahiti was like *before Laurence came.*

Sometimes when we got cold, we would lie in the burning sun on the white sand. Where possible we chose deserted islands so we could go naked. I found it very difficult to abandon the few square centimetres of material which were the legacy of my upbringing. Although there was no one for miles around I felt a thousand invisible eyes staring reprovingly at me, like the eye in Cain's tomb. I had never looked at myself in a mirror, and suddenly felt very embarrassed by my own appearance. Always fully clad, I had lost contact with my body, and behaved almost as if I had not got one. I am not the only person to feel like this, and if everyone had the chance to live on a desert island for a while with their partner, many marital problems would solve themselves of their own accord.

Nakedness puts us in our place. It engenders humility. We poor humans who have no fleece or shell to protect us from the cold or blows, become aware of age-old complexes which cut us off from the one we love. In a marriage there must be complete physical harmony. And for this you must first of all be in harmony with yourself, be at peace, at ease with yourself, or in other words, love your own body. To do this you have to cultivate it, as one does one's mind. You must swim, walk, climb, run, roll in the sand. The covering must be worthy of the mind inside it. Beauty, for us, is precisely this exact balance between mind and body, between the development of the body and the spirit. Nothing to do with copying glossy magazine photographs. From this direct and total union with nature stems a kind of purity, a state of grace.

One of the things I liked best, after fishing and sunbathing, was seeing Christian climb a coconut palm. My Polynesian heart rejoiced at it. He was the first *popaa* in my life I had seen climb a palm with the agility of an islander. Bernard Moitessier would be the second, but he is no more metropolitan French than I am. You have to climb twenty metres up a vertical trunk so rough that it could flay you alive, and 50 or 60 centimetres in diameter, with only your hands and feet to help you. I'm very proud of my dear savage.

These island traits are seemingly the only thing we have in

common, as everything else—character, origins, schooling—
were designed to lead us apart. And yet, if I had been asked to
imagine my dream husband, he would have had a smooth
golden skin, a strong, athletic body—like all the young men I
had grown up with in the sun. He would have loved the sea, the
wind, the hot sands and adventure. When you are born on an
island, you always dream, from an early age, of going elsewhere. Until I took the boat to France I could never see a
steamer leave the harbour without shedding tears; I longed so
much to go. To go no matter where, so long as it was somewhere else. In this respect our yacht is most satisfying. As for
Christian, if the girl of his dreams has long, soft, fair hair, she
also had to have a pleated-skirt-and-white-blouse naiveté and
submissiveness, while also embodying maternal warmth. So
that was why we both loved drinking the sparkling, sweet juice
of green coconuts from the same shell, why we laughed as we
devoured the *nia*, the pulp as delicate as fresh cream. Why we
left Tom and Nelly on the *Carmellia* reading their detective
stories, chain-smoking and drinking whisky or *Hinano* beer,
making cakes or sleeping, killing time somehow or other. We
had the sun and the sea. Their way of going round the world
was to use tins instead of the fresh fish and fruit which we
brought back from our excursions into the valleys. And their
favourite occupation was getting some friends on board with
guitars and crates of beer to laugh and sing until they had drunk
the lot.

Happiness at sea. We could feel it coming closer. The boat
was for us above all a way of getting back to our roots. We
longed for lagoons, greenness, rocks, waterfalls, and real people
—people who live their own lives. Not people who make films
and hash up legends for tourists. Like all happy people, Polynesians love laughing, and joking. They are born comedians.

The purr of a little outboard motor approaching: a swoosh as
the boat turns; a light tap of an oar against the hull of the
Alpha—ouch, the paint. It is Rick come to fetch me. With his
little engine which splutters and carries 200 kilos safely ashore.
What a luxury. One, two, three, seventh wave; we accelerate—
as long as it doesn't stall. I haven't too much confidence in the
machine—and we're over the surf. We pull the dinghy up the

beach and I put Laurence in the shade. Luckily the yacht club is under the trees.

Crouching on the two-square-metre slab of concrete, I soap and scrub for hours. The men made so many clothes dirty, between Saint-Tropez and Casablanca, when it was cold and stormy.

While I am bending over these clothes Laurence is judiciously setting out to discover the world. For the first time since she was two weeks old, she is on dry land, on something which doesn't move. On her red and white *pareo*, she progresses in little jerks like a rabbit. The sand is shiny and blindingly white. Such fascinating powder—rough and yet velvety soft—when you're only three months old. Our cabin boy wriggles forward and comes back to the *pareo*, over and over again, until she falls headlong into the sand. Her face is a picture.

Rick and Pierre come to my rescue. Rick takes a bag which his cleaning woman will wash for two dollars: she has a washing machine. Pierre picks up the baby and the clean clothes.

Many-coloured fish hang on a spit in the cockpit. My two Guillains are disappointed that they've only caught such small fish: they are only 20 to 30 centimetres long, my favourite size because it means there are a lot of heads to eat. Fish heads are so delicious.

While I clean and scale them Christian cooks some rice and in less than fifteen minutes the meal is ready. For dessert we have a papaya and some guavas. To think that my mother could never make me swallow an ounce of papaya and now I'm eating them whole. It's because one misses fruit so much at sea. But it's very difficult to pick a good one. The perfect time to eat them is when they drop off the tree of their own accord when you touch them. They can be revolting or delicious. Some varieties are floury or very dry, others sweet and juicy. We like them with honey or lemon—or both together, which is how I give Laurence hers. Papayas and guavas have more vitamins than any other tropical fruits. They are rich in pectin, and have the same regulative effect as apples: they are good for diarrhoea. They are also rich in carotene, and a good substitute for carrots, which are scarce and expensive in many sunny islands. Their black pips are supposed to have all sorts of properties.

4*

My grandmother had a liver cure which consisted of swallowing nine papaya pips every morning for nine days. And the leaves of the guava have a spectacular coagulant effect: to stop a cut bleeding you crush some leaves in your hand and put them on the wound. This should only be done if no other medical aid is at hand—as Dr Spock would say.

At times it is difficult to thumb a lift, when there are no boats. This happens in the afternoon when the yachtsmen, whether they are lucky enough to have an engine or not, take a well-earned siesta after a good meal at the Hilton or with friends. How to get ashore with Laurence, without a dinghy? After a month at sea we want to feel the ground under our feet, see damp grass, flowers, people.

Aunt Marinou's bath.

Four rolls of inflatable tube—it should float. Christian, who is always happy with a solution which makes life easier for him, puts on his flippers and waits in the water. I suddenly remember that the bath is tiny: 80 by 35 cm. And there are 200 metres to go, and the breakers. I have nightmare memories of waves when I was small. I turned over and over as if I was in a tumbler dryer, hitting the sand or shingle with my head, my feet, with my head again—and I thought it would never end. Finally I was thrown violently on to the beach and lay there dazed on the shingle. When I got up I was in danger of being sucked back by the undertow of the next wave.

Oh the terrible sucking sound a wave makes as it rolls back. One day I went under twice running. It was on the east coast of Tahiti where the sand is black and the waves very high: people surf there now. Of course the breakers here are nothing like that; but what if the bath turns over, or Laurence tries to stand up, if Christian doesn't notice in time, if she upsets it.

'Christian. No. Come back. No. Not over the breakers!'

I start crying with rage or exasperation, from fear or misery, I don't know which—or from misery which only needed some pretext to burst forth. I go on crying, and of course it's no help. I continue to cry.

There's nothing for it but to lower myself into the water too. Christian is already way ahead. He has slowed down and is waiting until the last big wave of a group has formed, before he

projects himself forward with his flippers. I have never found it
so difficult to cover 200 metres before. Then, when I at last see
him standing up, with the bath and flippers held above his
head, the first big wave of the next series is on him: he just has
time to run to the beach. What a drama.

Barbados. Didier's nocturnal escapades, when he got back
exhausted at six in the morning, and fell asleep as we were
getting ready to go out fishing with the *Vap*.

Barbados. Paradise Beach, which lives up to its name, and
where we took two very nice Swedes on our first charter trip.

And the boat we were lent one evening when we were expected ashore, which overturned in the surf. We recovered most of
our things: except two nappies and the little horsehair pillow,
which had cost so much money in Marseille. I had made a
mattress from an old dress, stuffing it with vegetable fibre and
the pillow with horsehair, being guided by the child-care books
and my liking for natural materials. I should add that Dr
Spock was for me the grandmother or older friend whose
experience is so reassuring, and who can warn you of possible
dangers. I had never seen a baby dressed from scratch, and the
textbook was very useful. A woman who lives alone in a flat
with her husband and baby isn't really isolated. She knows she
can call on her doctor, her neighbours, the social-welfare
people. If she's worried about a rash or abnormal breathing she
can always shout for help and someone will hear her.

But at sea I felt completely isolated. I had to be able to cope
with anything, know a lot about child-care and children's
illnesses, have a good stock of medicines and be good at first aid.
I needed good textbooks which I could learn by heart and keep
always by me. Above all I had to feed my baby until we got to
Tahiti. If I had lost my milk, we would have had to stop in the
first port we came to for a few months, because we wouldn't
have risked making a crossing with a baby being fed on bottles.

People have often told me I was irresponsible. But as I have
said, I was brought up in a country where babies are born and
grow up without any problems, often without any medical help
in the neighbourhood. I didn't see why I should be an exception
to this natural law.

Barbados. Fishing at night for flying-fish. Nine in the

evening: we are comfortably installed in our double bunk in the forecastle, reading by the warm glow of a paraffin lamp. The bay is calm, with only a light breeze which prevents us opening the hatch completely in case the lamp blows out. Suddenly, we become aware of things shooting across the water in every direction. Our two heads immediately pop out of the fore-hatch: five or six *gommiers*, the canoes without an outrigger but with fore-and-aft rigging, typical of the West Indies, are streaking across the bay in all directions.

They have only one sail, and obviously when you are poor anything will do to catch the wind: sacks, flour or salt bags, patchwork efforts or plastic leaves. There are two men on each. The helmsman brandishes a torch, of bamboo stuffed with rags soaked in paraffin, which he waves in the air. The fisherman in the bows, with amazing dexterity, catches the flying-fish attracted by the light with a large net on the end of the pole. Not a word is spoken; there is silence except for the slight swish across the smooth surface of the water. Tomorrow at dawn the whole catch will be sold in under an hour. Because here, as elsewhere in the Antilles, there are plenty of fish in the lagoons but little in the markets. This is surprising: you never see a lagoon in an inhabited area without at least one underwater fisherman, with a canoe following him, and women who fish fully dressed, standing in the water up to their waists with their fishing lines—not to mention nets which they swim out to position. A Tahitian legend says that men are young porpoises who were placed on the shore by their dying mother: one can almost believe it. Although another legend says that a spider, which is apparently a very intelligent creature, gave birth to men. West Indians are descended from Africans, a mainland people, who as far as one can judge are not great water lovers. Although the sea is warm there and there are not many sharks, they haven't got the sea in their blood.

'*Mamari*. Hullo, Ken. Good trip? How long did it take you?'

'Twenty-five days. No dead calms or storms. Marie is arriving by plane this week and we're getting married here.'

A scene typical of any port where seafarers meet: we recount the details of our Atlantic voyages between snatches of song, with the help of Barbados punch and lemonade, guitars and harmonicas. The *Solmar* spent two days with her mast submerged, during the storm we were in when we left the Canaries. The three tall strong bearded men admit they felt very small on their beautifully varnished hull which wouldn't right itself. All the contents had slipped to one side, and the water had begun to seep in. They pumped: the boat was heeled over at more than the maximum angle; it was impossible to steer, sleep, navigate or even heat anything up. They thought they had had it. Tonight they are laughing noisily like people who are delighted and amazed to have escaped alive. They talk of selling the *Solmar*.

Ken gives us some sad news: the Swiss *Rhâ*—a couple with a little girl of two and a half—sank off Cape Verde. They hit a reef in the dark. Luckily they managed to get ashore in their tender. The boat was fully insured. They will go back to Switzerland to build another. Two years later I would meet them in the Antilles, chartering their new boat. What faith— we haven't got their confidence.

I don't know if our spirit survives the death of the body, but a boat's spirit lives on and haunts us. It rises from the waves at the slightest provocation.

'Bring back, bring back . . . my Bonnie to me. . . .' It is good hearing the deep, warm voices tonight in the little cabin of the *Alpha*, while Laurence sleeps happily on. How awful it must be for a mother and small child to find themselves out in the rain and dark at two in the morning, in a tender going towards an unknown shore, towards a dry, barren and desperately poor land. Catherine Deshumeurs told me that she never dared throw anything away in the Cape Verde islands after she saw a child diving to get an empty sardine tin which he wanted to flatten out and use for building a house.

Would the little girl on the *Rhâ* have to live in a house made of tin cans? And the poor skipper who would feel responsible, and who would see his house, his shell—how can one make a landlubber understand this?—a part of himself slowly sinking in the dark water. It is traumatic for anyone when 'his' boat sinks: for Bernard with *Marie-Thérèse* I and II, for Marc Darnois with the *Valrosa*, Eric Deschamps with the *Railleuse*.

February already. And we wanted to be in Tahiti by the

beginning of July to take advantage of the best season before leaving for the Torres Strait. We're not racing; but we need to get to Tahiti soon to replenish the ship's funds. We're sure of being able to earn a bit there. It's sixteen months since we were last working and our budget has to be 'squeezed' to the bare essentials. I have already mentioned that this particularly affected me, because of my undernourished childhood and need to feed the baby.

Our stores are primarily composed of things it is essential to have if one is not to starve: large quantities of rice, corned beef, sardines or pilchards for the days when there is no fresh fish; potatoes, sacks of onions, chick-peas or split peas, pasta, lentils and haricot beans. The only sweet thing we've got is white sugar, although we should have a lot of biscuits, chocolate, tinned puddings, tinned and dried fruit, and sweets, so that we could nibble at them day and night to prevent us feeling exhausted: one is always on the go on a boat and always hungry.

However, in the meantime, on our last evening in Barbados we have our first Tahitian meal on board the *Alpha*: raw fish with coconut milk, yams, fried bananas, white and violet taro, breadfruit roast on the Primus, sweet potatoes and fried fish, and as much coconut milk as we can drink. It only takes a few seconds to get the fibre off the coconuts with a sharp point; then you cut the nut into two perfect halves with two or three short, sharp blows, and squat and grate the coconut to extract the milk. As the coconut grater is often fixed on a sort of stool, this makes a characteristic knocking sound. How often my sister and I had to stop fishing in the river when we were children, when this knocking started up all round us, telling that it was time for a meal: it is a sound as characteristic as the *angelus* in French villages.

Today we're so delighted at having coconut milk again that we rub it all over our bodies and in our hair, and Christian drinks half a glass of it.

'Take care—it's a laxative.'

The only large fish we have found is a shark. We've never tasted shark meat and Christian is keen to try it as they eat it here. It's a bit tough for our liking, but our guests fall on it eagerly. The table setting is very simple: a *pareo* with two big plates, two soup plates and four odd bowls, for the eight of us. As we've only got three forks, we have to use our fingers. We drink orange-leaf tea and lemonade. It's good to be sitting round a table with friends after a month at sea.

VIII

A Sailor's Paradise

LAURENCE IS LYING in the cockpit, staring at the mainsheet. As the trade wind always blows in the same direction, we continue to sail westwards. But we will come back to Barbados in two—or three?—years' time.

Today we start coasting from island to island, which is pleasant because we can come into a harbour every night, as on the Côte d'Azur. Eric was right when he said that the West Indies are a sailor's paradise. Wind all the year round, islands within sight of each other, white sands, green lagoons, coconut trees and sun, and hardly any tides. There are a few reefs, but they are generally round islands which rise steeply from the water. You just keep your eyes open and climb to the mast-head from time to time. The dangerous times are at night, when you're tired, or when you're sailing into the sun and the sea shines so brightly that you can't distinguish the different coloured patches which indicate a shoal.

I love arriving at islands which are sheltered by a reef. A bar of coral is a marvellous breakwater, protecting the land from the fury of the sea and its inhabitants from large fish. Without reefs many Pacific islands would no longer exist.

We have got to repair the sail, because while we were peacefully sleeping we gybed: the improvised boom, a broom handle to keep the jib sails boomed out, has cut right through the mainsail and torn it. We haven't a spare.

Didier is in the crosstrees to tell us the general direction in which to sail. From the foredeck I can take care of the details, signalling when to avoid small clumps of coral and estimating the depth of the water quickly. Union Island and Palm Island, a few miles apart, have the ring of white foam round them which indicates a protective coral reef. We nose up to the latter at a reasonable distance to find a way through.

'Hard-a-starboard.'

'Hard-a-port.'

What a slalom. The *Alpha* is like a toy. We play with her like a sailskiff, go about in a trice, skim over the sea, beat up to windward. Then the channel: fairly wide and with hardly any current. We tack up it in the grilling sun, without using the engine, to a wooden causeway where a friendly West Indian signs to us to moor. A line fore and aft to the jetty—a rare luxury which we don't often come across on our travels. The West Indian is the caretaker of the Union Island yacht club. It is surprising to find a yacht club in this small island which seems very primitive and thinly populated. There are a few sailskiffs drawn up on the shore and of course several water-ski boats in a beautiful boat-house.

Christian and Didier, armed with three-cornered needles especially made for use on heavy cotton sails and thread like meat string, are doing more harm than good to our mainsail: every time the needle goes through it tears the cloth in every direction. But what else can we do? We've broken endless fine needles doing a few centimetres of seam. Bernard had found a good solution; he had a hand sewing-machine like the ones you find in Casablanca. But we didn't take his advice: you think twice before loading a clumsy extra piece of equipment on a 9.50-metre boat.

Union Island rises gently to a wooded summit, which dominates the plain, where the grass is cropped like a lawn. Here and there are great brown patches of barren earth. There is little fresh food available—only tropical vegetables and fruit, at reasonable prices. Fish you must catch yourself, and you have to hunt your own meat. There are wild goats in the bush. Didier and Christian go to have a look with the caretaker, in hunting kit, with a gun. Instead of a goat they bring back a greyish iguana. The caretaker says it is a great delicacy, better than rabbit, and they give it to him as a present. Far from making it into a stew, I suspect he went off to stuff it and sell it to a tourist for 60 or 100 dollars.

Union Island, like all the Lesser Antilles, is a favourite haunt of luxury American charter yachts. During our 48-hour stay, several gleaming boats have stopped for lunch or for the night. Like the Trojan horse, they disgorge an army of tourists. With shrimp-pink skin, checked caps, dark glasses, white cardboard nose protectors, floral West Indian shirts, flowered shorts which don't fit, bare feet, and of course their cameras, which will enable them to take a good look at the scenery for the first time, when they get home.

On the beach, trodden by thousands of other tourists every day for years, the women cry: 'Oh darling! Look at this shell!' 'Oh darling! Look at this stone!' And they keep a broken shell or piece of coral to remind them of their unspoilt desert island. In the evening, after a hearty meal washed down with plenty of drink, the tenders are filled to bursting with this merry throng. They hurry ashore, the boat heels over precipitously, they scream and fall fully dressed into the water and go and sing on the beach, fortified by gallons of strong punch. The natural life.

It's the natural life for us too. As there are no goats, we stuff ourselves with crayfish, squid, delicious goldfish, washed down with coconut milk and accompanied by sweet potatoes and violet taro.

After two hours' sailing we reach Palm Island. A wonderful beach of white sand round a lagoon where some stilt-birds are standing. Four mountains plonked down in a dolls' house landscape look over the emerald green lagoon and the dark blue sea. On the slopes of the hills are four beautiful villas carved in the stone, which melt into the mountains. It all belongs to an American, whose son Jim is tall, fair-haired and bronzed. Christian and Didier spend hours diving with him.

I cross the lagoon with Laurence and make a tour of the island. Sea-fans spread their black lace on the white sand. Smoothly rounded bits of deadwood with shapes like animals, polished and bleached by the sea, look as though they are about to move: you could almost stroke them. The sand is so fine and white that it's a pleasure to see Laurence tumble in it. In the afternoon, after a stupendous catch, the three boys go out goat hunting. They're hopeful—I can't think where they will hide in this treeless landscape. I prudently prepare some fish—which is just as well because they come back without any goats and there are now five of them. They have invited a couple they met to share our second Tahitian meal. To complete our happiness, these two are flying to Paris tomorrow and will post our films to be developed and telephone our family for us. A telephone call, hearing the voice of someone who has seen us and shared a meal with us, is one of the best presents we can give our family during the voyage.

Still the marvellous trade wind. Ideal sailing weather. We've no desire to stay in port.

Bequia is one of the prettiest of the Grenadine Islands. We are approaching it by moonlight, slowly, all ears and eyes. Tonight the full moon has kept me awake. It's good to think in the vast silence of the night. A silence filled with an intense but diffused humming, so that one doesn't know if it comes from within oneself or without. This uncertainty, the way one's organic and spiritual life mingle with the natural world around one, gives rise to ecstasy, and a great sense of anguish—pain at being infinitely small in the immense universe where we are both masters and of no more consequence than dust. At such moments, at sea, one feels as though one is losing all consciousness, existing beyond thought. But in a quiet harbour you hold your breath and enjoy the sensation to the full. When you are safe you can afford to feel scared.

'Hi, *Alpha*! Are you French?'

Admittedly you couldn't tell from our flag now: the red has unravelled, thread by thread.

Catherine is dark with lovely blue eyes. She is a professional pianist. They've been working for eighteen months with an agency which sends them tourists. A boat of 13.40 metres, which can take two people and four if necessary, can be hired out, according to the standard of comfort it offers, for between 500 to 700 US dollars a week. Plus six dollars a day per person for meals. It seems too good to be true, but Jean and Catherine are longing for a real holiday. We would understand what they felt like only too well when we had done this kind of work ourselves, on our new boat.

It's an endless infernal round. 5 am get up. While the tourists sleep, you do the housework quietly, wash the deck and prepare a proper full-scale American breakfast. This takes about two hours. Breakfast lasts till nine-thirty. Then the 'guests' get dressed at their leisure and go on deck. Meanwhile the skipper has completed the departure formalities, checked that you have enough water and fuel, weighed anchor and hoisted the sails. His wife has washed up, made the beds and tidied the cabins. At about ten-thirty or eleven o'clock, iced whisky is served on deck and Catherine prepares lunch, a cold meal which will be served on deck at about twelve-thirty. More washing-up, and you drop anchor in a pretty bay. More manœuvring, formalities, etc. You then take the tourists ashore in the tender and lead them to the 'souvenir' shop or leave them on the beach for a while. Catherine gets in fresh food, bread. When she gets back to the boat it's at least three o'clock. She has to get tea, which means a home-made cake or biscuits, for five o'clock. You fetch them all back to the boat, then transport them out again. Catherine dashes back to peel vegetables, prepare the meat, make a cake. Because in the evening there's the sacred dinner-hour—or rather the damned dinner-hour. There must always be an elaborate meat dish and a home-made dessert. This entails a lot of work, especially on a boat. The tourists have time to change, set their hair and do their make-up, arrange the shells they've found on the beach. The meal goes on till 11 pm. More washing-up and then you have to chat or play cards with them, before you can go to bed.

That goes on for months and months without a break, with no private life except for a few hours together between midnight and 5 am. After that you need a holiday.

The bank comes today. The bank here is a little wooden boat which comes round twice a week. This morning it's moored alongside a schooner which is unloading cement. We leave our anchor chained to a buoy, and go alongside to change a traveller's cheque. The bank boat can't be more than twelve metres long and looks rather old and rotten. When I think of the difficulty involved in attacking the English bank train. Jumping ashore, I go to get some bread from a nice fat old West Indian woman who makes it the French way. A lovely surprise—it's hot and smells delicious.

The sun is setting. There are some old schooners lying aground on the beach with their beautiful long black hulls. Streaks of green cut across the pink-and-red sky. The colours change every minute, melting and fading into one another. At the instant when the sun disappears behind the horizon, when the sky is still bluey-green and the vegetation already black, a red flame seems to leap from the silken surface of the water for a few seconds, licking the motionless boats, changing them into dark shadow-lantern silhouettes against the green sky. Then the light suddenly vanishes, leaving the sky dark and studded with stars.

I always bring Laurence up to see the sunsets. At five months old she would point to the fiery horizon of her own accord, her eyes shining with delight.

It's so easy to learn how to be happy.

At St Vincent, having completed the arrival formalities, we go fishing in a bay with very steep cliffs. On our return we moor at the quay which is high, and difficult to reach. The town is completely dead by 6 pm, very ugly and dark. There are villas which were clearly once pretty but which are now seedy, left to rot by their occupants. The people in the street look aggressive; there are no Whites. It's the only West Indian island where we had the strange and unpleasant sensation of being a hated race who were not wanted there. It was a great relief to get back to our home, our *Alpha*—our little bit of France. All these British islands which have obtained their independence are extremely poor. The plantations taken over by the West Indians have been abandoned and there are hardly any schools. The young are bored and some of their ways of passing the time are not very healthy. There are still lovely coconut and banana planta-tions. But no social organizations.

The island is very green, the valleys deep and wooded. There are apparently wild goats there. I'll believe it when I see one. We have to hug the coast for a bit as there's not a breath of wind. We find a deep bay running back inland, with two peaks towering above it—La Souffrière Bay. It does have a sul-phurous atmosphere. We drop anchor 50 metres from the beach with a stern line round a coconut palm. Luckily there is a little river there. While Laurence plays with mossy stones, I wash our sheets in the soft water.

All hands on deck at 7 am. The wind has got up early but is blowing from St Lucia, where we are headed. The *Alpha* is sailing well into the wind and we make for our last Grenadine Island. Coming into the bay of St Lucia we meet the *Anjerro*, a charter boat. We've caught an enormous red mullet, the finest we've ever had—60 centimetres long, 25 across and 12 centimetres thick—and are invited to join the barbecue on the beach, adding our catch to the lamb and chicken.

The next morning, although we got to bed very late, Laurence wakes us as usual. At nine, as the wind gets up, our sails are hoisted and the *Alpha* is off again.

As we go along the coast towards the port of Castries, we discover a channel which seems to disappear inland. You can see the inlet coming from St Lucia, but it must be invisible coming from Castries or Martinique. Curious as always, we go about and sail up the channel, which leads to a marvellous deep, wide bay, at the foot of an almost uninhabited valley—Nelson Bay. It was here that the admiral hid his entire fleet, surprising the French as they sailed from Martinique.

No great sailing ships or warships today, but a comfortable motor-boat with some friendly French people on board. We share our lunch. Jean-Pierre is returning to Paris this week: he will telephone Manouche, Christian's god-mother, to give the family our news.

Perfect weather, sailing as if in a dream. With a good wind on the quarter and the sea almost flat, we skim along at six knots towards Fort-de-France.

The sea and happiness.

You have to really take in this weather—feel it, absorb it, in silence, and let it be engraved on your memory so that you'll remember it for a long time. The sails are full, the wind doesn't waver, Gigi purrs contentedly on her pins, the sun is just the right heat.

At Fort-de-France we find the *Erna*, the *Inconnu* which we left behind at Cannes, the steel *Pingouin* which we haven't seen since Casablanca—and our post. Civilization.

Two thirds of the 30 or so letters waiting for us date from the time of Laurence's birth, and Christmas. The questions about the preparations for our voyage are meaningless now, and I think the only appropriate reply we could make would be to quote from the telegram from our Uncle Pierre: 'Bravo. First lap safely over.'

This has been the easiest part from the point of view of navigating. Perhaps the hardest for Laurence and myself. The problems everyone experiences, in a relationship, the gulf between me–Laurence, Christian–the boat, mean that I often feel neglected and alone. I have often, I must admit, like everyone else I imagine, asked myself if I hadn't made a mistake, if I wouldn't do better to go ashore, earn my living somewhere, with my child, rather than leading a life in which I had little time left over for Christian. I find it hard to remember these doubts now, my desire to escape. I remember one day, when I was particularly tired and discouraged, I was only deterred by the thought that if I went ashore, and found work, I would have to put Laurence in a crèche and wouldn't see her all day.

Because in fact the harmonious and united family that we are today—Christian, our two daughters, the baby we are expecting and myself, our family of *Call of the Sea*—was only created after the vicissitudes common to everyone, and not easily or as a 'matter of course'. I see our life as the slow and difficult formation of a couple, of a family unit which the boat and the sea have helped us to create, and now enable us to guard jealously.

Fort-de-France. Didier and I are looking for work: our funds are at rock bottom. But it's rather difficult to present oneself and say: 'I live on a boat. We don't know when we'll be leaving —possibly in a week, or a month, or six months.' Because the skipper doesn't know and doesn't want to know. When the wind is right the *Alpha* will sail on towards the sun again.

After about three weeks Didier is taken on as a rep for a wine company, and we two give sailing lessons. So one fine morning, with Jacqueline, Marie-Odile, Jean-Claude and Jean-Pierre on board, we set off to spend the weekend at Pigeon Island, a little island to the north of St Lucia. Our friend Ricky had told us how to approach the island—we have no chart. It's easy in daylight, but you mustn't make a mistake and approach it from the north, where there is an easily identifiable rock, instead of the south. In our hurry to be off our little plan gets lost.

The day goes well. No one is sick, it's lovely weather and we get to Castries at about five o'clock. There's nothing attractive about Castries. We are unanimous in deciding not to spend the night there. Pigeon Island is quite near and we re-set the sails. Ricky talked of white sands, palm trees and marvellous places for underwater fishing. The *Alpha* is nosing towards Pigeon Island, when the tropical night—there is no twilight in the

Tropics—falls suddenly and completely. There's no moon until midnight or 1 am.

Pigeon Island is a black line against the black sea and sky, directly ahead of us. How far? We have no idea.

At about nine o'clock, getting more and more anxious, I start boldly humming jolly sea shanties and, very discreetly, anchor Laurence and her cot securely. You never know—a sudden bump; Laurence is only five months old.

The wind has dropped slightly and to save time Christian has got the engine going. A one-cylinder diesel in a steel hull makes quite a noise. We sing at the tops of our voices on deck, in the dark. Jean-Claude peers into the darkness from the fore-deck— one can't see anything at all. And it's the first time he's been at sea.

The din of the engine, and the crescendo of our voices.

'France, do you remember from which side one should approach the island?'

'I think there was a dangerous rock on the north.'

'What are those lights over there? Boat masts?'

'Oh, we'd better not make for the lights, there probably isn't a harbour there. They'd confuse us.'

And we swing round to the north. Where the rock is. It's incredible how stupid one can be.

And crash—a thunderous noise, of metal crashing against a reef as hard as granite. The waves throw us violently to starboard, right across the rocky ledge.

No one speaks. Except me. Of course, I have to cry, 'Christian, Christian!' thinking 'Laurence . . . ' But I am at the tiller, with the engine full astern, the tiller hard a-port.

The waves have subsided a little, but we have to hurry because they won't be like that for long. Christian jumps into the water, and heaves with all his might while I rev the engine. My heart's in my mouth. Laurence is still asleep and not crying. That's the most important thing. The *Alpha* moves off the shoal of rock, and I can breathe again. A fairly small breaker knocks us back a bit. Christian shoves as hard as he can, and climbs aboard, dashes past me to the tiller. There is the roar of a huge wave as it forms—the *Alpha* cuts through it neatly at right angles, and we are saved. We must have hit the rock at least six times, hard.

I slam open the roof and go down to the saloon to light the storm lantern. Shout: 'The water's coming in.' It's up to my ankles.

Laurence is still peacefully asleep down there. We take up the floor and begin handing a chain of buckets, which are quicker than our bilge pump. It's exhausting work, especially when the water never goes down. We can't stop for a second. We pass the buckets from hand to hand, twenty centimetres from Laurence's cot and still she doesn't wake up. It's a great blessing, because I don't think I could bear to see her cry just now. But she wouldn't know what was going on. The fact that she's asleep gives me strength and I feel reassured, as if nothing terrible could happen while she's sleeping. Which is illogical.

Anyway there's no time to think. Bent over the bilge I fill two buckets one after the other without a break—a red 10-litre one and a smaller blue one. The person behind me takes the red bucket and passes it to the 'emptier' in the cockpit. Jean-Claude, in front of me, takes the blue bucket and empties it through the forehatch. We change places every quarter of an hour, because it makes you feel giddy. Christian is at the tiller and doing all he can to force on the *Alpha* towards Castries. The water has stopped rising in the cabin, but is not getting any lower. We reach Castries at about midnight. The water's stopped coming in and the bottom is dry. The mud has stopped up the hole, which seems to be in the keel. But where? And how big is it? We'll have to wait till tomorrow to see.

In the meantime, after a good clean up down below, we hold a meeting over which the skipper gravely presides. There are several possibilities for getting back, if the *Alpha* has to be laid up in Castries—which might be difficult anyway. Then the skipper says that in the circumstances no one will be expected to pay their share of the expenses. But he is immediately interrupted by protestations: 'We wouldn't hear of it.'

'It was a risk we all took.'

'It was a great experience and we don't regret it at all.'

'You must let us pay our share. It's your job.'

I shall never forget these words.

Then we go to bed. Laurence, who has been constantly shoved around, amidst all the uproar, is still sleeping soundly. She's never known what a quiet room is like, or been by herself with her bed always in the same place, and stationary. She's always slept anywhere: on my lap in a restaurant, in a knapsack on my back on excursions, on a *pareo* on the sand, or the floor of the cabin or the steel deck. I have noticed that she has a marked preference for wood, and only likes something soft for her head. There's no reason to dissuade her. Tonight she's in the forecastle with us.

Christian and I have nightmares all night, about huge holes in the hull, water filling the cabin, Laurence still asleep in the water and the boat going down, in the dark, with water everywhere, all round us. Yet it's the first time the *Alpha* has been so still, with her keel firmly stuck in the mud.

Next day it's as fine as ever. As soon as it's light Christian dives down to see what the damage is. Some dents on the starboard side, below the waterline. A tiny crack about a centimetre wide in the root of the keel, right in the bows. That's all. The cement round the ballast has come away from the steel and the water came in.

Ideally the part of the keel containing the ballast should be isolated from the rest of the boat by welded steel plates: the water wouldn't have come in then. The crack is two plates up. It's always there that we hit anything first. We must reinforce it.

For the time being Christian dives down and applies a bit of hot pitch to the crack and it sets hard and fills it beautifully. We've got off lightly, but what is more annoying is that the rudder-post is out of true and it's difficult to work the tiller. We'll have to go into dry dock to put it right—and that'll be expensive. Just for good measure the accelerator lever is broken. Christian fixes a pulley and a length of nylon rope, a system which we use for a year, after several unsuccessful attempts to solder on a lever.

Now there is no risk of sinking, we set off for Pigeon Island again in blazing sunshine. Seeing the place in daylight, we are amazed to have escaped so lightly. A wooden boat would have been splintered to pieces between the ferocious waves and the iron-hard rock. Our steel hull saved us, and yet we only had three millimetres of freeboard above the waterline. Anyway, one must obviously approach the bay from the south, where we saw the yachts yesterday. Ricky had warned us—it was just one of those stupid accidents.

Back in Fort-de-France, we decide we must dry dock the *Alpha*—but how are we to pay for this? Beach her, like the Grenadine schooners? It's an idea—but there's hardly any tide in Martinique. We need a sheltered beach where we can get her welded—and we'll need electricity. It also means we'll have to empty the boat of most of her contents, and live elsewhere for a few days. And then there'll be problems with the mast and rigging. It's far from an ideal solution.

We go to tell Geneviève and Ricky our troubles and ask their advice. We have a fruit-juice cocktail before dinner, submerged to our necks in a heated swimming pool at their lovely villa. The pool is the only daily relaxation Ricky allows himself. He's an extraordinary man: when he was still taking his baccalauréat he spent the long vacation underwater, cutting metal posts with a blow-lamp. It's extremely hard work for which you must have an excellent constitution. It was in this way that he got his first boat—a *gommier*. Since then he has started numerous businesses, one of them being *Jalousies Martiniquaises*, which he manages, while bringing up his large and charming family at the same time. Geneviève and Ricky are an exceptional couple, and our dinner with them was immensely soothing.

Of course Ricky has welding equipment. Of course he has men to work it. And he also has a friend, Mr Grant, who has a yard where the boat can be hauled up. He telephones him at once to ask if we could pay a special rate. We are given to understand that it would be about 150 francs if we don't take too long. 150 francs is incredibly cheap, but it will make a terrible hole in our budget all the same. We say we'll think about it.

At dawn, the *Alpha* is hauled up the slipway and into dry dock. We've got 24 hours in which to repair and careen her. Ricky is going to send us his welding gear for the keel, and his men will also take care of the rudder. Armed with scrapers, Christian and I scrub and scrub—we remove seaweed, moss and barnacles which have stuck to the boat in spite of the anti-fouling we put on in Casablanca. Laurence sleeps or plays in the cabin, unperturbed by the noise and heat of the careening.

After the scrapers, we use wire wool, then sandpaper, and finally scouring powder and a scrubbing brush. It doesn't sound very difficult, but with only the two of us at high speed, in the tropical heat, it's gruelling work. You have to keep bending over and reaching up to rub and scrape. When the hull is clean, we put on two good coats of quick-drying minium.

By eleven the three men are there with the welding gear. While they are strongly reinforcing the root of the keel, Christian pours some pitch between the cement and the hull to prevent any risk of corrosion, and puts a new layer of cement in the bilge.

At midday the crew of a large fishing-boat, which is also hauled up there, bring us some hot food—a kindness which I can only repay with smiles, because they speak in a bastard South-American Spanish. And Mr Grant brings us a magnificent lettuce from his garden, with the air of one apologizing for bringing so little. But in the torrid heat of the dry dock, nothing could have been more welcome than the sight of the crisp green leaves.

At about four o'clock Christian takes out the rudder and tries to straighten the post with the help of the men. We'll put it back later. Meanwhile I finish putting on a coat of white paint with a roller.

Mr Grant can hardly believe we were on the Pigeon Island rocks: 'In twenty years, I've never known a boat get off them. One can see from the dents that you hit the rocks hard, but there is hardly any damage, it's incredible. And not a spot of rust or electrolysis on the hull, although in parts the paint obviously wore off long ago.'

'That's thanks to Bernard Moitessier. He advised us to place anodes all round the keel, fore and aft. As rust is caused by electrolysis.'

At nine, after another meal from our neighbours on the fishing-boat, we put on the second coat of white paint and paint in the waterline. What a day.

Next day at 5 am, we put on the anti-fouling. When Mr Grant opens the yard at seven we're ready to go. The *Alpha* is hoisted in the cradle, all newly painted and gleaming. The slipway is free for us to pass. And when Christian asks what we owe him for the slip, Mr Grant says simply that there's nothing to pay.

I shall never forget his kind expression, how sweet he was with Laurence, and his generosity towards us.

Nothing is worse on a yacht than having to sail on a date set in advance. When you've chosen to live on a boat, you are irrevocably committed to the caprices of the wind, the sea and the seasons. They give the orders, and decide when we can leave, not us. We have the opposite attitude to the man who has subjugated nature, who crushes a mushroom under the wheels of his Jaguar, defies time and space in his plane or counteracts a headache with a pill. At sea man becomes insignificant. You have no control over a wave, or the wind. You make yourself small, erase yourself, wait till the storm is over, trying to control your boat as best you can, and yourself as best you can, doing your utmost to stay alive.

You don't challenge the sea, or defy her. You listen, try to feel her mood if you can, and guess what she will do. You can love her, passionately, but she can make you afraid, and harm you; she can be cruel. Even when you think you know her, you can never tell what she has in store for you.

But go we must, because Jacqueline's holiday begins today and she has decided to go sailing with us for a fortnight, and to go as far as she can with us. We embark at eight in the morning in the quiet little harbour behind the fort. There are some white horses outside—we're in for some fun and games.

Geneviève has given us a complete medicine chest and a large tin of Tonimalt. En route for Dominica.

On rounding the point, we find there is a fresh breeze. There are flurries of wind all round us, but the strong gusts are from the east. It's odd seeing the wind making circles round us, ruffling the surface of the water in a strange way.

As soon as we are in the 'channel' between Martinique and Dominica, the wind increases and we have to lower the jib quickly, hoist the storm-jib, and reef the mainsail. The *Alpha* heels right over. Finally, we lower the mainsail, and reef the storm-jib. Seasickness attacks all hands—only Laurence is spared—and I take some Marzine just in case. The troughs are three to four metres deep, but the waves are going in practically every direction, and we are shipping a green sea. In spite of his oilskin and three sweaters Christian is drenched to the skin. Didier too.

There are gusts and squalls with bright intervals all day. We're thankful to drop our trusty CQR anchor in La Souffrière

Bay in Dominica. The water is very deep, right up to the shore, which we reach by swimming. We munch some sprouting coconuts which can be easily opened as soon as a shoot is growing from the husk. Inside there is a spongy, sweet and juicy substance—the seed—which is called the *uto* in Tahiti. My father calls it sugared cotton-wool. Children love it, and so do we.

We are rocked mercilessly by a heavy swell all night. When we have a charter passenger on board, I always feel guilty if we can't offer them fine weather, particularly during the first few hours, because there must be nothing nastier than starting one's holiday by being violently seasick. I feel as embarrassed as if it were entirely my fault if there is bad weather the day our guests choose to come aboard. How can one explain that it's best to wait for favourable weather, that one must never feel hurried or pressed for time—that one must be like Saint-Exupéry's Little Prince, who said: 'If I had 53 minutes to spare, I would walk quietly towards a fountain.'

In the morning Jacqueline insists she's had a very good night, and seems delighted. I feel reassured.

The rigging was severely strained in yesterday's wind, and the sails have come unsewn in several places. We have to spend over an hour mending them. While I wield my needle—which is tough work in this material—I remember Bernard Moitessier's sound advice to us to reinforce the fabric where the seams meet and at danger points. How stupid of us to be so careless. One always hopes that these things will happen to other people, not oneself. So instead of swimming in the clear water here, we have to sew on patches. It's the chore I like least of all on board.

Now we're in the wide bay at Portsmouth. It's very deep, with a beach of dark grey volcanic sand. Ragged little children swim out to sell us a few oranges and bananas, and shrivelled tomatoes the size of a gull's egg. Touched, we buy everything except the tomatoes. The kids seem to be only five, seven and eight years old. They carry their wares in transparent nylon bags.

I suddenly see that the smallest is in tears on the beach. The two older ones look at us silently and despairingly. The bag

with the tomatoes is being carried out to sea by the current, and
has just got as far as the *Alpha*. I immediately jump into the sea,
but quickly realize what the matter is : a horde of small jellyfish
bite me all over. Poor little children. I manage to recover the
tomatoes and the bag, and set out with Jacqueline and the
children to a nearby village.

By the side of the trodden-earth path, pathetic hovels made of
old packing-cases, boxes and rusty corrugated iron, propped
against each other in miserable rows, provide scanty shelter for
ragged children with distended bellies. The adults sit by the
path and gossip. It's a fishing village, but they only fish from
their boats, with a line or net, or more often, as everywhere in
the West Indies, with traps : the fish swim into a lattice-work
cage and can't get out.

Dominica has a very fertile volcanic soil where things grow
well. There are plenty of trees and coconut palms. I can't
understand why the people are so listless. One could live well
there on hardly anything, if one wanted to, with very little
effort. So why don't they bother? Here too I got the impression
that the Africans brought here long ago had never been able to
adapt to their surroundings.

This morning Laurence has got her first tooth. It's amazing,
because I hadn't noticed it coming. She hasn't been dribbling
or crying or seemed upset recently. Then this morning I saw
this little hard white thing on the pink of her gums. Rushing to
my child-care books, I see she is of legal age for a first tooth,
that all is well and she has been spared a lot of trouble. This
little tooth makes her seem very grown up all of a sudden. How
quickly babies grow old. And yet I'm longing for her to be
bigger.

A fairly strong wind takes us from Dominica to Les Saintes in
three hours, and we get there just after sunset. The village of
Terre de Haut is like a dream : Breton fishing-boats of every
colour are drawn up on the sand all along the beach. Everything is in soft pastel colours, clearly delineated, clean and
charming, gay or sober, simple but heartwarming. One has an
irresistible desire to see it close to.

We go ashore to get bread. Little concrete paths wind
between old French houses, each surrounded by a very low wall
and a well-kept garden. There is nothing rich or ostentatious

about them. Everything has the air of having been lovingly made, with a passionate desire to keep up the traditions and life-style of ancestors who came here 200 years ago. The Bretons never mixed with the West Indians from Terre de Bas. They intermarried and kept their blond hair and blue eyes, but they have also become rather inbred. Which is why the French warships which call here on their way to Tahiti are welcomed.

At six in the evening Terre de Haut is as lively as a fishing village in the South of France. Every night the sailors crowd into the only café in the port, to drink or sing, round large red or green-clothed tables, or hold animated discussions. The children are simply dressed, but very clean and well cared for. The young people have retained a certain distinction. They are not cowlike or soft, or alternatively brash. The determination to remain French in the West Indies is in their blood. They have the fierce patriotism of people who are cut off from their homeland.

When we've finished shopping we come round to anchor on the other side of the island, at Pain de Sucre. It's much more sheltered here than at the village. We moor alongside a wooden landing stage standing in two metres of water. The landing stage leads to a very white sandy beach below a lovely coconut plantation. Under the palms is a large colonial-style house with wide verandahs, and outbuildings dotted here and there among the trees. It is very elegant and one can imagine a lady in a crinoline lying languidly on a chaise-longue with a little negro servant waving a large fan. It's the only sad spot in this dream-like haven. The house is shut, but they say that a family comes here once or twice a year for a few weeks.

We'd like to spend a fortnight in this sheltered bay. The lagoon is green, and when there's a wind, everything looks wild and tormented, with crude colours which contrast strangely with those of the evening before. We feast on fish, crabs and lobsters.

But if we want to get to Tahiti this year we must press on. As we are heaving up the anchor a Zodiac comes alongside with officers on board from the *Rhin*, a French warship which is on its way to Polynesia for the second series of atomic tests, the Force Alpha No 2. It's an emotional moment for us meeting the *Rhin* in Les Saintes: when we were knocking off instant photos

in Tahiti to get our boat, there wasn't a sailor who didn't have one of our colour photographs, of himself with a Tahitian girl and garlands of flowers, in his wallet. So seeing the *Rhin* again is like coming full circle: we're back where we started, having realized our dream. And the Force Alpha give us another present—a tin of ship's biscuits. The sailors call them war bread, and look surprised when I refer to them as little cakes. As we're dining aboard the *Rhin*, we decide not to leave until tomorrow.

We sail from island to island on our way to Antigua, one of them a desert island where we feel like Robinson Crusoe, and where Laurence can play for hours in the water. At Antigua there's an airport and Jacqueline will be able to fly back to Fort-de-France. We say *au-revoir*, and sail on.

And at six o'clock on Thursday 25 April we reach St Barthélémy. It's a French port. The population is Breton and West Indian. Unfortunately it's a grey day and we have only dispiriting, 'depressed' memories of our last island in the Antilles. Yet the people there are extremely pleasant. It's upsetting; one wants to get them all away from there, away from their monotonous and limited existence which isn't actively harmful but which doesn't make them very happy either.

At last we're on our way to Panama, to the Pacific. We begin to feel we're making a long voyage. The adventure is just beginning.

5

IX

Patience In The Doldrums

OUR ONLY CHART of the Caribbean is an Index Chart—
showing winds and currents—given to us by a cargo boat. We
won't sight land again until we get to Panama. At least that's
what we hope. Ricky has strongly advised us not to get shipwrecked on an island belonging to Venezuela, because we
could end up in prison. It happened to one of his friends not
long ago.

On our way to Tahiti at last. Still a bit more of the West
Indies, Christian points out, and I flinch. I've had time to
forget what it's like out on the open sea. It's incredible how
many boats which have set out to go round the world finish up
in the West Indies. Hundreds who have set out on the great
adventure have stopped there for good, attracted by the easy
life. Not to mention those who have been disheartened by their
first long passage—across the Atlantic—and who have put
their boats up for sale and begun to dream about mountain
chalets.

Now the serious part is beginning.

We are in the Caribbean and hope it will be less daunting
than the people who gave it their name. Judging by the Index
Chart there'll never be a lack of wind. There should be a strong
prevailing wind of force four or five along the whole route,
with about nil per cent of calms. The currents are mostly
favourable to us. But the area is very crowded—a funnel in
which steamers, yachts and merchantmen congregate from all
sides, going towards the canal. You have to keep your eyes
open. We know from experience that a light is not enough.

Christian tries in vain all day to get Washington on our old
radio receiver. He can't get a time signal from anywhere. We
must know what the Greenwich Mean Time is, because the
only chronometer we have is a watertight watch.

We get back into the rhythm of a long voyage, nibbling ship's biscuits and wishing we had a whole cargo of them. They relieve seasickness, anxiety, and that hollow feeling in your stomach.

We can get Cuba clearly on our receiver, and are lectured all day about the horrible Yankees, but can't get a time check. We must try something else—it's getting urgent. The skipper reckons we are about 90 miles from the last little Dutch island. We have two compasses. One is inside, at the head of the captain's bunk, the other on deck. The latter doesn't work and swivels crazily in all directions. We can't think why.

Laurence feeds hungrily. I have to rest more, and fight desperately against my growing lassitude. Laurence has a perfect grasp of the ideal way to spend the first few days at sea: eat and drink well, keep warm and sleep as much as you can. She's never sick. She has a seawater bath every day in the cockpit.

Oh dear. I had put her bedding out on deck, with the empty cot on the cockpit bench. When I go to get it, it has disappeared. I'm terribly upset. Luckily there's still the mattress. I sew some strong material on to it and a bit of fishing net, which I hook on screws. It's less attractive and comfortable, and not even transportable. And we can't buy anything else until we get to Tahiti. And I had so longed for a child's pretty bedroom. I've stuck some simple drawings on the varnished ceiling which is only 30 centimetres above her head, to brighten it up a bit. Her only toys are a plastic counting-frame, three rings on a chain and three little rubber animals.

Nothing on the wireless. A broken connection, probably. The days pass. The sea is stormier. It's miserable in this weather not to be sure of our bearings, which Christian can only judge from the time we had before. We could be 20 or 30 miles from our estimated position, that is nearer to the coastline with its islands and dangerous shallows. Our badly patched sails are straining in the wind. Will they hold out as far as Tahiti?

Opening the hatch is out of the question. Every time we open it a crack to crawl out, the skipper's bed is drowned in a flood of water.

But we don't regret being here for a moment.

Gigi is straining in the stormy sea. Because as well as being steep, the waves often hit us broadside on. The *Alpha* has a violent movement, and our muscles strain all the time. We can't sleep properly.

So that Laurence can play in safety, I have fixed some sail-cloth right across my bunk, and she holds happily on to it. She jumps on her fat little legs, but never loses her balance. Even when she walks about in the cabin, she never falls, in spite of the rolling motion of the boat which makes us all hold on tightly. The waves are sweeping over the deck all the time, so she'll stay down below while this lasts.

Now the mainsail is tearing. We lower it immediately and as sewing is out of the question today, we hoist a red boomed-out storm-jib. Christian takes the radio receiver to bits and finds a wire has come loose. Didier gets out the gas soldering iron, but loses the cap while putting in the refill. Overboard. So there's no hope of mending the receiver. A good example of how important an object can be at sea. The loss of this piece could cost us our lives.

All we know is that we don't know—within twenty miles—where we are. It's not at all funny. The sea is growing more stormy all the time and it's very difficult to keep one's course. The waves crash against the bows. Didier has moved his bedding on to the floor in the saloon.

Should I have forced Laurence to lead this life? The permanent din, the violent jolts which the human body was not made to withstand. But is it worse than the métro rumbling under Paris all night, the cars and polluted air, and frenetic people rushing about in towns?

In the week since we left St Barthélémy, we've lost two good towing lines, a black oilskin, Gigi's spanner, Laurence's cot, two booms, and a torn jib. The engine has stalled, Gigi has just broken and we can't mend the radio. It would be difficult to have a worse run of luck in so short a time.

We're taking turns at the helm—it's absolutely exhausting.

As we never sleep deeply, my nerves are in shreds. And no one can understand that who hasn't experienced it. You have to have felt like that to believe it. Why don't I regret having come? Why does the temptation to go ashore and live elsewhere remain only a vague impulse? Because adventure runs in my blood. Because I'm too tired to think. It was only later that I would understand that basically it was because I couldn't imagine life any other way: you can't put a price on a sunset in the northern Galapagos Islands; it is worth a lot of sacrifices.

The bread's finished today: the rest is all green and must be thrown away. The bananas are finished. And so is the large fore-sail: I took the tiller aft while Christian took our bearings. Two waves in quick succession came up behind me from astern. I didn't react quickly enough, we gybed and the jib split in two right down the centre seam which came completely adrift. I need hardly add how angry the skipper was. An interlude in our married life. Luckily the mainsail has been mended meanwhile: we hoist it at once. But it seems very fragile in this weather. Where are we? The thought obsesses us.

This morning we got to within 30 metres of a German cargo boat which must have been on its way from Panama, to ask them where we are. Some men on the deck stared at us through their binoculars. Christian made signals which they didn't understand. Finally I went on deck with Laurence and semaphored SOS. They went calmly on their way, leaving us to it. If we had been urgently in need of help I don't think they would have acted any differently.

It's even more depressing because the sky is overcast, the wind is increasing in strength, and the sea is rising, rising. The water is dirty, muddy, and full of all kinds of débris: bits of packing cases, plastic bottles, treetrunks on which seabirds perch with shrill cries.

We have only got our ten square metres of canvas, two storm-jibs goosewinged out, one on the forestay, the other in place of the mainsail, held by a firmly secured broomstick. But with the wind mostly force eight or nine, this frail boom will probably break and tear the sail any minute now. So the skipper takes off our only boom, the proper one, but makes a false move and the spar falls into the water. And we're running before the wind.

'CHRISTIAN!'

He's in the water. I scream at the top of my lungs. My voice gets lost, piping in the wind which is howling like a pack of wolves. A fearful agony constricts my throat, no, my stomach, oh I don't know, it's too painful. Every tenth of a second counts, and yet I do nothing. I do nothing because any movement would be time lost, lost for ever because I can still see Christian.

As if my seeing him could prevent him disappearing, keep him within our grasp.

Didier and I have thrown him the mooring line which is always coiled in the stern. By some awful mishap it wasn't secured. I thought Didier was taking care of it and he was probably counting on me to do the only possible thing—take a turn round the mooring cleat. But we found ourselves clinging, like two idiots, to ten centimetres of line, unable to save Christian.

It's a foolish story and we come out of it very badly. But it's a true story. Our two storm-jibs were boomed out forward. There was a strong wind and the troughs of the waves were six or seven metres deep. The *Alpha* was riding out the gale well, with her ten metres of sail. It was impossible to heave to at once without sheeting in the sails. And it was out of the question to luff up and go about in this weather: even hove to, the current was so strong that we'd be no better off. We could see treetrunks sailing past us.

Each tenth, hundredth of a second is vital now. I am panicking and my thoughts and reflexes are frozen. Everything rushes through my head wildly: rope on the box bunk—it would take time to go down for it, I'd lose Christian from sight; throw anything that will float—the buoy in front of me—but my body won't respond. Why? Didier isn't doing anything either; he must be numbed too, or panicking, it comes to the same thing.

Christian has caught hold of the log. The log-line, a nylon line a few millimetres in diameter, secured to the boat by a small bit of metal, is not exactly designed for hauling a man on board. Why doesn't one of us throw a line to him now? Because we both think that the log-line will give? That it will be too late anyway? Why? But was I capable of thought at that instant? Aware of the fact that Christian's life hung on a log-line?

I didn't even think 'man overboard', which as far as I am concerned is synonymous with certain death. It's a black hole, nothingness. I am outside time. I've even forgotten Laurence.

Christian is an exceptional swimmer. He is gaining centimetre by centimetre. His muscles will break. Luckily he's only got bathing trunks on, and strong lungs. He raises his head from the water as little as possible so as to offer the least resistance, in the raging, glaucous, dirty sea.

The sky is black, the wind whistles in the rigging and the *Alpha* is straining. Each second seems like an hour. I can't breathe, I'm not trembling: I am beyond all reaction.

I stand unmoving, my eyes on Christian.

My mind and body are frozen.

Christian climbs aboard. It all goes cloudy.

'Why didn't you take a turn round the cleat?'

He doesn't even seem angry. Did he realize the position he was in?

Why did he jump overboard to rescue the boom in such a heavy sea? Why did he obstinately do it without warning us? He wanted to get a line round the boom in the water and haul it up. There's always a line coiled in the stern: why wasn't it made fast? It all happened so quickly that it seems incredible. Why didn't we take a turn round the cleat? It was an unpardonable, inconceivable error.

Christian is safely on board.

Christian is safely on board.

Christian is safely on board.

One's impulse at times like this is to shout 'Help!', but no one could have heard and one realizes how helpless one is in the middle of the ocean.

Was it our tiredness which was responsible? We knew very well what we ought to have done, it was quite easy, and yet we didn't do it. We foresaw everything except the panic which hits one like a sledgehammer and paralyses the nervous system.

The broomstick of course breaks as expected, and we hoist and reef the mainsail. But one of the main seams gives: will we reach Panama? Everything is sopping on board. Our sweaters are dripping wet in spite of our oilskins. Didier is very tired and beginning to feel seasick. Christian replaces him at the tiller to give him a chance to rest. We still don't know where we are. The weather's appalling with squall after squall, and it's impossible to get a true navigational fix because the sky is perpetually overcast. If only it would get better. We are merely surviving on board—trying to think as little as possible and not to talk, because at such times one can only talk about one's worries.

But we are cheered by Laurence with her smiles, her chattering, the progress she makes each day, her radiant health, her childish voice and two little white teeth which gleam like pearls.

When we wake up it's dead calm, which seems incredible. It's like being in port. We go up on deck in the sun. Christian starts the engine and repairs Gigi. The log indicates that we are doing four knots under power: the hull is covered with weed in spite of the speed we've been making and the anti-fouling. Next day the wind gets up a little. We pass two merchantmen who signal to us that we're on the right course, which reassures us a bit.

We're brusquely awakened at 2 am. Christian has started the engine. Before us, only one or two miles off, in the brilliant moonlight, lies the rocky coast of South America—black and aggressive, like a sinister tomb. So we must be twenty miles from the position we calculated on the incorrect time. If Christian had been asleep we would have landed up at the edge of the dense forest—which smells, surprisingly strongly, of chlorophyll—far from civilization, and help. But our skipper always instinctively scents danger.

Unable to sleep, we hug the coast until dawn. As it grows light we see several boats are on the same course as ourselves, and we reach Panama safely.

The canal zone is a bit of America dumped down in the heavy, humid equatorial heat. It rains there every day. We make ourselves at home for the evening in the Christobal yacht club, a wooden building with a large verandah-restaurant which extends on to the landing-stages. We have a lovely hot shower to get the salt off our skin. The next day the two men go off: by law one must have five adults on board to go through the canal, and a special pilot. Christian and Didier are helping a neighbouring yacht, the *Fugue*, who will help us tomorrow.

I seize the opportunity to clean the boat. The oil lamps and Primus smoked a lot crossing the Caribbean, and the ceiling is grey. Meanwhile Laurence explores the deck on all fours. I'm not afraid she'll fall overboard because she never goes anywhere without testing each handhold carefully. She's incredibly careful, and she's still only seven months old.

But I have to retrieve her from the *Skaffie*, a seven-metre yacht of 4.8 tons, belonging to Dee Dee and Jim, who have decided to sail to the West Indies with two little kittens—it was

the kittens that attracted Laurence. The *Skaffie* will have fun if
they meet the same weather we've just had. I don't think we'd
have the courage to go back just now. It's a bit reckless of them
to sail in that direction at this time of year, when there is a
99 per cent chance of a strong head wind.

At seven o'clock, as the men are not yet back, Dee Dee and
Jim invite me to the yacht club for a French steak: a 400
gramme steak with chips and a green salad. Delicious.
Laurence, sitting in a high chair for the first time in her life,
watches us and covers herself with a delicious potato purée
topped with grated cheese and fresh butter.

At about eleven, the men have all arrived back by train, and
want to go to bed at once because it will be our turn early in
the morning. I learn that the *Fugue*, which left at seven, arrived
at Balboa at 6 pm, and that in the last lock the current wedged
them against a huge barge and they couldn't get free. It was
funny in retrospect. It took them an hour and a half to get back
by train, and cost a dollar each. It costs eleven dollars for the
boat to go through, which is very reasonable, because one
might be the only boat in a lock, and we make as much work
for the canal as a steamer.

Wednesday, 15 May. The pilot comes on board. It is obligatory
that we should be stationed as follows: Didier and one American each with a line in the bows, Christian and the second
American each with a line in the stern, with myself at the tiller.
The pilot directs operations and takes over the tiller if any
difficulties arise. So Laurence will have to spend the day below,
in the cabin, in spite of the torrid heat. It's impossible to keep
her on deck and she can only come up to be fed.

After our 600 locks in Europe, we're not too worried about
going through the canal. And Christian and I have also been
through it several times on steamers. It's familiar territory for
us. Which doesn't detract from the violence of the currents or
the back-wash.

We feel terribly small in the vast lock, with hawsers which
seem to go on for ever; the safety of the *Alpha* depends on the
strength of these strands.

Christian is on edge when he has to give the tiller, in this
strong current, to a pilot used to large cargo boats, who admits
5*

it's the first time he's taken a yacht through. Right in the middle of Lake Gatun, we run out of fuel. We continue under canvas, while the pilot asks for a refill on his walkie-talkie set. Less than two hours later, a motor-boat brings us twenty litres of fuel. We haven't lost very much time. Lake Gatun is very turbulent, and we'd hate to fall in the water for fear of hungry caymans.

We get through the locks without a hitch, and moor at the Balboa yacht club at about six. We can stay there free for ten days. A motor-boat with a pilot—also free—is at our disposal to take and fetch us ashore from seven in the morning until seven at night. But tonight we've no desire to go ashore—we only want to sleep.

We've got a very crowded programme for the ten days we can stay in Panama—because the visa given to us for going through the canal expires after that date. We need: a visa for the Galapagos Islands; a radio receiver which works; to change the jib halyard; learn about lights in the Galapagos from a neighbouring boat; fill up with water and fuel; and stock up with provisions for at least four months, because we can't be sure of finding what we want in the Galapagos. We ought also to take advantage of the tide to careen the hull, find a good boom, fishing lines. Quite a full programme.

As far as the visa is concerned, we certainly ought to have got it elsewhere. As both Ecuador and Panama change governments fairly frequently, the Ecuadorian consul never gets paid —so he pays himself. It's quite a comedy. Normally a visa of this sort only costs about three dollars.

The consul is squat, plump and thick-lipped, and the price of a visa in fact depends on his mood, his degree of lucidity at the time and the yachtsman's appearance. Christian must look far too healthy because he starts off by asking for 35 dollars. We are told by our neighbours that one man had to pay 50 dollars for a minute sailing boat, and another fifteen for an eighteen-metre schooner. You have to bargain. But the little man won't listen to us. I go there with my husband and daughter and explain in Spanish that I've got a baby, that I might have to see a doctor in the Galapagos Islands, and that anyway we can't pay 35 dollars. He shakes his head, stubborn and churlish as a mule: 'There's no doctor in the Galapagos.'

Which is incorrect, anyway, because there's one at the American base. In an emergency a plane can fly you to America straight away. And the little man continues: 'All right, 30 dollars.'

We leave, deciding to abandon the Galapagos and go direct from Panama to the Marquesas Islands. We write to all the family telling them this. But on the evening before we are to leave the consul suddenly says it will be seventeen dollars. We ask for a receipt, but he goes scarlet with rage. So we decide to leave it, although it's at least half what he first asked. Very strange.

Panama turns out to be a very friendly port for us. An extremely distinguished elderly gentleman with greying hair and a kind face comes to visit us on his tender. He asks discreetly: 'Do you want to do any shopping with your baby? I can take you if you like. My car is at the club.'

He's so kind that we accept at once. The gentleman, Russ, stops at the club for a minute to telephone. A few minutes later we are in a large American store, where everything is much cheaper than in Panama. We write down the price of everything we are interested in in a notebook. We are not allowed to buy anything here. You have to have a Canal Zone resident's card. Russ gets some fresh food for us to eat this week. Then he asks, almost timidly: 'Are you in a hurry? Have you got something fixed for this evening? If not, I'd love you to meet my wife, Polly.'

We accept again, and ten minutes later, Laurence is stroking some thick green velvet chair covers. She puts her cheek against the material and smiles—it's soft. She seems amazed at this new world which doesn't move. She opens her eyes wide in her little bald head, and Russ christens her 'big big black eyes'. Polly and Russ have the serenity of a couple who have lived their lives to the full, but they also seem extremely young although they have numerous grandchildren. They sail, fish and their holidays are very adventurous for a leading canal official. Polly asks us to share 'a simple dinner—take pot-luck with us'. This civilized existence is very refreshing after our stormy crossing.

Another advantage of civilization. For 2.50 francs, which I

put in the club washing-machine, I can wash eight kilos of clothes—everything we've got. Meanwhile Christian is bargaining in Panama. He comes back with a good radio and a guitar. Cigarettes are only seventeen centimes a pack. At about eleven, Russ and Polly take us in their speedboat to Toboga, a very attractive little tourist island which has managed to keep its primitive character. There are delicious, cheap pineapples there.

Next day, taking advantage of the low tide, we moor alongside a wrecked cargo-boat on the bank opposite Balboa, at the other end of the famous Panama Bridge. The tide goes down more than two metres. We take up our scrapers, brushes, scouring powder, minium, paint and anti-fouling once more, the last with no great confidence. By seven we've finished and the tide has turned. As it gets dark we suddenly find we're itching all over.

'Nonos!'

But it's too late to take cover: they must have surreptitiously injected their poison into us as soon as the sun went down. They are little midges which you can hardly see, and seem much more venomous here than in Polynesia.

Laurence? I go aboard at once, but by some miracle she seems to have escaped. We hastily swallow some insect bite pills and use up two tubes of Phénergan in the night. At about 1 am, in broad moonlight, we leave the wreck with no regrets.

Christian spends the remaining time making up a list of useful provisions to take with us. I go on foot to Balboa with Laurence every day; and she chatters away in her pushchair. I pick up *atoni* mangoes from the beautifully kept grass along the roadside, just fallen off the trees and deliciously ripe. Laurence loves them and I'm delighted to be able to introduce her to trees, leaves, grass.

Balboa is clean, tidy, prefabricated, immensely well kept and hygienic. Shops and cars are air-conditioned and dogs don't foul the streets. In Panama City on the other hand complete squalor and total poverty go cheek by jowl with sickening wealth and the utmost dishonesty. Panama has its own smell, which is heavy, over perfumed or fetid, humid and suffocating, bigoted and depraved. By a shop selling plastic religious souvenirs, an urchin of twelve sidles up to you to offer his fourteen-year-old sister for a dollar.

I was in Balboa a year ago. Some friends who had decided to go to Panama by taxi, asked how much it would cost: 'Town centre? Four kilometres. There are five of you so it will be three dollars.'

That was correct. But the taxi, instead of taking them to the main square, as they had asked, took them to a villainous street nearby and stopped by a vicious looking bar. 'Here you are—ten dollars.'

'But——'

The driver took out a flick knife. 'Ten dollars.'

They paid up at once.

Panama—slums, stolen passports, duty-free shops where people haggle over the last sou. In some streets you shiver and get the feeling you are surrounded by murderers. Not necessarily mean, dark streets. Streets with smart flats, and villas with gardens surrounded by railings, where it is deathly silent even in the daytime. There's no one about and murder is no illusion: there's one every day. Panama is in a state of semi-permanent revolution. At present, for instance, the Americans from the Canal Zone don't dare go there for fear of being gunned down.

An American friend living in Panama City shows us the town, and also Old Panama, which was sacked and burnt by Morgan the pirate. David has been here several years and has a marvellous family, who are all musicians: the eldest girl plays the harp, the eldest boy the flute, the third the violin, the fourth the viola, their mother the piano, their father the organ. The youngest is courageously having a go at the 'cello. Having heard me say I couldn't find a rubber sheet, only plastic ones, David scours Panama all day. He finally brings me one.

We are supposed to be leaving tomorrow. Some friends are getting in the provisions for us. We take care of water, fuel, paraffin, bags of sugar, flour, potatoes, onions, all in twenty-kilo sacks. We wonder how we'll get it all in the lockers. When we arrive on board at four o'clock, we are surprised to find a large case of provisions we've ordered; plus all sorts of presents: little jars of food for Laurence, packets of cigarettes, biscuits and chocolate. With a note from Mr and Mrs H, who we have only met briefly once or twice: 'When our children go to Europe this summer, many people whom we will perhaps never meet will give them a helping hand, in one way or another. This is our way of thanking them.' We are very touched, and sad not to be able to see them again to try to tell them how grateful we are.

And the next day, Sunday, Russ asks us to accept a case of presents: 50 little jars for Laurence, rusks—and for us, detachable stainless steel heads for the underwater guns, cartridges for our .22 LR rifles, cigarettes, an enormous bag of sweets, and at the bottom of the case, a twenty dollar note 'in case you need it in the Galapagos'.

But we haven't got a visa.

We go back to the blasted Ecuadorian consul, who still wants seventeen dollars. We have to leave because our time is up. But we are a bit worried because on 27 May the headlines in the leading American newspapers read: 'CIVIL WAR IN FRANCE'. 'Eight million strikers in the streets of Paris.' 'Paris besieged by students and communists.' 'Paris is dead. Everything has come to a standstill.' And the Americans in the streets go about with smug smiles.

It's very upsetting when one can't do anything about it. What is our 'duty'? What possibilities are open to us? Not many. It would be at least a year before we could get back to France. Will Didier and Christian be called up? We feel there is nothing we can do except continue on our way to Tahiti, and see there what we can do. But we're worried about our family and friends who are besieged in Paris. I can't help thinking about all the horrors of the war, which my parents often described to me, and which still haunt my nightmares.

We go to see Fergusson on the *Serena*. Fergusson is a law unto himself: every year he spends several weeks' holiday on the canals of Patagonia and Tierra del Fuego. He insists that the fantastic beauty of the scenery makes it worth the effort. It makes us want to see it for ourselves. He gives us 200 metres of best quality nylon rope, and some very supple terylene to patch our sails with.

At 9.45, after a last communal shower in soft running water by the yacht-club landing-stage, we set sail into the Pacific.

At 10.45, Russ joins us in his motor-boat: he's brought Polly

and a young couple. We leave the *Alpha* in the care of the self-
steering gear and all go aboard his boat. It's most impressive
seeing one's yacht sailing along with no one on board. A
phantom boat. If this engine fails—goodbye *Alpha*. There's an
auxiliary engine, but all the same. Then at last it's time for
Russ to go back, before the sun sets. He leaves us with an ice-
box full of milk-shakes, frozen chicken, butter, coca-cola, beer—
and he has tears in his eyes when he says goodbye to 'big big
black eyes' who can't stop smiling at him. We feel tearful too.

One day passes, then another. The south wind is very feeble and
it's the south we are heading for. We are making no progress
and it never stops raining. None of us dares say what we are
thinking: the doldrums.

We are at the end of the period of favourable winds, and
consult our manuals. Most navigators take ten days to a fortnight to reach the Galapagos. They go south more or less along
the coast of South America.

We are still only a few miles from Panama, becalmed in the
Gulf. But we can get the Washington speaking-clock on our
new radio and it gives the time every five minutes throughout
the day and night. Modern technology is really amazing. We
could determine the boat's position with an ordinary alarm
clock.

All the fresh food goes off very quickly in this heat: pineapples, avocados, bananas, tomatoes, peppers, ripen in three
days. So we try to catch a turtle to console ourselves—with no
success. We also lose a dorado, which got off the hook at the
last minute.

Everything in cardboard packets—Laurence's cereals, porridge, semolina—gets damp. One should have everything in
hermetically sealed tins with desiccator bags. But eggs coated
with vaseline will keep several weeks if they are fresh to start
with.

We are hardly moving at all, and we don't man the tiller. It
should be peaceful—but the annoying thing is that our living
space is so reduced. The forecastle is taken up by Didier and the
vegetables. The washroom is stuffed with provisions and
unusable. The cockpit is unbearable in this heat with the
burning sun. Which leaves the saloon. Laurence takes up the

whole of my bunk: there is only the skipper's to sit on. We can sit or lie down on it and that's about it.

It's difficult to imagine. We three adults, plus a baby who is beginning to climb everywhere, which cramps us even more because we have to be careful all the time not to trip or fall over her. She's seven months old and can climb out of the cabin by herself, even at sea with the boat rocking. The exit ladder is a vertical plank 1.10 metres high with two little steps fixed across it. Laurence pulls herself up by her arms and installs herself flat out on top of the engine to sleep like a kitten, choosing the most stable part of the boat.

I have already said that our happiness, which was the result of our chosen way of life, was not easily come by. I can't pass over in silence what is now only an unhappy memory. There will be other black spots, many more, before the happy days in which I am writing this.

Our close quarters, combined with the dead calm and equatorial heat had a disastrous effect on our nerves. Christian and I fought incessantly. Didier remained remarkably calm, reading and doing an hour's English every day.

It's extremely difficult for two or three people to be cooped up together day and night on a very small boat. The lack of privacy is unbearable for a woman. It is terrible never to be able to be by oneself, and even if there is a curtain or door as a physical barrier between me and the others for a minute, everyone is aware of every detail of my toilet. It is rather like an indecent assault going on for months on end.

And all these small things end up by being detrimental to a marriage.

When you are living under these conditions you can't hide anything from your partner, and he can't hide anything from you. You have to really be able to live together. And, when you have already said 'everything', you still have to be able to find something to say to each other. In fact you don't talk any more, or discuss things. Sometimes you hold a long monologue. You concentrate on surviving, on tiring yourself out as little as possible.

I remember all the people we have met in various ports, who envy us and say: 'You *are* lucky.' It strikes me that if they had been in our place they wouldn't have got very far. You need to be lucky when you embark on an adventure like this. A voyage isn't exciting and intoxicating every day. You have to weather a lot of blows before you can enjoy a nice beach or a superb sunset. It wasn't without good cause that Miles Smeeton gave his book the title *Once is Enough*! It speaks for itself.

Our Caribbean crossing wasn't very tranquil, and didn't begin well. But I can't imagine life any other way—even when I feel I am weakening, I tell myself: It would be unbearable to live ashore with a husband who goes off at seven in the morning and comes back at seven at night, exhausted by his day's work and having spent the best part of the day with other people, doing things I can't take part in.

I still think that love is the pleasure one shares in being alive, having a roof over one's head, not dying of cold or hunger, having a child whom you bring up together. Above all sharing the same risks permanently. In modern life we don't share the same risks any more. But between these two extremes of existence, there must be a happy mean?

It's raining and there's not a breath of wind. A shoal of tunny fish swim round the *Alpha*, which is trailing along no faster than the current. Some bonitos pay us a visit. The heat is torrid and humid and we think longingly of the trade winds. The washing doesn't dry: even when it isn't raining the air is too damp.

Suddenly, at about ten o'clock, I see Christian creep down to get his harpoon with the detachable head. He comes quietly back on deck, with a strong bit of rope. Didier takes the rope without saying anything. And—they've got it. The detachable head has gone into the only soft part of the turtle, in its neck. An ordinary tip would have got twisted. Christian tows the turtle, which gives Didier time to pass a line round it. A few minutes later the beautiful green-backed creature is on deck: it must have been incautious enough to take a nap floating on top of the water.

Although I've often seen it done in Tahiti, I find the cutting up very distasteful. Even after hitting it on the head, the turtle's still alive. You put it on its back and run along the soft edge between its shell and stomach with a large knife. There are streams of blood everywhere and the insides are still alive while you are cutting them up. It's sickening. Yet one has to kill to eat. And turtle meat is the only red meat we get at sea. We can't miss the chance.

We have real steaks for lunch—lovely thick, red steaks. In the evening a stew with vegetables. As there's no wind and no chores to do, we celebrate. Large old turtles have a strong fishy taste which can be most unpleasant and put you off them for good. But a young turtle, especially if you have time to purge it in clear water for a few days, can taste of any meat from beef to pork, including veal and horsemeat.

The one we've caught is a bit too old, especially as Didier has never tasted it before. Turtle-meat is good, but there's a lot of it and it goes on for a bit too long. We've already eaten it four times in two days and there's plenty left. We take our bearings to cheer ourselves up: 120 miles in a fortnight. It's our record for slowness. And there's still no wind, only a cross sea, and we're making no headway, in spite of the engine, in the grilling sun.

Christian harpoons a second turtle. The beast. But the turtle gets the better of him, because it goes off with the detachable tip and the nylon gets caught in the engine propeller. And several sharks appear just as he's about to dive down and investigate. As soon as they look like going off, Christian bravely gets into the water and untangles the nylon line in record time, while I keep a lookout.

The vegetables are rotting, the fish won't bite. We're all sick of turtle, except Christian. The wind is against us. We have noticed that porpoises make a sucking noise, like kissing. As soon as we hear it we go on deck and a few minutes later they appear. Laurence recognizes them and is wild with delight to see them leaping and playing only a metre away from her.

Didier has finished his tobacco and redoubles his efforts to learn English with me. Christian is worried. We mend the sails nearly every day and we're making no headway. It's getting desperate. We begin listing everything on board which could be made into sails: old sheets, *pareos*, and a ten-square-metre tarpaulin.

I hope that we won't be reduced to this; there's no hope of getting any sails until we get to Papeete. And we've still got to get there.

One day passes, then another. A nice surprise. When we wake up we see Malpelo ahead of us. A fortnight to get to Malpelo, it's incredible. It usually takes three to five days. But don't let's celebrate too soon, it's still only on the horizon. The rock, less than half-way between Panama and the Galapagos Islands, is inaccessible and uninhabitable, right in the middle of the sea. It's an important landmark—at least we're on the right track. It must be awful to be stuck there, miles from anywhere, in the doldrums.

It's very chilly and we get out duvets, sweaters and trousers. At this time of year the Humboldt Current brings an icy stream, which the whales love, from Cape Horn. The wind is still fairly strong, still against us.

This morning Malpelo is still ahead of us. We begin to ask ourselves if it isn't a mirage, an hallucination. It's discouraging going so slowly. Especially as the wind is wearing out our sails to no purpose. If it doesn't change, will we go back to Panama or proceed very, very slowly to the Galapagos? There must also be a very strong cross current. The wind changes all the time and it's a real struggle to keep our course.

We gaze in silence at the infernal zig-zag route we have been following for over a fortnight. Again our only chart of the Pacific is an Index Chart which stretches from Australia to South America. We have a chart of the Galapagos and three of the Marquesas Islands. When one sees all that water without any land, one wonders how many months this voyage will last. In the evening, when the sun goes down, Malpelo is behind us at last.

Friday 14 June. The *Alpha* is a year old. It's a shame to be in the doldrums for her birthday. We've given up counting the days or the distance still to cover. And where are we going anyway? We'd like to know. Will we do 3,000 miles at a speed of one or two knots?

What a night. No moon, gigantic waves and the lugubrious sound of the tiller threatening to break at any moment. The wood is split along almost the entire length. Christian has mended it as best he can with nylon rope, but in this sea the rudder thrashes about and wrenches at the lashed tiller. The waves constantly wash over the bows, and at about 1 am the jib goes. Didier and Christian change it again in the pelting rain. Then it's the mainsail's turn. We furl it for the rest of the night. Our poor skipper can't go to sleep again. He keeps sitting up and then lying down and turning over again, worrying about the sails.

The boat is perpetually submerged, the gunwale under water. The *Alpha* rides nimbly up and over the great waves, and sometimes breaks through the crests or goes under. She's too heavy, too weighed down by barnacles. The sky is still grey, menacing; we've had enough of this weather. Why don't we call in at Cocos? That would break the voyage for us. It will be marvellous if we take as long doing Cocos-Galapagos as we've taken doing Panama-Cocos. Anyway the wind seems to be pushing us towards Cocos.

When I was going by steamer to France, to rejoin Christian, we passed this island. An extract from the Sailing Directions was pasted up, with comments: 'It is said that it was on this island that Captain Morgan hid his treasure after he had sacked Panama.' All those who had gone there to hunt for the treasure were said to have died mysterious deaths. There was talk of giant spiders, huge poisonous mosquitoes, millions of snakes—and monkeys. The Sailing Directions stated that the island was infested with poisonous red ants, and surrounded by sharks. It didn't sound very attractive. But we can rest in a quiet bay and mend our sails properly—only there are still 160 miles before we reach Cocos. At the rate of twenty miles a day it will take us over a week. Eight days to do 160 miles. It takes a steamer less than two days, a plane only a few hours.

X

Our Own Island

THE SEA IS making an incredible din. A sound of tumultuous
torrents. Currents are eddying in every direction, like great
rivers crashing into each other all round us.

But life goes on much as usual in the cabin, as if we were in
harbour. Christian writes; we are rather like shipwrecked
mariners but we must keep up an appearance of normality.
I force myself to keep the boat clean. Our life is organized down
to the last detail as usual. It's vital not to let ourselves go. Our
English lessons with Didier are important for keeping up
morale. It's important to learn and work at something, to
nourish our brains which have no outside stimuli. We're like
caged animals at the zoo. And we haven't even got people
staring at us to distract us. I gaze in horror at the tracks the
weevils have made in the rice, semolina, pasta and porridge.
Laurence is entranced by the little holes running through the
dried peas. Christian is staring at a spot no bigger than a
pinhead on our Index Chart of the Pacific—Cocos Island.
We've decided to call in there.

And the dead calm continues endlessly. Doldrums, notes the
skipper. We've said it now. The weather doesn't correspond
with the true definition of the term, since the doldrums means
an area without any wind at all. But a contrary wind, powerful
currents and calms in succession have just about the same effect
on us. Twenty miles a day, for weeks on end, is quite something.

We don't say 'when we get to' now, but 'if we get to Cocos
Island'. Each object on board has taken on vital significance.
We can't waste or lose anything. We have to economize on
writing paper, the soft rubber for the charts, the paraffin for
lights and cooking; we mustn't lose pencils or cooking things;
we have to count our provisions. We won't be able to buy
anything for a long time.

Our conversations with Christian become daydreams which ramble on for hours. We could live like Robinson Crusoe on a desert island for six months. After all, what they say must be rather exaggerated, to keep off gold diggers?

Yes, of course. But we've got to be very careful because of Laurence. And we come back to reality: shampoo our hair in salt water, scrub ourselves all over, give Laurence her twice-daily bath. Oh dear. She's fallen in the soapy washing-up water. Jelly-fish the size of peas which are ordinarily invisible and harmless, secrete long filaments of a lovely turquoise blue if there's any soap in the water, and these sting. It's a sharp pain but it doesn't last, and the red mark left by the burn soon fades.

Fishing for dorados continues, and we always eat them raw. All our clothes and bedding dry in the sun, thanks to the calm weather. The water we shipped only two days ago has made everything damp and there's a smell of mildew everywhere. Christian estimates our position exactly, which puts us back at a point behind our yesterday's position, but we hadn't taken astronomical bearings for a week. We were covering so few miles a day.

Three o'clock. Christian suddenly leaps up: a large object has jolted roughly against the stern on the starboard side. There's a second heavy scratching, like the sound of a grater against the barnacles. Only sharks behave like that. There are about a dozen of them, the smallest one at least two metres long. They've come to rub their backs on the hull.

Luckily the whales don't seem to have the same idea. The *Alpha* seems rather low in the water when one thinks about all those sharks, and remembers how far they can leap after their prey when necessary. It makes our flesh creep.

In spite of all our plans, we can't help thinking that this life can be sheer slavery. A yacht is a constant worry. Everything has to be kept in perfect repair on board: the guardrails must be well greased, the mast and cross-trees regularly inspected, the shrouds kept taut. You have to keep an eye on the sails when they begin to get worn, spot the smallest seam tearing before it comes apart completely. The *Alpha*'s hull also presents us with various problems: how can we scrape under the seams if it begins to rust?

Then, apart from highly sophisticated and carefully guarded 'marinas', there are practically no harbours which are 100 per cent safe. There is always a risk of theft, or bad weather. But isn't the whole of life full of such obstacles? We have chosen these particular ones in order to be able to enjoy our desert island—I only hope we get there. To enjoy turtle hunting, eating crayfish grilled over an open fire—until we can't eat any more—to enjoy sunsets of unparalleled beauty.

Nothing is for free, and we are having to pay for these things by our own efforts and patience, doing our twenty miles a day. Sometimes I think we're completely mad to let ourselves be buffeted like this all day, and all night. To ship a green sea; stay transfixed at the helm. But in the long run it doesn't depress me as much as catching the métro at six in the evening, my alarm clock going off at five or six in the morning and setting off in thick, icy fog for a badly lit and stuffy office, where everyone nurses their grievances in communal misery. I am taking an extreme example, to compare it with living on a boat, which is itself an extreme example of pleasure cruising.

Having grown up in Polynesia, before aeroplanes and the atomic bomb, at a time when it was easy to fulfil one's needs without living crammed together and coldly dependent upon one another, I find our large sophisticated cities growing sadly more and more like the human zoo which Desmond Morris describes so well. I feel incapable of voluntarily bringing up children far from the natural world, far from sun, with no sand and water to splash about in.

Disaster has struck tonight. The boat is yawing as usual in the wind, and Christian gets up to put her back on course. But this time there is an awful crack as the skipper swings the sail across to the other side.

'Didier,' he shouts hoarsely, 'quick, give me a hand.'

Didier, roused from a deep sleep by a jerky movement of the *Alpha*, is on deck in a matter of seconds.

'Blast!'

The mainsail is torn right across, in tatters from one end of the boom to the other, by the first reef.

In the hurly-burly, I find myself on deck to inspect the damage just as the skipper lowers the sail. I could weep. The canvas is rotten, swollen with salt and burnt by the sun.

We have no spare sail and can go only 150 miles at most with the engine. When we had to choose between 100 extra litres of fuel or drinking water, we didn't hesitate: we chose the water. And we have about five months supply of foodstuffs on board. But can we hoist our sheets and *pareos*? It's out of the question to mend the sail at sea, because it has to be stretched out flat. As a temporary measure the skipper reefs the sail. The torn part is rolled up and securely fixed to the boom but the area of sail is greatly reduced. The wind is moderate and the hull is covered with weed which trails like fins down the sides: when will we get to Cocos? At dawn I cry in a nightmare: 'A needle, a needle!' I'm completely swamped by an immense white sail I'm trying to mend. I've got kilometres of thread which is all tangled, but no needle. I need a huge needle.

We've been at sea 26 days already. We would possibly have reached the Galapagos long ago if we'd sailed due south, using the engine. There is not much fresh food left. Only a few lemons, a lot of onions, and only a kilo of potatoes. We'll have to eat vitamin pills. We've got enough drinking water for a month. If it rains we can collect some more in Laurence's bath, under the mainsail.

The skipper says we'll reach Cocos tomorrow. There do seem to be more birds and the wind seems a bit stronger; but seabirds can go long distances. We have seen them everywhere, even 1,500 miles from the shore. Quite small birds, who have to spend many nights at sea. But today the skipper puts the points of the dividers with one on our position, one on the spot representing Cocos Island. There are 50 miles to go. I can't believe we'll hit it exactly right. We all bend over the chart. Laurence smiles at us, her four baby teeth pearly bright in her little round head.

This little bit of woman takes up all my time. I realize that everything I do or think is qualified by her existence. I need to stand back from her. I sometimes think it must be bad for her always to live with her father and mother; I'm afraid she'll become spoilt or capricious. But so far there's no problem. She smiles and laughs all day long.

At sunrise, we catch a glimpse of the unaccustomed contours of an island in the morning mist away to the south-west. We see a mountain sharply delineated for an instant, then it melts away. Are we imagining that a cloud is an island?

But the sun gradually rises behind us. Cocos Island is clearly visible directly ahead—but the wind is no stronger. In the afternoon Christian decides to start the engine so we will get there before nightfall. And then the crank-handle snaps. He tries to mend it. The engine won't start. It hasn't been used for too long and is useless.

'Damn and blast!'

It's enough to dampen anyone's morale. No sails, a boat weighed down with provisions and covered with barnacles, a tiller which has to be held at an angle and which doesn't respond properly even then—and now this wretched engine. It's maddening, when you're only a few miles from land, to be so helpless and unable to get there.

By the end of the afternoon it has started to drizzle. The sky gets more and more overcast. By sunset we are one or two miles from the shore, but the weather is terrible and we can't possibly land in the dark and mist on an island for which we haven't even got a chart. We were to learn later that Cocos Island belongs to Costa Rica. One must have an authorization from this country to go there, to get which you have to promise on your honour not to look for Morgan's treasure. All we're looking for is a bit of peace and quiet. We have bad dreams all night, and keep getting up, and Christian tacks out to sea, then back towards land, towards the sea, the land. In the morning it rains more and more, with gusts of wind followed by a dead calm. We're a bit worried about landing on the island and some pop music from Radio Washington cheers us up.

A current drives us along the coast. It's tricky without an engine. More than once I think we've foundered as gigantic black rocks tower over us, or the cliff, which seems suddenly to be all round us. Christian has wisely got some empty jerrycans ready, which we can use as a raft to drop anchor out at sea if necessary. Sometimes the current takes us directly towards the cliff. So Didier and Christian paddle with planks two metres long. What a blessing the paddles are, but they're so slow.

At last we're there, we're anchored. We scraped the bottom

with the keel and had to pull up the chain and anchor. Finally we dropped our good old CQR successfully in a marvellous sandy bay.

The sun is shining, tinged with the reds and orange of sunset. The colours of the island come alive. We see great scarlet balls in the trees: edible fruit? But the 'fruit' fly off. Christian Zuber told me later that we were lucky enough to arrive just at the frigate-birds' mating season: to attract the females the males swell out a huge red sack under their neck and beak.

We inspect the luxuriant vegetation in vain for a last lingering monkey or poisonous snake. There are only the frigate-birds, boobies, egrets, and every kind of seabird, as far as the eye can see. They all squawk in unison. The boobies dive straight down as if they had been fired from a gun, with their wings flat against their bodies. They never fly up without a fish in their beaks.

We are about 1,000 kilometres to the west of Panama, and 700 kilometres north of the Galapagos Islands. 'Our' little island is about 200 metres high and must be about 20 to 30 kilometres in circumference. The cliffs are sheer above a deep sea. There are bare black rocks rising from the water beyond the two arms of the bay, on either side. It seems difficult to penetrate into the interior of the island. We can see five waterfalls from the deck of the *Alpha*. All that fresh water going to waste. I can feel the water on my salt-dried skin. What is the secret of this cursed island? It is so like Polynesia, with its soft exuberance.

On examining the bay more closely—we were later to learn it was called Chatham Bay—we see a small watercourse which seems to indicate a rift in the mountain. The colour of the vegetation, the way the trees grow, suggest—is it a valley? We're delighted at the idea.

There are dozens of sharks. Are they fonder of human flesh than those of the Tuamotu Archipelago or Bora-Bora? As we're uncertain we decide that the 'women and children' shall stay on board while the men go and investigate before it gets dark, which will be fairly soon. They load into the inflatable bath: camouflage outfits bought in the Puces market, socks and gloves, anti-mosquito cream for their faces, caps—and the gun. Wearing their bathing trunks they get into the water in the midst of the sharks' fins. Some small ones come and sniff the bath, and the flippers of the two valiant swimmers as they do a frantic crawl to the beach, 150 metres off. Ten minutes later Laurence and I can see them standing correctly dressed on the sand, which seems unreal to me because I've seen nothing but water for a month.

They inspect the beach, scrutinize the trees from which the snakes should writhe—or some nice little monkeys. They are ready to tackle all the dangers promised by the stories about Cocos Island. They dig around and turn over dead leaves and treetrunks looking for red ants or harmful insects. Suddenly Christian raises his gun: at the far end of the beach a goat is staring at him quite unafraid. Our skipper presses the trigger, but he's forgotten to release the safety catch and the goat trots calmly off into the thicket.

The animals on the island must be descendants of those which were brought or abandoned there by the pirates whose lair this was. For tonight at any rate our two hunters will dream of the thousands of oysters they have seen clinging to the rocks at low tide, of egrets which would be delicious on a spit, and of the squealing of wild pigs on all sides. We are longing to taste fresh meat again.

In fact, this beautiful wilderness, gilded by the last rays of the setting sun, is not at all frightening. One feels that if one has no fear, and lives at its own rhythm, it will be a friendly island.

Laurence doesn't seem interested in the birds which wheel above us with loud cries, but she watches fascinated as the tip of the island is silhouetted darkly against the flaming sky. As always in the Tropics, night falls abruptly, twenty minutes after sunset. The incessant chatter of the birds dies away, becomes a whisper, a rustling sound: the silence is filled with intense night-time activity. There's always a fish leaping, a bird flapping its wings in the branches. The sea rises and falls, taking pebbles with it and murmuring on the beach. We are right in the middle of the calm-belts which the sailors of old dreaded, far from all civilization. There are no humans on the island. But there is fantastic animal life—and the air is filled with heavy, exotic sounds.

We spend a peaceful night in the motionless boat. Have a proper meal, at the table, with plates. We get out some clean

sheets and install ourselves in our cabin in the forecastle. Didier
shares the saloon with Laurence.

After our dinner of corned beef with rice and onions, we sit
on deck and the skipper plays some flamenco on his guitar.
We finish the evening with lingering Tahitian melodies which
die away into the night. Then, in the silence, the nocturnal
rustling becomes an uproar. When I was a child this humming
both fascinated and upset me. I forced myself to dissect what
grown-ups called silence. But it rapidly gave me a kind of
vertigo, a feeling of a bottomless precipice. So I would pick up
a little sand and tell myself quietly that the night was exactly
the same as the day time, but without any sun. And yet the
night is quite a different world.

Towards midnight, a heavy bump wakes us up abruptly from
a deep sleep. Then silence. Then another bump. We've run
aground. As the tide is very low and must be about to turn, the
skipper decides to wait for high tide to move the *Alpha*.

At six o'clock the first rays of the sun, already blazing and
burning hot, turn the cabin into an oven. Luckily the pure
brilliant white of the boat beats back the heat: even when the
sun is at its height the steel of the deck is cold to the touch.
Thanks to that and the good ventilation of the hatches fore
and aft, we have always, luckily, had to have bedclothes at
night, even in the Tropics. At the first blaze of light, I push the
blanket to the end of the bed and Christian opens the hatch.
Our two heads bob up from the forehatch. We have to half
close our eyes in the blinding light. The sea sparkles, it is warm
and the water looks lovely. The birds have been awake and out
hunting for hours. They dive down beside us, come up with a
fish, are chased by one of their kind, lose their catch, snatch it
back, lose it again—squawking loudly.

Oh how lovely it would be to dive naked into the clear water.
But it is still full of sharks, of course. Didier and Christian have
their first swim while I make some griddle-cakes with flour, oil,
baking powder and water. I use a glass to press them flat with,
and for an oven, put an aluminium plate upside down on the
Primus, with the frying-pan on top covered with a saucepan.
The boys are swimming round the *Alpha*. The fish seem never
to have met human predators before, invading their lagoon.
They come sniffing round the two strangers. A shark with a

long dorsal fin and a tail with white marks on it brushes past the tip of Christian's gun. A few metres farther on, some scad come leaping with a flash of silver from water thrashed into a whirlpool by the sharks' flippers. I call the others back for breakfast. The griddle-cakes are a bit hard on the teeth but taste delicious after our diet of stale, mouldy or green bread, followed by rice with powdered milk, then rice with water and jam.

We free the anchor from the coral it has got caught up in and make our way between the clusters of coral with our makeshift paddles to a deeper anchorage. This will mean there is farther to swim, through the sharks, to get ashore.

The sun is getting higher and it's time to think about getting some food. The fishermen can take their choice from the vast aquarium of fish of every colour and kind. I place my order: 'A sole for Laurence and two red mullet for me.'

Christian will probably bring back two or three large scad for himself, and Didier some groupers. Fifteen minutes later I have cleaned and scaled them and they're sizzling in the pan. The sharks are fighting over the entrails nearby.

After our surfeit of dorados and turtle-meat, we really appreciate these small inshore fish, with their delicious tender flesh. There is no oil or mud or sewage here. Laurence conscientiously finishes up the brain and eyes of her sole: how has she managed not to swallow a bone? She hasn't made any fuss, at any rate. She's now eight months old.

This afternoon I can enjoy putting up a twenty-metre line to hang my washing on. The sheets, towels and nappies stretch from stay to shroud and are drenched with sun as they flap in the wind. There's nothing nicer than a sheet dried in the sun after a month of damp sleeping-bag soaked in sea water. While I'm enjoying this very basic and prosaic pleasure, Laurence is discovering maths. She's busy passing three rings on a chain from one hand to the other, in different ways that help her to appreciate space and distances.

Her favourite pastime is carefully and conscientiously collecting everything that doesn't get swept up each day: grains of rice from a crack in the floor, crumbs, hair, down— which she unfortunately puts in her mouth. As I am trying to forestall her with a damp sponge, on all fours, under her

indignant eyes, there's a loud rapping on the grating of the
cockpit. A moray nearly three metres long is thrashing about
frantically, its tail beating against the seats like a whip. Its skin
is dark brown and amber coloured. It opens its jaws fiercely,
revealing sharp teeth, and the round, menacing eyes in the
smooth, shiny head are obviously looking for a prey. It rears its
neck up like a snake and makes for anything which moves.
It's quite the finest moray Christian and Didier have ever
caught.

One day in Tahiti I saw one three times smaller, which had
bitten off the finger of a child of seven. This one could easily
bite through a wrist. Its savage and evil expression looks truly
prehistoric.

Perched on the engine canopy, Laurence watches it. As the
great mouth snaps in her direction, she gives a nervous cry and
then laughs. She has the confident air of a baby who knows
she is safe and points her chubby little finger at the 'thing'—
which will make a tasty soup, a West Indian *blaf*, and some
delicious steaks grilled over a brazier.

My two savages get into the water to attack the barnacles
with a scraper. The 'scratch, scratch' resounds through the
hull. Fish appear on all sides, not in the least afraid of these
intruders from another world. They come and sniff the humans
and gobble up the shells from the *Alpha*'s belly in passing. And
suddenly, miraculously, dozens of them rush at the hull and
snatch greedily at the barnacles. From inside the boat one can
hear little scratching sounds, which get louder and louder,
coming from all directions. Didier and Christian watch the
underwater feast for a while entranced and then come up,
delighted to be able to throw away their scrapers. It's a nasty
job underwater. And the fish go on feasting all night, while we
dream of a smooth, clean hull, gliding soundlessly through the
transparent water.

How lovely to be here on our own island.

The underwater fishing recommences. When Christian has
caught his first fish, a little grouper comes up to him and he gives
it a bit of his catch. The grouper gobbles it up. After that it
obviously feels it has been adopted and follows its new friend
everywhere, like Jojo the Grouper in Captain Cousteau's film.
It's there when Christian dives down from the boat, waiting for

its little bit of fish. It would be his faithful companion for nineteen days.

Our skipper is amazed that his childhood dreams should have come true like this. Robinson Crusoe's desert island, Cousteau's *Silent World*—and with his little family beside him.

'It is good to be able to realize one's dream,' he writes tonight. 'It is even better if one can realize it without sacrificing family life.'

We feel free because we've followed our choice to the end. We could have made a soft city life for ourselves, with running water, a shower, electricity—which are luxuries as far as two-thirds of the world are concerned. We could have taken out all kinds of insurance policies, against sickness, death, on our lives, and installed ourselves in comfort and security, which are certainly greatly to be valued. We could have been content with our dreams as we walked hand in hand along the quays, thinking of wonderful voyages, and quietly envying those who had the 'luck' to be able to go on them. We could have been satisfied with what others had shown us in books or in films.

But we knew that you can't describe a ray of sunlight. That beauty, like happiness, is untranslatable. That poets spend their life trying to describe the emotion they feel, an emotion which cannot be grasped because it is human, living, ever changing.

We felt confusedly that only an adventure we had lived could satisfy us, excite us. But it wouldn't be easy to achieve it. We had to work hard for months on end to buy our boat. And afterwards our life was a battle with nature which cost us continual effort. We knew no one would give us encouragement, or help us, because 'it wasn't a sensible thing to do'. The nicest of them would merely smile gently, incredulously. But we would live our dream together.

And today here we are, experiencing our adventure, on this desert island.

An intense excitement pounds through our veins. Our bodies are intensely aware. The sun licks us with its warm caresses, enfolds us. Our eyes aren't large enough to bear all this light. Our ears are alert, our eyes rove ceaselessly, our nostrils quiver at strange scents. The morning of the third day dawns.

We went to bed with the sun and rise with it. As soon as it's light Christian takes our bilge pump to pieces, which we bought in Cannes for ten francs. It's a real ten-franc pump, and gets blocked up all the time. Luckily we don't have to bale out more than ten litres of water every two months. It leaks in insidiously as on all boats, through the stern gland.

While I'm scrubbing the deckhead, where the paraffin lamps have left a grey sediment, Christian fixes an extension to the bilge pump, intending to pump up the 80 litres of diesel oil which he put in a reserve tank. He starts pumping, but only water comes up. We all remember the oil which made the after-deck slippery on the port side of the boat when the boat listed as we left Panama. We thought that there was a tiny leak, a few drops escaping from the join between the deck and one of the cockpit back-boards. The whole 80 litres has been gradually replaced by sea water, as diesel oil is lighter than water. Christian stops up the hole with cement and empties the tank. That will mean 80 kilos less to carry—but also 80 kilos less diesel oil, our only reserve supply. There's only the ordinary tank, which holds 40 litres—that is twenty hours at six knots, or 120 miles.

When the *Alpha* is clean and tidy, we start mending the sails. The most difficult part is sewing on a piece almost the length of the mainsail boom. The tear isn't very straight, and also the terylene sail is a bit misshapen and stretched, so that it's impossible to mend it without making pleats which will make it weaker than ever. And to make it worse the two pieces are very frayed. We use triangular needles which cut through the threads of the material. But what else could one use to get through five layers of stiff terylene, hardened by salt and sun? We push with all our might using a sail-maker's palm. The needle is pulled out with pliers on the other side. You need strong needles and it's a man's job. I leave the heavy sewing of the large patch to the men, and strengthen the worn seams, taking care to use the holes which are already there.

After three hours of this work in the gruelling sun, we all dive into the water. And while the two fishermen go off, followed by their little grouper, who now always accompanies them, I sit on a clump of coral, a large round mass of about a metre and a half in diameter, convoluted like a brain and the colour of pale honey. Here and there in the crevices, the 'jaws' of clams—red, green, blue, sulphur coloured, phosphorescent—

open and shut. I sit there without moving. In a few minutes I'm surrounded by fish. First come tiny luminous blue ones, with a black stripe down their back. They must be about two centimetres long. They have come out from under the coral reef, spreading out in a cloud, and swim round my legs in a shoal, without touching me, but razor close. They have a good look, inspect me thoroughly, then return to browse under the coral. I can hear the sound they make quite clearly. Then come flat, oval fish, luminous yellow in colour, with a wide black stripe. They are about ten or fifteen centimetres long, and come from another clump of coral. They too swim round me, opening their mouths just by my legs as if they wanted to taste them, but without touching me or brushing against me. Two gleaming scad do a somersault. A grouper almost touches my mask, stops and looks at me and then swims away. Then I see two little sharks about a metre long, motionless on the surface, watching me. I beat at the water to drive them away, and make for the beach. As I stand up in the water after taking off my flippers, I feel something rub against my right ankle, and turn round to see three fins scudding out to sea. Those damn sharks aren't afraid of anything.

Happiness at sea. It's an indescribable pleasure to feel one's bare feet on sand again, after the long, weary weeks when we felt we might never get here. Deep down inside us, in spite of all the experience of those who have gone before, in spite of the fantastic progress made in navigation, each crossing seems like a gamble. On the one hand, in these days of progress, it seems quite natural to be transported from one side of the world to the other. On the other hand one feels almost astonished to be alive and well, and on dry land, at the other side of the ocean.

The sun is already high and Christian is waving a superb crayfish. The skipper reports that he aimed at two young sharks but that the arrow slid off their hard skin. He also encountered a fine thornback. Didier brings back some groupers. It's sad we can't take any underwater photographs.

We've been at Cocos Island for four days now. The days pass, and, as everywhere, one day is much like another. But on land there's no need to navigate. The first few days the skipper

6

automatically made a time check three times a day. But gradually, because hunting for food often takes hours, we have forgotten about time. Our automatic watch has stopped because it hasn't been worn. In any case we've taken the time from the sun for a year now, because the watch only shows Greenwich Mean Time. Soon we've forgotten the date too. And wonder how we ever knew what day of the week it was. The sun wakes us every day at six, and sets at six in the evening.

For the present we're living from day to day, as if each day were the last we will spend on the island. We're taking as much advantage as we can of this place—but are ready to leave at short notice. And at the same time we're making plans to build a log-cabin and stay here six months.

It would be ideal if we could lay up the boat and if we had vegetables to sow. We could be picking tomatoes in less than three months. My Polynesian childhood comes flooding back to me. We've got matches, firearms, and enough food to give us time to discover what there is to eat on the island. There's plenty of fresh water, game, fish and almonds. But wouldn't Laurence need cereals? And the difficulty is the family would worry when they didn't get news and would send out search parties, which would be ridiculous. It's a pity we're not absolutely free.

Our daily life is much like everyone else's: with eating our chief preoccupation. We fish, hunt, scavenge, in a manner worthy of our ancestors. But they were tougher. They say that my grandmother of the New Caledonian pioneering family, whom I have already mentioned, went to the market in Nouméa every week on horseback, riding the twenty kilometres from their plantation. One day when she was in the final weeks of pregnancy she set off on her horse, went to the market, had her child, and rode back the same day with her baby and the things she had bought. One feels very feeble in comparison with such an indomitable figure. And yet, as I said, she was by no means uncivilized. She knew how to make lace and taught her children to write, read, do arithmetic, history and geography. She knew the medicinal properties of plants and all about birds. A little of this lore has come down to me via my mother and is invaluable to me. But there are many gaps in my knowledge.

There must be many edible plants on the island, but which

are they? At which stage should they be eaten and how cooked? People who know that taro corms can be eaten and try them raw without cleaning them in running water, get a nasty shock. Taro corms contain a kind of tiny crystal which prick like needles. It's essential to know they dissolve in water. And anyone who has been unlucky enough to taste a green olive from a tree will understand the problem we're faced with. Besides which, if one makes a mistake about a plant or fruit one can end up dead.

No supermarkets here. No steak in cellophane, or frozen vegetables. The meat is still leaping over the mountainside. The almonds—*auteraa*—from the balsams, have a very thick, tough shell. You have to hit them hard between two stones to crack them, taking care not to hit your fingers. Cracking *auteraa* by the roadside on the way back from school was one of my favourite childhood occupations. If the fruit were still ripe, with their lovely plump red skins, my stained hands and clothes would earn me a spanking. But the little kernels extracted with so much care were so good, that I couldn't resist the temptation.

On Cocos there is no fishmonger to clean, scale and skin fish. Your fingers get pricked and sometimes your hands cut because scales can be razor sharp. These fish are used to swimming about among the sharks, and are a far cry from frozen haddock fillets. They taste different too.

Then you have to cook all this food. You collect wood and puff at the fire with your eyes streaming—three times a day. It all takes time and patience, and then you have to start all over again. It's impossible to put on fat or develop a tummy. You eat enough for ten people and stay thin, don't put on any weight.

One soon realizes that what one thinks of as a nice holiday venture—'the natural life' as it were—becomes a strain, and very exhausting when you're not used to it. But life on board is a good preparation for it. It's a revelation to Didier. For me, it brings back memories of the *faré himaa*, the hut apart from the house destined as the kitchen. The smell of smoke wafting towards the sea as we came home from school. Followed by the smell of coffee or tea with a little coconut milk. You dipped bread with apricot jam or tinned butter in it, and that was your supper. Then it got dark. There was no electricity. The more determined children studied by the light of a paraffin lamp.

Others waited till the morning. So as soon as it got light you would hear children chanting their multiplication tables or their history prep at the tops of their voices.

But I can remember all the household chores this 'natural' life involved. If you do everything yourself, you soon find there's very little time left over for anything except sheer survival. After a day like that you need rest. And we have got some of the advantages of civilization. We've got harpoons and guns, matches. In the old days Polynesians, who had no flints or sulphur, made fire by rubbing two specially shaped bits of wood together, one convex and the other concave. For hours on end. One can understand why the guardian of the queen's fire was sacrificed if he let the flame go out.

After such tiring work, it's impossible to read or write. Even one's thoughts are gradually limited to the necessities of daily life. The body has to be liberated from too much labour, before the spirit can expand freely.

Why do we like this life so much? Perhaps like children who are told 'don't do this, don't do that, you're too small, you'll hurt yourself, you're doing it wrong' we're happy to be able to do anything we like without anyone stopping us.

Perhaps too, to be fulfilled, men need to make something with their hands. Apart from an élite who have chosen a trade or vocation which allows them to some extent, to be creative every day, people work to make money, thinking more about the profit they'll get from their work than what their work will demand from them. And work like this, which entails no initiative or sense of responsibility, which is incomplete, an uninspired link in a chain of which it is not even aware, no longer satisfies people. It is good to start from scratch and make something completely. Which is why craftsmanship is so satisfying. But the worker on an assembly line needs a lot of imagination to get any pleasure from his work.

Hunting a wild boar, cutting it up, cooking and eating it is highly satisfying. It's the first time we've really been hunting, in the true sense of the word. The animals are completely free, in every way, because they've never seen men or guns. But it's a law of life that one has to kill to eat. Whether it's a plant or an animal, one is forever taking the life of something which only asked to be allowed to live for as long as possible.

There's plenty of game on Cocos Island: wild pigs with long snouts, chestnut skin, and two tusks; short-haired goats; countless birds of every kind. Animal noises, especially from the boars, resound all day long. You see the feathers of large birds, which have no doubt been eaten by the pigs, on the paths the animals make. We already have our hunting ritual: hunting kit, boots and guns are put in Laurence's bath and floated ashore, through the sharks. This has to be done at low tide. The beach stretches far out then, and you can get a good way round the island, without a tedious climb. Then the hunters start climbing, cutting their path metre by metre with a machete. After three hours hard work they reach a plateau which forms the most extensive part of the island. Animal tracks run across it in every direction: the earth is sometimes churned over and ploughed up over several square metres. The vegetation is equatorial with virgin forest. Giant creepers fall from great corkwood trees. The dark undergrowth is covered with damp green foliage. When you turn over the warm leaf-mould with your foot, a large cockroach or shiny centipede glides away. There are a few mosquitoes, but no giant ones. Birds make a wild squawking in the palm trees. The sun can't penetrate the thick foliage and you are blinded when you emerge into the light once more. Your feet, unused to shoes, and in spite of thick woollen socks, get covered with blisters from all the walking and climbing, and the blisters then burst and leave your skin raw.

But it's a real joy after a month at sea, to be on this plateau surrounded by greenery and animal life. How lovely the damp earth smells. Beside a stream, the skipper finds a very old bottle, of green blown glass. Perhaps from the days of the great navigators, of Spanish galleons. Very exciting.

An expedition to the interior of the island takes all day. Coming back, when the tide is up, it's dangerous. You climb down holding on to the creepers or using the rope which the skipper had the foresight to bring. However, the day's excursion doesn't result in any game—and it would be difficult to get down the cliff carrying a dead animal anyway. But at the last moment 100 metres from where the expedition began, a sow and two piglets come to drink at the stream. The hunters take aim—and the animal is cut up on the spot; they get back with four joints of sucking-pig. While the pig is being cut up, clouds of flies suddenly appear from nowhere. The meat has to be hurriedly stuffed in gunny bags.

Four joints: four meals. We are longing to taste the red meat.

If you want to hunt, it's no good going to the interior of the island. The best and simplest way is to hide in the long grass by one of the many streams by the shore. The animals come there to drink throughout the day and you only have to decide what size and shape you want. In nineteen days we've killed seven animals. We try to preserve the last one—which is quite an experience. I've never preserved meat in my life and have no book to tell me how, except the SEB cooker book, which says you need preserving jars, which I haven't got. But I've got some little baby-food jars: they've got screw tops and are sealed with a synthetic band which seems as good as new. I cut off some of the best meat and cook it for an hour in the pressure cooker with a little water, salt and pepper. I washed the pots in salt water but didn't sterilize them. I push the meat well down with a little gravy on top. Then pop them in the pressure cooker with a little water, and heat them for fifteen minutes.

When I take them out the tops are blown out which is quite normal. But when they're cooled down, if they still have raised lids, it means they are bad.

The little jars hold an amazing amount: I got a whole pig into twenty of them. And they last over eight months. They might have lasted longer, but we finished them after eight months in Tahiti. They taste much nicer than corned beef, and will enable us to vary our menu after ten or twelve days of dorado meat.

Even on Cocos Island fish is often on the menu. From choice rather than necessity. If you don't mind swimming through sharks it's an underwater fisherman's paradise. Didier and Christian always bring back far too much.

We eat some of the many thousands of oysters clinging to the rocks, on the spot. There are also hundreds of dark-grey crabs. They're quite unafraid and you can get close enough to them to give them a sharp tap on the back with a stick—and pop them in the saucepan. We fill the pan with them and simply steam them in salt water, and they're delicious.

The rivers are full of langoustine. We catch some with our hands but haven't got the right equipment—and are too lazy to make it. In Polynesia they have two different methods of catching them. The quickest—the classic method—is to use a little harpoon made of a thin lemon tree branch with iron barbs. You go upriver at night with a Coleman lamp which blinds the langoustines, and spear them one by one. The other method, which children use, takes time and patience. You take the rib of a coconut-leaf foliole, the *niau*, a brown stalk about a metre long which is very thin and supple and quite strong. Then you get a length of fibre about fifteen centimetres long from the coconut husk and make a little rigid lassoo with it which is fixed to the end of the *niau*. Then you crouch silently at the water's edge and try to tickle the end of the langoustine's tail. When it's frightened, it leaps back and is caught in the lassoo, which tightens round it. You pull it up and begin again. My sister and I spent hours fishing like this when we were children.

Laurence drinks out of a glass, and likes picking up her food by herself, in her fingers, which is good. She eats a little of everything. She can't distinguish small objects at a distance yet, and doesn't appear to see the birds which fly overhead. She crawls around and tastes everything: sand, dead leaves, grass, and the moss on stones from the river which she particularly likes. I'm often horrified to see a centipede 30 centimetres long under the damp leafmould, but I don't let Laurence crawl there.

Her favourite toys are hermit crabs. She follows these funny little creatures which live in shells abandoned by other animals, and seizes the shell delightedly, and is then puzzled to see the crab has disappeared. She scratches at them with her fingers, but it's no good. The little crab has curled up and shut his home with his flattened claws. These attractive little things can pinch hard. You can use them, without their claws, as fishing bait. When you arrive on a beach, the sound of footsteps drives them into their shells, but if you stand still and whistle softly they come out one by one.

The beach, this whole island, is a joy. We have marvellous cold showers under the waterfalls and drink our fill from the springs. All the meat, fish, almonds, fresh water make us forget more sophisticated pleasures. So we are keeping the carton of cigarettes Russ gave us to barter in the Galapagos or elsewhere.

We've only got twenty dollars and three bottles of rum, and Tahiti is a long way off. The skipper notes that if we manage to reach the Galapagos we'll be saved because the trade winds will carry us towards Tahiti. If not? Well if we have to stay on Cocos Island we can always do what our ancestors did and cut the *Alpha*'s name and the date when we arrived in the rock. You see the names and dates of sailing-boats on gigantic boulders: 1673, 1740, 1863. We, too, must seem like castaways to these stones.

1 July. We decide to fill up with fresh water. But how can we transport 500 litres of water in an inflatable bath? The easiest way would be to get as close to the source of supply as possible, i.e. to the beach. We could then carry it in jerrycans. Also, with the boat hauled up on the beach, we could give the hull a lick of paint. No sooner said than done. As soon as we wake up, at high tide, we draw the *Alpha* up on the beach with her keel in the sand, and with one anchor out at sea, and one on land. It's marvellous to be able to go ashore without getting one's feet wet. As the tide goes out the *Alpha* is left lying on the sand. So we can only put 140 litres of water in the tank which is in the keel. However, we seize the opportunity of painting the starboard side of the hull. The tide goes out from six to midday and comes in again from twelve till six. We wait until six to take her out to sea again, and have a boar roast over a fire for dinner meanwhile.

While we're sitting round the fire we suddenly see a fishing boat which looks as though it's putting out its net. It must be from Ecuador. It's impossible for them not to see the fire and the *Alpha* with her tall mast on the sand. We think up all sorts of deals we can do with the cigarettes and rum. Exchange them for paraffin or rice? We finally decide on paraffin, flour and sugar. But it's a fantasy. We haven't got a dinghy to get there in, and it's too far to swim. They seem to have no desire to come and see us. I feel indignant: we must look like a shipwrecked boat and they ought at least come and see. Didier and Christian shout 'Hi!' to no avail. When it grows dark they haul up the net and disappear over the horizon, followed by a cloud of birds which we can hear crying. We haven't seen another human being for over a month.

The tide is up. Operation launch, and we all go aboard. The *Alpha* doesn't want to know and clings obstinately to the sand. We start the engine but it's no use. The high tide, with its waves, must have pushed her farther up the sand and she's sunk into it. Christian drops an anchor at sea, secures it with a line to the top of the mast and tries to make her heel over by pulling with a pulley. If he succeeds in heeling her over enough he will reduce the draught and will be able to work us towards the anchor. But the two men pull in vain, the mast threatens to crack and nothing happens. We'll have to wait and hope the next tide will come up farther.

At about eight we're all in bed as usual and try to settle down for a good night's sleep. But the *Alpha* begins to bump hard. The tide's going out and the waves are knocking us about. The two men tighten the line to breaking point and try once more to get her to heel over, but with no success. They've got great blisters on their hands from pulling on the pulleys.

The forecastle becomes unbearable. Christian moves to the quarter-berth on the starboard side and I take Laurence to the port berth in the saloon, and she howls each time the keel bumps on the sand. Poor baby. I take her in my arms.

Christian is terrified for the mast, but what can we do, except wait? When we list the water is forced up the sink, which we immediately shut off. The *Alpha* lists more and more, which gives the waves free rein and now they're coming in over the tilted cockpit and drench Christian's and Didier's bunks. I'm on the opposite side to the lists and have to keep moving with Laurence. It's awful not to be able to sleep because of the violent jolts, which make us fear for the mast. By about eleven-thirty when we're on dry sand again, Laurence and I are lying on the bunk-board at right angles to the ceiling. I get up in the dark and step on Didier. To get into the cockpit you have to pull yourself up by your arms. It's impossible to use the stove, which isn't on gimbals.

At about one-thirty the nightmare starts all over again.

But as the tide comes up the waves are bigger. We have to take in Gigi, who is being buffeted, and shut the door to the cockpit as the waves besiege the boat. One breaks the tiller. At four the sea is fairly high and the two men subject their hands to further torture trying to get the *Alpha* off. Instead of tying

6*

the line to the top of the mast they tie it at the level of the crosstrees and pull with a whole series of pulleys. After half an hour's straining, the *Alpha* finally works free.

Phew! We really thought we'd have to end our days on Cocos Island. But the engine refuses to start again. We have to creep along in the dark between the coral reefs, using our famous paddles. We finally fall asleep at about six-thirty, exhausted, and wake at midday. It's raining. When it rains we do housework, play Scrabble, baccarat or dice. Christian always wins at dice and I at baccarat.

The engine is working again. The list of what we've got left on board is all too brief: two litres of paraffin, three kilos of sugar—enough for a week.

From 2 July onwards it rains from time to time. On the afternoon of the third, after some showers in the morning, the sun comes out at about four while we're playing Scrabble. I suddenly hear a strange squawking and get up and go on deck.

'Christian!'

There's a very peculiar, gigantic object ahead of us, about a dozen yards away. It's like a series of huge trunks floating in a line on the water at regular intervals. Hundreds of birds are perched, clinging, on this shiny black cylindrical object. Each time all the trunks go underwater all the birds fly up making a great din and go and perch on the new trunks which appear. We don't doubt for a minute that it's some huge creature: 20, 30, 40 metres long? It seems to be like a giant eel in shape, at least a metre in diameter. We can't see its tail or head. How can such a large *thing* get so close to the shore, through the coral reefs? It must take up about a dozen metres of water.

'Shall we go after it?' suggests Didier, delighted at the prospect.

'Count me out,' says the skipper, thinking of the monstrous seven- or eight-metre sharks which he's seen recently on his underwater fishing trips.

'You're mad,' I add.

I would rather be a little bird. And I keep thinking: 'I hope this huge *thing* doesn't mean us any harm.'

How long did it stay there? Ten minutes, an hour? We stood watching it, petrified, and it was with immense relief that we saw it turn towards the entrance to the bay, very slowly, with all the birds perched on top, and clearly silhouetted. If only we could have photographed it. Is Cocos Island, alone and un-inhabited in the middle of the Pacific, a refuge where the giants of the sea can emerge?

It is raining harder and harder. The rivers turn yellow, then brown, and colour the bay. On 10 July, in the middle of the afternoon, a gust of wind snatches off the forehatch just as a heavy swell gets up. It's enough for us to get our sailing orders. I hurriedly take down my washing lines and Christian starts the engine, and it's goodbye to Cocos Island.

A joint is slowly roasting over the cinders on the beach. Another is hanging ready and waiting in a tree. No matter, we'll have to leave them there. We've got to go because we don't know what the bay's like in bad weather. It's not very nice leaving only an hour or two before dark, but it's a question of safety. We make for the north of the Galapagos Islands, and don't dare guess how long the crossing will take. But we have to pull on our old salt-stiff sweaters, trousers and oilskins again, and do balancing feats. We sail round Cocos Island for the last time. There are huge waterfalls everywhere, from the recent heavy rains. Deep valleys and barren ridges follow in succession. There are coconut palms here and there. We are a little dis-appointed not to have seen more of it. Particularly as we didn't find a single coconut on the island named after them. And green coconuts are so good. We'll come back with nuts and vegetable seeds and plant them there.

The wind is squally and keeps changing direction. The currents have become rapids. But the *Alpha* is clean and makes good progress. The sails are all patched, but they're strongly sewn. Huge sword-fish leap in the air by our side. The birds which are following us dive-bomb us and Laurence smiles delightedly.

XI

A World In Fusion

WE ADOPT OUR sea-going rhythm once more: sleeping like watch-dogs with one eye open, and our ears pricked. If this wind continues we'll be at the Galapagos in under a week.

We are in excellent humour and so relaxed that Christian is caught off guard——'Hell! Gigi!'

When Didier reaches the stern, all he can see is a white blob, sinking in the tremendously deep water. Gigi is dead. Gigi has gone, for ever. Gigi has been swallowed up and is sinking three or four thousand metres or more into the unknown and vasty deeps. Gigi, our best crewmate, our helmsman. Gone to the bottom of the Pacific, taking with her our precious spanner. I saw it topple over just as Didier, who was sitting down, cried out. We shiver, because Gigi is almost human and we subconsciously feel she's part of us: we are reminded that it is certain death for anyone who falls overboard.

We take watches once more. The two boys do the greater share, but I go on deck from time to time to allow Christian to take our bearings. My main job is to make life easier for them while they are on duty: more carefully prepared meals, hot drinks during the night, breakfast at four or five in the morning for the helmsman, occasional snacks. You have to take care of your helmsman if you want him to last.

After their first night on deck the boys seem quite happy. They were getting bored on their bunks, they say. They had finished their supply of reading matter and were reduced to reading the small-print ads—while I am struggling to get everything done in the day. From eight till midnight I keep Christian company, and watch the sea and stars. There are great phosphorescent patches of plankton on the water, and huge, phosphorescent fish, which we can't identify. One of them, which seems to be there every night, is at least eight

metres long. At the tiller like this, in the cockpit, you realize
you're not *on* the sea but *in* it. Sitting on the cockpit seats you
can easily lean out and touch the water. If the wind increases in
strength, the deck is swamped and you're drenched with icy
jets of water. We are *touching* the sea. Laurence also has this
very strong impression: a little later on, from the deck of a
steamer, she would say: 'Mummy, I want to touch the sea.'

A nice surprise: our position is only 150 miles north of the
Galapagos. Ordinarily, we would follow the rules and approach
them from the south, at San Cristobal. It is the same for all
archipelagos: each group of islands has a main island where you
make your 'entry' and present or request a visa from the
authorities. However, that being said, it's not always possible
to do what you want, when it's a question of wind and sea.

I'm the only one who has any idea what these mysterious
islands are like. Alain and Anne Hervé of the *Aventure* showed
me some colour transparencies in Tahiti by the light of a
paraffin lamp.

'They are like a desert,' I said. 'Just stones and cacti, and it
looks all black.'

'There's nothing else there,' Anne replied. 'But you should
see the colours. The sunsets, the moonlight, the animals. It's
very striking. You either love them or hate them.'

Laurence is nearly nine months old now. Her hair's beginning
to grow—a few blonde wisps. She's got two upper teeth, which
makes six in all. She can get out of the cockpit alone, at sea,
which means 50 centimetres vertical climb, using arms and
legs. It's nice, but it means I have to be even more careful,
because there's nothing to stop her falling in the water. Sometimes when I see her performing all these acrobatic feats I
wonder how she'll ever learn to walk. I feel the movement of the
boat may retard her in this respect: ordinarily she should start
walking at about a year. We'll see.

We are very near the Equator and will soon be in the
southern hemisphere, but it's as cool as spring in the Mediterranean. It's the time of year when the Humboldt Current
brings the polar ice from the southern seas. One has to wear an
oilskin even in the middle of the day, over sweaters, and
mittens, and caps and scarves at night. There are sperm whales
swimming in shoals, which is unusual. The great creatures

surface all around us. There are some quite a way behind us, and some ahead and to port and starboard. It is frightening when you see them rear up vertically revealing their great black bodies, with their open mouths complete with enormous fangs gaping towards the sky. A human would make one mouthful. The terrified dorados huddle round the boat as if seeking protection. The birds, which grow more and more numerous, fight over their prey above us.

We are approaching the first islands in the north of the Galapagos. There are no lights and the currents are numerous, dangerous and unknown, with only the Wenman rock directly ahead of us, to land on. We pore over the chart. The skipper indicates the most direct route to San Cristobal, where we are supposed to go first. The island is right at the other end of the archipelago, going diagonally across it via Santa Cruz, where we have a rendezvous with Bernard on the *Klis*. So we'll make for the latter, passing Isabela on one side or the other. Each island has at least three names—Ecuadorian, English, French— which often bear no resemblance to each other. Isabela is Albemarle; Santa Cruz, Indefatigable; Pinta, Abingdon; Marchena, Bindloe, etc.

We sail round the rocky cliffs of Wenman. The island is a great plateau of rock 253 metres high, with steep cliffs rising precipitously from the sea, which is very deep there. The vegetation is sparse. It is said to be the place where there are the most species of birds in the world, for such a small area. We can see penguins, frigate-birds, boobies, albatrosses, petrels. The current is very strong round Wenman, but we sail round it, at a distance of about 30 metres, looking for an anchorage, particularly for a beach or crevice which would enable us to climb up. However, there are only the steep cliffs all round the island, with caves here and there, and the deep ultramarine blue sea below. No goats, apparently. The bird droppings give off a very strong smell.

The morning mist is clearing. At first it's all flat and dark. Then the stone becomes a bluish grey and you can see vertical ridges. Then it changes to pinky grey, and you can clearly see the different layers of rock. Finally it becomes a brown grey, then violet. The birds wheel overhead with great deafening cries, filling the sky. Christian takes in our drag line in case a bird should get caught in it, but it's too late. A booby has bitten the spoon and got caught on the hook. We lift it gently on deck to free it. It huddles in the stern, looking defiantly at us, and won't let us touch it. Its great beak could cut a finger in two. The two men finally both hold it down, and unhook it, and it flies off.

At the foot of the cliffs there are some very dignified little penguins, which stare at us as we go past. A little way away some turtles which are asleep on the surface of the water, dive as we approach. Laurence can see birds overhead now, and smiles as she points at them. I attach her harness to the pulpit in the bows, and she watches the sea, so full of turbulent life, bearing us along.

In the morning we find ourselves opposite a lunar landscape, with white rocks and jagged streams of lava. A hellish, burnt-out, deserted, raw, volcanic, menacing coast, with no bay or creek where one could shelter for the night. Oh for Cocos Island.

A miraculous catch consoles us a little. The pelicans try to snatch our fish. There are sea-lions on the rocks, and they drag themselves heavily along with their strong tails and flippers. The oldest among them, the 'grandfathers', remain motionless, keeping a look-out from the highest rocks. These appealing animals are as quick as lightning once they are in the water.

Just as we finish fishing, the sun appears on the horizon and a few rays lighten the overcast sky. It is all suddenly illuminated with fairy-like colours. We are transfixed. The island looks immense, warm, beautiful. The black lava, the sea-lions—dark violet, gleaming. Half an hour later it's pitch dark. The birds are silent. The sea-lions set up their raucous barking, which goes on all night. I hope the anchor will hold.

Next day we sail into submerged craters, which form part of the cliffs. It's very strange; we go a few hundred yards up the crater and go about to sail back. In the evening we drop anchor on a huge beach of black sand in Black Bay, just by the strait which separates Isabela and Fernandina, which we reach next day using the engine. Fernandina is just a bare, burnt-out, lifeless cone. At Santa Cruz we learn that less than a month ago it was wooded and had a lake, which was shattered by a volcanic eruption while we were at Cocos Island. We might have seen our last firework display over this volcano which everyone supposed to be dead. André de Roy would tell us later that two seismographers were also attacked by a pack of wild dogs there. They instinctively stood back to back—wild dogs are supposed not to attack you from in front. They didn't know how long they stood there. It seemed ages until the dogs went away.

Still the black lava. The scenery doesn't make you want to stay there, but it does make you want to come back, again and again. It has a slow, magnetic, powerful, irresistible attraction. It is perhaps this which is the charm of the Galapagos, of these heaps of stone.

We'll never forget the crossing to Santa Cruz, to Academy Bay. The strange voyage, carrying on our family life as usual, using up the last of our supplies in our floating capsule, sailing through the frightening lunar landscape. The days passing slowly and the night watches a strain, with a strong wind against us and the dangerous currents and coast.

None of us sleep properly. We all want to get away from Isabela as quickly as possible. We are suffering from complete nervous exhaustion, and have just decided to stop at a small island twenty miles ahead, when Didier thinks he sees a port. The skipper takes the binoculars. A miracle. There's a jetty and a few houses. We pass the binoculars from one to the other. Half an hour later we can see the light at the end of the jetty.

We prepare for our arrival. Didier sees to the deck while I tidy up below. We hoist our quarantine flag and courtesy flag, which is apparently very important in the Galapagos.

We drop anchor at four-fifty. A launch immediately speeds towards us with the local officials on board. Luckily we have arrived before five o'clock, or we would have to pay the supplementary tariff. An expensive administration, with a base here on Isabela just for 200 inhabitants—and a few madmen like us.

The officials are charming. The language here is a mixture of Indian and Spanish. Sugar is the local currency, and is worth twenty centimes, in French money. You can buy 25 packets for a dollar. And 25 packets is the price of a live goat here, which you can resell in Ecuador for 100 packets. It seems incredible when you think that you've got to walk for over twelve hours up a mountain to get the goats. They hunt them with dogs and catch them alive, as they do the wild bulls. Villamil, the little port we arrived at, only exists because of the hunting. It was built three years ago and most of the houses are prefabricated. A boat comes once a month from Guayaquil with supplies and to collect the goats and cows. It's due in tomorrow morning. We'll have to wait to get our stores, because there's nothing left in the village.

At about ten in the morning the *Guayaquil* moors a little way from the port, because the harbour is too small for her. She's a narrow little cargo boat, very high in the water. She rolls dreadfully—you feel sick just looking at her. Boats shuttle to and fro, navigating the dangerous channels, loaded with bricks, cement, wood, paraffin, flour, tins of food. We spend seventeen of our remaining twenty dollars on fifteen kilos of rice, fifteen of sugar, potatoes, five gallons of paraffin, a tin of yeast, fifty pounds of flour.

The loading of the goats and wild cattle is a curious and sad procedure. The goats are hoisted up from the launch to the boat with ropes attached to their horns. The cows are the most upsetting. They are too big for the launch and are dragged through the water to the boat. This is done by hauling them by their horns and tail, so that they are lifted out of the sea—otherwise they'd be full of water and no good, the men say.

This evening, the Villamil officials have given us a large piece of dried beef, some cocoa, some oatflakes and lemons. The people are so nice we would like to spend a few days here, and go hunting. But the mooring is so unpleasant, and it would be very difficult to get ashore with Laurence. And we're still hoping to find a lovely green island. Surely, Santa Cruz, with its famous Academy Bay which everyone visits must be better than the others, because people from all over the world have chosen to live there.

Santa Cruz. Black lava again, and sea-lions, and forests of bare cacti, like sinister candelabra. Then suddenly a marvellous bay with a beautiful white sandy beach—gleaming white. There's a little shoal with waves breaking to starboard, a few miles from the shore, but Christian is irresistibly drawn by the white sand and turquoise water and wants to get closer. As if by some

presentiment I fasten Laurence securely, shut all the hatches
and shout: 'Not so close, Christian!'

And at the same instant an enormous wave gathers under the
Alpha's keel and lifts us up. I hold my breath, and stay close to
Laurence who is peacefully asleep. A second breaker passes and
thunders down only a few metres away. Christian is con-
centrating hard at the tiller; Didier is very tense.

A third breaker is gathering by the *Alpha* on the port side, and
the seconds seem like hours. The green, translucent water curls
over us as we list—I feel sure it's the end of the voyage for us.
The wave gathers with a terrible crackling sound and breaks
almost directly under the *Alpha*'s keel. I feel weak. We're
saved. Didier and I were speechless with fear, and we saw our
skipper's legs tremble for the first time.

But the sun's still shining and we reach Academy Bay. The
Klis is there.

'Wow,' says Didier. 'If this is what the Galapagos are like—
remember Cocos Island?—What the hell are we doing here?'

Bernard Moitessier is on his six-metre trimaran, shouting a
welcome through his foghorn at the top of his voice. There are
a few other boats there: the *Gearra* belonging to the young
English couple with the kittens; the *Tahiti*, Karl's ketch; Fritz
and Gush's boats. The sea is opaque, rough, angry. The shore is
rocky, with only bare cacti as far as the eye can see. The headland, on the side of the bay where we are moored, is dominated
by Karl's house—imposing but blending perfectly into the
landscape.

In the middle of the bay there are a few other houses—the
village. Nearby is the Darwin Station, where a rich American
has built a hotel—still empty apparently.

Bernard takes us ashore in his dinghy.

'It's the custom on arrival here to have tea with Marga.'

Marga. A small woman with grey, curly hair, bright blue
eyes and slightly over-pink cheeks.

We sit in a large room overlooking the sea, round a big
table, with the little band of immigrants. They live on the
headland, a quarter of an hour from the village by rowing boat,
or an hour on foot through the cacti. A lady of 80, Marga's
mother, presides over the teapot. The three Angermeyer
brothers—Gush, Fritz and Karl, Marga's husband—sit next to

her. Fritz's wife and the de Roy family complete the group. The children aren't there.

This little gang live quite on their own, isolated in their ivory tower. They have their own society with its own customs, but no leader, judges, police or employers. Everyone works and lives for himself. This doesn't mean you can't render anyone a service but the rule is: every man for himself, providing it doesn't harm his neighbour.

The first ones to arrive had difficulty in finding good hunting grounds. It sometimes took them months to find a spot regularly frequented by goats, and, once found, to be able to find it again with the aid of landmarks or by marking the cacti. You can easily get lost in the forest of cacti which covers the coast, and go round in circles for hours, and die of thirst. So each person has his own hunting ground or grounds and guards its location jealously, especially as the goats are now less numerous and more easily frightened. It takes several hours to find them, but there are enough for everyone. Until recently the Ecuadorian government gave the immigrants the land they developed. Jealous people are now contesting the rights of ownership of the little colony, but these are only petty local quarrels of the kind which can exist anywhere.

We all feel very close, in an expansive mood, and we invite them over to the *Alpha* for 7 pm. This just gives us time to tidy up a bit and put Laurence to bed. From six-thirty onwards, as soon as it's dark, the boat begins to fill up. Gush brings us some carrots, some potatoes from the mainland, and some papayas. There are soon fifteen of us sitting in the *Alpha*'s cabin, as it's cold outside. Christian picks up his guitar, and we all sing. The three Angermeyer brothers have very fine voices, and sing German songs. We all join in, in our own language. After we've run through our repertory of songs, the skipper lists the various problems we've got to tackle: we've got to make a new automatic pilot, mend the tiller, careen, and build a makeshift dinghy for our stay here, because the water is icy.

The dinghy: Karl will lend us a corkwood raft. The tiller: there's plenty of strong wood, you only have to cut it. The automatic pilot is more of a problem. There's nothing in the village except cement and bricks. No welding gear, no metal tubing, no plywood. It would take a month to order it from Ecuador:

there's only one boat a month and the last one left yesterday. We can't wait that long, because we must cross the Pacific before the hot season, when the trade winds are succeeded by cyclones and torrential rain.

At 9 pm, only the de Roys are still there.

'I've got some reinforced concrete,' André says. 'And an oak plank about 1.50 metres by 1 metre. We'll see—it ought to be possible, even without welding gear.'

A ray of hope.

'Is it true,' Christian asks, 'that the government pays for every goat killed?'

'It was true until a few years ago. They didn't give you much anyway. The goats had multiplied to such an extent that they were becoming a danger to the rare fauna and flora of the Galapagos. In particular they ate a very rare plant which was indispensable fodder for the famous giant tortoises, which were threatened with extinction. The situation was so grave that the Darwin Station organized mass slaughterings of goats. It was horrible, deplorable. At Barrington, for instance, they killed the animals and left them on the spot. The carcases slowly rotted in the sun and in that heat the smell was unbearable. The buzzards were bloated and the other goats were frantic and didn't know what to do with themselves. People who needed to hunt for their living had to give it up: it turned you up to have to walk for hours through carcases. And besides, the goats which had escaped fled and hid far up the mountain. It was months before people could look for new hunting grounds. It's a day's expedition now. You have to leave at five or six in the morning, before dawn, and walk fast for several hours. You get back just before nightfall.'

We're going hunting.

Brrrr—Brrrr. 5 am. It's a long time since we were last woken by an alarm clock.

'Brrrr,' Christian says, getting up. 'The alarm clock going off so early and the cold remind me of setting out for school on grey Paris mornings.'

Without more ado, half asleep, we pull on woollen socks, canvas shoes, trousers, shorts and sweaters. Laurence is wrapped up snugly and put in her knapsack, on top of her bundle, with only her head and arms sticking out. She looks surprised but delighted. Didier and Christian carry guns and gunny bags.

'I can buy some hunting shoes,' André's daughter Tui had said, 'with the money from a skin.'

We all jump on the corkwood raft to go across to the de Roys, who have invited us to breakfast. We have to climb up the *barranco*, the rocky fringe of ancient lava which forms the bay. Some iguanas, startled by this early morning invasion, scuttle into each other, their hard skins rattling over the rocks. We go round the cacti and take the cliff path which leads to a little bay.

The dawn light is tinting the white sand and exposed twisting roots of the mangrove trees a pinky mauve. Everything is still somnolent, peaceful. There is only a grey heron, standing gracefully on our path, looking out to sea. He doesn't deign to move aside for us. Then we turn our backs on the sea to go up to the de Roys. The track winds between two lagoons, almost dry at this time of year. An ibis is asleep, with its head tucked under its wing. The cactus forest begins again above the lagoons, and we climb up some steps cut in the earth, then up a little stone stairway leading to a wooden bridge. From the bridge you can see right over the bay, which is blue now, streaked with a very pale orange. On the other side of the bridge is the de Roys' house. Some startled finches flutter up from the terrace.

There's no time to lose; it's nearly dawn. We leave the breakfast things and our two families set off. We go at a good pace, with Laurence in the knapsack on my back, walking between the cacti and over basalt stones in precariously balanced layers. They shift as you tread on them, and if you stretch out your hands to save yourself, there are the cacti.

Laurence tries to get hold of them. They're almost like trees with their great trunks and branches four or five metres high. Although it was cool by the sea, it's stifling in the forest. We've brought water and a little food, but the de Roys don't usually take anything with them, even on an all-day trip. The basalt stones are very jagged and sharp, and cut through our rubber soles and tear the canvas. You can easily wear out two pairs of tennis shoes in a day's hunting—which makes it an expensive sport in the Galapagos because everything comes from the mainland and it's difficult to earn money there.

After walking for three-quarters of an hour we cross a rocky crevasse. A further hour and a half of cactus and we're beside the sea again, walking across jagged lava until we finally reach Turtle Bay. The beach is blindingly white, the sand so fine and powdery that it clings to your skin like talc. We rest under the mango trees. Laurence crawls off and swallows handfuls of white powder, which doesn't appear to be indigestible: the sand is made of madrepore shells reduced to a fine powder by the sea. It's pure calcium.

By one of the forelands of the bay there are piles of marine iguanas one on top of another, warming themselves in the sun. They're like big lizards—the largest I've seen are 60 centimetres long—and are very gentle and easy to catch. Laurence can crawl faster than they can and catches them by their tails. Their skin is very hard and their backs covered with great spikes like a dorsal crest. The first time you see their large mouths full of teeth you are very impressed. But André explained to us that they are like lizards and when they are afraid they immobilize their adversaries by seizing them in their jaws but don't hurt them unless they try to pull away. A friend of his had to leave his wrist in a land iguana's mouth for 24 hours, and could only wait patiently until the animal was ready to release him. Marga's mother goes to sleep every night with three iguanas in her bed.

We walk—and walk. Tui catches a kid but sets it free. Twice Christian sees some goats which the others haven't noticed. He fires. André immediately carries out a surgeon-like dissection. He carefully opens up the animal and takes out its entrails, taking care not to cut into the internal organs, as otherwise in this heat the soiled meat would be spoilt at once. He delicately extracts the heart, liver and kidneys. And the buzzards swoop down. They squat a few metres away and fix us with a terrible bright, piercing stare—waiting till we've gone. The flies are less ceremonious: they swarm in their thousands over the viscera with a muffled buzzing sound.

When the animal has been cleaned it's put in a gunny bag which one of the hunters carries over his shoulder. If it's too heavy to be carried in one piece it's cut up. The skin is removed with care, because Tui will scrape it and dry it to sell. Then the meat is cut into four joints, with the undercut, brain and tongue.

The offal is put in a little separate bag. The rest is left to the buzzards.

The billy goats are not shot unless they are very young, because they have too strong a flavour. One avoids killing the females who are feeding their young or in kid. Tui is fourteen. She cuts up the animals as neatly as her father, and carries home a 30- or 40-kilo goat on her shoulders like a man, running between the cactus plants and over stones for hours on end, without eating or drinking anything all day. Which doesn't prevent her being slim, and very feminine—a fourteen-year-old teenage girl, in fact. Happiness at sea is also meeting people whose lives are different from other people's.

On with the hunt. Didier bags a goat. Then Tui. There's more cutting up. Finally, as Christian has shot four, we call a halt. We rest in some underground caves where the water is almost fresh, hardly brackish at all. We can quench our thirst and get cool—it's so hot outside.

On the way back, near Turtle Bay, we see some very tame wild duck, stilt-plovers, wild fowl, a wild ass—oh that adjective which describes everything here and which is so great a part of our happiness.

We get back exhausted. Laurence is worn out after her long day and asleep in the rucksack. Jacqueline walks beside me to support her head. When we reach the de Roys' house at about six o'clock, the setting sun is turning the cacti violet, then purple. The sea shines like molten gold, and the silhouettes of the mangroves are as black as the lava and iguanas.

The grey heron, in the lagoon, is now a delicate pink. He takes a few, dignified steps, his head held high.

Every morning, Christian goes to André's workshop to work on Gigi II. It's a slow job, because there is no electricity or welding equipment. Each flat iron bar has to be cut with a hack-saw, then bored several times with a hand-drill. It's important not to break the drill, which can't be replaced on Santa Cruz. The iron fittings are shaped with a vice, hammer and tongs. The counterweight of the wind-vane is molten lead in a jam tin, which will solidify on the end of the iron rod supporting it. It's six days before Gigi II finally arrives aboard, painted white.

There were other goat-hunts with Tui. And other islands—

we had to try out Gigi II. On Barrington, we watched the old
male sea-lions keeping their young in order. The latter obey as
soon as the old ones lift up their heads and beat their flippers,
reproving the flighty youngsters who want to frolic in the water
with us. The little ones rush off as fast as they can to rejoin the
others, looking like guilty children caught in the act. The order
to assemble is given as soon as they scent danger on land or sea.
And there is plenty of danger around, as one can see from the
great bites, like amputations, which have been inflicted on the
sea-lions and seals. In the Galapagos, sperm-whales, orcs and
sharks abound, even near the coast.

Once when I was washing clothes in sea water, on the beach,
I turned round to look for Laurence who was crawling around
—and she wasn't there. I instinctively looked in the water, all
along the beach. No sign of her. I went towards the group of
sea-lions. Laurence was right in the middle of them. As soon as
I approached the old males moved menacingly towards me.
What could I do? Call to Laurence? It might upset the males.
So I did as she had done. I took off my bikini and knelt on all
fours. Then watched the sea-lions' reaction. They hadn't
budged. I advanced slowly, taking care not to lift my head so as
not to frighten them, and managed to reach the herd and
recover Laurence. We crawled away together on all fours,
which Laurence thought was huge fun.

The days pass, spent with the splendid de Roy family who
hunt for and classify shells and send them off to collectors and
museums all over the world. In fifteen years they've shaped a
life for themselves in this forgotten spot, a life of records and
books, happy children and grown-ups.

Christian finishes the new tiller; the wood's so hard that when
you're drilling you mustn't stop or the drill will stick. Tonight
he's finished, and we take our poor old patched sails aboard.

We're sad to be leaving the de Roys, who are a real family, as
we hope to be, but we are happy at the thought of setting off
again. How good it is to be poor and unencumbered, free to go
where we like in our little *Alpha*—our small boat, with our baby,
now ten months old. The boat is all we possess. If we lose her,
we'll build another.

Yes, tonight, it feels like a departure.

Where can we get fresh water?

'Go and see Forest Nelson,' André tells us. 'Tell him you've got a baby on board and need a little water to cross the Pacific. He's got quite a big supply, he won't say no.'

Forest Nelson makes us a present of a full 350-litre tank-full, plus 100 litres in a canvas water-carrier. To get it aboard we have to get close to the village and shuttle between the boat and the shore with cans in André's boat. It takes us all morning.

As we want to take some fresh food and a few bags of rice, flour, etc. with us, we've got to wait for the *Cristobal Carrier* which is supposed to be due in soon. We can wait a few days. But how are we going to buy all we need for three dollars?

So we start swopping and bargaining. Christian auctions off a manilla hawser, an old oilskin, some nylon cord, for 65 dollars, and Fritz buys the starter motor, dynamo and battery, as Christian prefers starting the engine with the crank, which is more reliable. Then Fritz gives us a cast-iron frying pan, which I had always wanted. It was lying rusty in his loft and will be most useful. He exchanges a Primus with two burners, on gimbals, for our Camping Gaz. As his stove's an old one, he also gives us five dollars. So we are now ready for the *Cristobal Carrier*.

We buy our stores by the sack-load on the crowded deck. At this time of year oranges only last a few days, so I spend the rest of the day making marmalade. We haven't alas got time to make lemonade. But it's very easy to make: you just put a little sugar in a bottle, pour on the juice, hermetically seal the bottle and keep it in a cool place where it won't get shaken up, i.e. on land, not on a boat. It will keep several years.

Didier has left on the *Klis* with Bernard. We're glad to be on our own for the long voyage ahead. Laurence makes less work now she's ten months old. She eats a little of everything, but I'm still feeding her as well. There's not much for a baby in the Galapagos. Jacqueline gives us some tins of Quaker Oats, petits-beurre biscuits, eggs, milk—and some books. Christian gets our passports back from the harbour-master's office and goes to Jimmy's to buy the stores: he finds a box of vegetables, butter, and a magnificent cheese and a large bunch of bananas waiting for us there. And a letter from Mme Horneman apologizing for not being able to offer us more, and wishing us *bon voyage*. We're very touched.

8 September 1968. We set out. The de Roys are there at 7 am, with their boat full of presents. Several hot loaves come aboard, some goat fat, a beautiful cake made by Tui, who also gives us a goatskin and a little toy rabbit for Laurence, which she's been secretly making for the last few days.

We hoist the sails in glorious sunshine, with all the de Roy family on board. They go a mile with us, until we are beyond the bay, and then go back in their boat.

'The difference between you and us,' Jacqueline says, 'is that you're going, and we're staying.'

'*Au-revoir.*'

'Write and tell us you're safe.'

Laurence waves a chubby little hand. She probably thinks she'll be seeing Gil and Tui again shortly, as usual. But soon the boat is only a dark speck on the waves, while before us stretches the vast, empty Pacific, gleaming in the sunlight.

XII

Apotheosis Of The Pacific

THREE THOUSAND MILES—nearly 5,600 kilometres to go
without seeing land or a boat. The *Alpha* cuts through the
waves, leaving her white wake behind her, glad that she's got a
month of clear sailing, day and night, ahead. It's marvellous to
be skimming along at five knots with the wind in our sails, while
Gigi steers us and we get on with whatever we like in the
cabin.

The sea and happiness. For a month we'll only have sea and
sky, sun and wind as our companions once more. Every day the
sun will rise behind us, and set ahead of us, so that we can
check our compass by it.

Happiness at sea. How miraculous it is, to be carried at will
by our little watertight steel boat to the other end of the world.
In a month's time we'll be in the antipodes of France, having
gone half the way round the world, and Laurence will be
eleven months old. We will be in the middle of the largest ocean
in the world—and at home.

I'm tired and doze on my bunk. Laurence, little early riser
that she is, comes to have her feed. My eyes are shut and she
doesn't dare wake me. But she's hungry. She comes so close that
I can feel her breath. Then she taps me softly. When I open my
eyes she smiles broadly and climbs on the bunk. Afterwards she
waits for me to get dressed and go ashore. She can't understand
why we're still in bed when the sun's shining.

Sail on *Alpha* towards the west. Last night the wind increased.
At daybreak we lost sight of Fernandina, the last island. There'll
be no more land until the Marquesas Islands, and there are no
merchant shipping lanes. Our only chart of the Pacific Ocean is
the Index Chart for June, July and August which a cargo ship
in Panama gave us; it is not very detailed. The Marquesas are

indicated by small dots. But we've managed to do Panama-Cocos-Galapagos with it, so we ought to be able to get as far as the Marquesas Islands.

Christian leaps to resecure Gigi who is leaning overboard. I put Laurence in the cabin and take the tiller. With this strong wind behind us I'm uneasy. One of the pins of the plate which anchors Gigi to the boat has sunk to the bottom of the Pacific. Christian looks for another in the galley drawer, which is overflowing with kilos of nuts, bolts, screws, nails, small fittings—taken from old bits of wood, attics, or just picked up in the street. In three months' time, true to family tradition, Laurence would be able to pick up all the nails and bits of iron which she found on the quay in Papeete, putting them carefully in her little bucket—'for my Daddy'.

Christian finally has to get into the water to fix Gigi's plate with a new bolt. In the icy sea.

Still the same perfect weather every day when we wake up, the same regular existence which follows the sun. Christian lies on his bunk for hours on end, reading. He glances at the compass by his side from time to time, at the mainsail overhead, and at Gigi: there's no need to get up. We talk more and more about our next boat—or, if the worst comes to the worst, the changes we'll make to this one.

The de Roys had a marvellous idea—they gave Laurence a pile of old newspapers to tear up and make into confetti. She's already been at it for three days with praiseworthy results and has just learnt something very important: you must never throw anything in the water. She was playing in the cockpit, and picked up a bit of crumpled paper and threw it overboard. What a marvellous game. You throw it, and watch where it drops, and with a bit of luck it will float and bob over the waves before disappearing. I had to smack her hand to show her she mustn't do this. Otherwise, Daddy's tools, Mummy's crockery, clothes—and anything else—would all end up in the sea. She has never thrown anything else overboard and quickly understood that everything which falls in the water is lost for good.

I should love to know what she is thinking when she watches a school of flying-fish leap out of the water and spread out in a fan before falling back a little farther on, then leaping again, and again. Unfortunately birds sometimes get mixed up with them, and the poor little fish get the worst of it.

Sunday 15 September. Our seventh day at sea. We've done 900 miles, which makes 128 miles a day. It's still fine, but the wind is stronger and is on the quarter. We're being buffeted about and the boat is often swamped by a huge wave which hits us broadside on and makes us heel over. Laurence turns her back to the waves, in the cockpit. But each time a large one arrives, she crouches down and holds on as tight as she can, as if knowing she could be washed overboard. Except that I'm close beside her of course.

Last night, one of these wretched waves crashed through the open hatch into the cabin and drenched Christian, and inundated the quarter berth. This morning I must dry the lemons, onions and cassava.

One day follows another, uninterruptedly. This pleasant monotonousness gives Christian and I a chance to rediscover one another—because our dream is coming true at last: we are alone on our boat with our little daughter, who is getting bigger every day.

Happiness at sea.

During these long peaceful moments we can look back over the past few years to our meeting one evening at the Bounty in Papeete—it has all gone so fast. We haven't had time to take it in properly. Three years have passed in a rush, and we hadn't really begun to grasp that we were two people, and now three, whose destinies are linked for always. It is only now that we are stunned at this realization, as if it had all happened unbeknownst to us, in a dream. Oh, our happiness at sea, our little daughter who makes it all come true for us, our feeling that we have never been a married couple, but lovers who meet now and then and steal a little space of time from life.

We feel free for the first time, with a chance to think. But in fact we don't think. We let ourselves drift to the rhythm of the boat, in the sun, taking as much advantage as we can of each day which passes.

This crossing is the last long stretch before Tahiti, where we will stop, and fill our ship's coffers before going on again.

Tahiti. It's our loadstone, our starting and end-point, the island to which we always return. Tahiti. The only port we love between America and Japan. When one thinks that it only takes nine hours by plane to get from Los Angeles to Papeete, and often over a month on a yacht, one sometimes wonders why we chose this life.

Every night the cockroaches have a bonanza. Dozens of them appear from everywhere and gnaw anything they fancy. They particularly like sugar. One has to take care not to leave milk or honey stains on one's clothes—they eat right through the material. What is worrying is how much they must be doing which we can't see. There isn't a great deal for these Panamanian stowaways to eat: our sweet things are in jars or tins. So what are they living on? The things in the lockers: books, charts, clothes? They stain everything and leave a sickening smell behind. They're still small. But when they're bigger, will they come and nibble our fingers and toes, as Christian tells me they did on the *Walborg*?

The wind is much stronger, at least force seven, and the *Alpha* is going at a terrific pace. From time to time the jib collapses for a few seconds and then suddenly fills again with a tremendous crack. Gigi is shaking badly. How long will she hold?

But this morning the sun is shining as usual, and Laurence is kicking in her bath. Our noon position shows that we have done 270 miles in 48 hours. A little too far south perhaps, but what a pace. We sing with joy. Christian plays the guitar and Laurence dances.

Crrrraaack! It is I who catch Gigi this time. It's the fitting which fixes her to the deck which has broken for a change. As it was welded we have to think a moment how to replace it. While the captain cogitates by his junk collection—the galley drawer—I hold on as best I can to Gigi, who seems to be fed up with steering on her own. Laurence howls. Christian secures Gigi to the stern pulpit with a bit of metal rod. But the wind increases in strength and two hours later the rod breaks.

I take up my position on guard again, and at the same moment the mainsail gets a two-metre tear. What a joyride. Then Christian gets a bit of stainless steel wire left over from the rigging and fixes Gigi, who has never worked better. She doesn't rock or shake at all, and is beautifully supple.

Now to work. We lower the mainsail, removing it completely.

We mend the sail until midnight, drunk with tiredness, and finally hoist it, before collapsing on our bunks. What will the next disaster be?

And the days pass, bringing a dead calm. You have to be able to take anything on a long crossing, and to have nerves of iron. Day after day we continue our slow and painful progress, unable to do anything, except wait for the wind to get up.

We have to be on the watch all the time, without a break— with no Sundays off. I shall never forget the butcher-woman in a little village who said to me: 'When you're sailing for a month, you anchor at night, surely?'

I was tempted to reply: 'Yes, with eight or ten kilometres of chain!'

A crossing means a month's ceaseless struggle to reach your goal.

Laurence has sunstroke, a temperature of 38 degrees. After eleven days with a good wind and the hope of arriving quickly, Laurence's fever makes us take the calms and light airs as bad auguries. Each of us, silently, remembers possible dangers: the baby falling overboard, inadequate suit of sails, danger of appendicitis and so on. But we neither of us say anything and keep up an appearance of calm optimism in front of Laurence.

Note in the skipper's log:

A small boat is sailing through the night at a few miles an hour, leaving behind her a long phosphorescent wake under the starry sky. It's very dark and there's no one to see this little speck of light bobbing over the waves. In this moving 'capsule' live a little family, who hope and fear, and sing, 3,000 kilometres away from the nearest land. Thousands of kilometres of sea to cross, alone, in a 'tin can' projected by a few square metres of sail rotted by a year's sun, sea, rain, wind. But today I feel unusually at ease. We'll be in Tahiti in a few weeks' time: we'll be able to swim for hours in the warm sea, lie on a white sandy beach surrounded by trees and flowers. What bliss, what a joy after these months of hardship.

Laurence is always disappearing now. Yesterday I managed to

grab her just as she was calmly climbing over the rail. Terrifying. I didn't scream, but last night, at about two in the morning, she woke up sobbing as if she'd just had a nightmare and went to cuddle up against Christian, much to his surprise.

The fishing is no better than the wind: the Pacific is as disappointing as the Atlantic was generous. It isn't that there aren't any fish but there are probably too many big ones which snatch our catch before we've had a chance to draw it in. We've already lost two spoons. As often as not there's only a bit of the head of our fish left on the hook, after it's been stolen by a larger one.

I really think I've learnt more in this year at sea than during my whole youth, notes Christian. This life enriches one, even if it sometimes seems empty and pointless.

Meeting the de Roys gave us a lot to think about. If we decide to go back to civilization and live ashore, who will bring up our children? School, television, posters, youth groups, evening classes, pediatricians, and, in ever increasing numbers, psychologists. When will we see them? In the evening when they come home to wash, eat and go to bed; in the morning when they're getting ready for school. Which leaves Sundays. But it's difficult to carry on a conversation from one Sunday to the next with one's children, especially when parents and children are not sharing the same life. Home becomes almost like a hotel for grown-ups and children, with the mother in most cases being reduced to general dogsbody. What it in fact means is that the father and mother are working for children whom they don't have the pleasure of bringing up, whom they don't have the pleasure of seeing enjoy the best part of the day— and the children become more and more deprived. Parents and children no longer have any work in common.

We don't believe that this is what family life is about.

On land it's very difficult to escape the system. The only solution is the one the de Roys have tried—find a desert island. But even that isn't a complete solution because children need to rub up against each other, get to know the advantages and pitfalls of society, so that they can choose the kind of life they want. It's up to us to give them the chance to live happily in whatever way they choose.

Living on a yacht enables one to combine various possibili-

Living on *Alpha* is like living in a house; but open the doors, and
there's the Ocean

Pygmalion: the floor
was 2½ by 5 metres;
three or four
couples could dance
on it easily

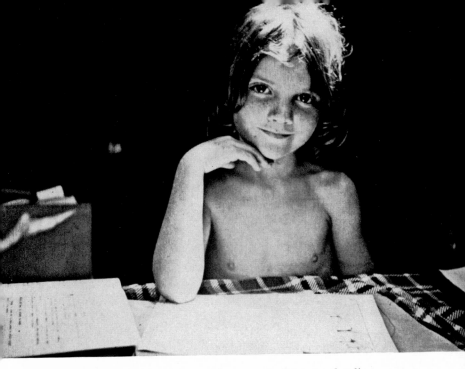

Laurence and her wonderful 'sea school'

Turtle: a juicy steak in mid-Pacific

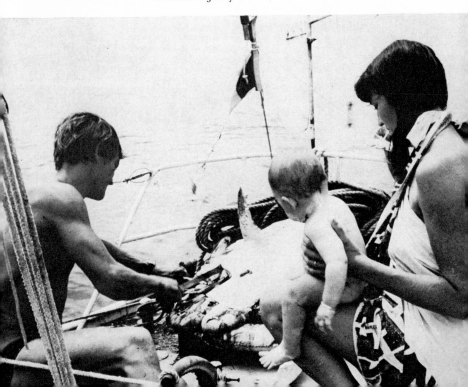

ties. We can live and work in a large town for a year without leaving the boat, and then live in a village for a year. There are excellent school correspondence courses. I've discovered a marvellous one which is very modern and adaptable, as its name implies: *Pédagogie moderne*. I'll write more about it later. And there's nothing to stop one sending the children to school for a few months from time to time, to learn a foreign language or come into more direct competition with others.

Meanwhile we're still at sea and I continue to work at my English and am also conscientiously studying graphology. An enormous whale—larger than the boat—surfaces only a few metres from the *Alpha*. We keep absolutely quiet so as not to frighten it, and stare fixedly at it. The monster dives down right beside us several times, going under the *Alpha*'s keel and reappearing on the other side. If it judges the distance wrongly it will give us a very nasty jolt. But luckily, it doesn't touch us— and hasn't come to scratch its back on the hull like the sharks. It keeps us company until the sun goes down, and disappears when it grows dark.

In the Antilles, Eric Deschamps told us: 'We were in the Virgin Islands recently. It's lovely there, more like Polynesia than anywhere I know. And I stroked a whale.'

'Stroked a whale?'

'Yes, a real, live one, in the sea. You see, we decided at about two one afternoon to spend the night in a lovely deep bay, quite near. We were still out at sea when I suddenly saw a black shape lying motionless on the water. I glanced at the chart, but there was no shoal there. The *Erna* sailed closer. We looked through the binoculars. It was a whale—fast asleep. But what was it doing there? It was the cool season and it must have got lost trying to follow a cold current. I sailed a little way off in the *Erna*, which I then hove to. A friend and I jumped in the Zodiac with our flippers and masks, and went up to it quietly so as not to wake it. Then we got into the water, and studied it closely for a while. You couldn't see much because it was so big. But what surprised me most of all was its skin: it was like an old tyre that has been in the sea for years. There were shells and weed and grass sticking to it.

'It finally began to move. We immediately got back in the Zodiac, which seemed minute in comparison with the whale.

7

It was no good telling oneself it wouldn't harm us, I felt most uneasy. After going a little way in silence we started the engine, softly, so as not to frighten it. But it was now wide awake and following us, and had great fun diving under the Zodiac. Brrrr! It went off at last, and we got back aboard the *Erna*. We felt safer there than in the dinghy.'

The *Alpha* advances about 100 miles every day, in spite of so little wind. It's marvellous to know that we're making progress.

'Do you realize it's only 600 miles more?'

Apart from our mail, which we won't get until we get to Papeete, I'm in no hurry to arrive. I feel I am on holiday for the first time in my life. My household tasks seem easy, almost non-existent. On the other hand I read and continue my studies all day. I can enjoy watching Laurence's progress, how she's trying to say new words. 'No' is easy. How wonderful for a child to discover a new means of communicating with others: your first smile, the first syllables you discover when you learn to read, your first love—and the wonder can last a lifetime.

What a difference between sailing here and in the Mediterranean [it says in the ship's log]. Here our oilskins are rotting in the forecastle, under a bag of shoes in which I've also hidden the bottles of Côtes de Provence I brought from the Mas du Mournaï so that they could go round the world. I regret the time about three weeks ago, when it was still cool enough to wear a sweater because of the Humboldt Current. But I have no regrets for the Mediterranean at all, probably because my boat's no longer new and I'd like to refit it throughout.

We can't hear Radio Tahiti yet, but it shouldn't be long, because there's a relay station in the Marquesas Islands. It's good that the moon is waxing, because we shall arrive by moonlight as we did in Barbados.

It smells like arriving, like land.

While we write a few letters, Laurence jumps about, sings and does all sorts of dangerous climbs. She's impossible, as always when we're getting close to land. There it is. Christian has got Radio Tahiti—we're there. It feels like home when we hear the familiar voices. We leave the radio on for the pleasure of hearing French and Tahitian spoken and sung.

Suddenly at about 3 am: 'France, come and look.' A black shape is visible on the great barren expanse of the ocean, where there has been nothing for 26 days: it's Ua Huka. Our throats feel tight and we can't speak. We are both thinking the same thing, and a phrase goes round and round in our heads, dizzily repeated like a crazy jingle on a poster: We are in Polynesia. It is the *Alpha*'s moment of triumph, the moment when the film music crescendoes at the close of a story which might have ended sadly but which is triumphant.

What a night. We don't want to slow down because we want to get to Nuku Hiva quickly. The two most important centres in the Marquesas Islands are Atuona and Taiohae. We have friends at Taiohae who will certainly have news of the *Klis*, of Didier. So we'll go there.

Christian continues going on deck every half hour through-out the night, but we don't sight land again until 6 am. When the sun rises, we're not dreaming, Nuku Hiva is there before us. A long way off, on the port side, we can just make out Ua Pu, the island with mountain peaks which look like the fingers of a hand. There are no reefs in the Marquesas; the islands rise sheerly from deep water as in the Galapagos. Luckily the wind is just strong enough to allow us time to identify each bay and cape. We pass the deep inlet at Taipi or the Baie du Contrôleur, and at 2 pm enter Taiohae, skimming past one of the Guardians —the two black rocks which stand one on each side of the entrance to the bay, like giant statues.

The anchor is dropped at last on the black sandy bottom, and we furl our sails. We are in the Marquesas. They give us a warm welcome at the *gendarmerie*, because they were anxiously awaiting our arrival: our friend Jacques, in Paris, horrified that our family had had no news of us for over four months, had asked for search parties to be sent out by the French navy, who were in Polynesia for a series of atomic tests. Luckily the navy doesn't panic and is used to the ways of yachtsmen. They waited a bit and Didier, arriving on the *Klis*, told them we were in the Galapagos. But Didier had been gone a month, and the *gendarmerie* were anxious to see us arrive.

The Marquesas Islands are typically French Polynesia, with

all its softness, limpid beauty and natural delicacy. You really live there. There is time to live—to breathe. In Italy, or Spain, or Morocco, or the Galapagos, you hardly ever see girls or young women in the village streets, but here you see them everywhere. Lightly dressed in gay *pareos*, with pretty flowers in their beautiful dark hair, and smiling, open faces, they are proud, but not cheeky, with a natural grace—and by their side are well-built young men who are just as beautiful.

The old lady with long white hair, sitting on a stone by her doorstep smoking a badly rolled cigarette, the naked child playing at her feet, have a calm serenity, and smile in a relaxed, friendly way, with no trace of nervousness, or fear or complexes. The only thing which matters is to live, without complicating life unnecessarily. Hunting, fishing, keeping one's house clean, sculpting, working, are things which one does unhurriedly, without continually watching the clock, without continually complaining how hard life is. It is no less hard than in other countries. But here one always looks on the bright side. Even the colour for mourning is white.

In Europe, if two bicyclists crash into each other there is a torrent of abuse. Here, they sit on the ground for a minute, and laugh loudly—even, or rather especially, if they happen to have hurt themselves. It is said that morals are loose here: this middle-class stricture, full of insinuations which may or may not be true, describes rather an attitude to life. The family is very much alive in Polynesia, and it is sacred. It is put before everything else, including conventions or laws. You hear people say: 'They don't love their children because they don't mind giving them away'. How false the accusation is. In Polynesia there are no orphanages, or centres for homeless children or unmarried mothers. There is always a grandmother, or aunt, or a friend, who will welcome a baby with open arms—or a mother who is too young and who thought a passing sailor loved her.

Children are not 'cosseted'. They are treated with affection but as people in their own right from the age of one upwards. You see little fishermen of three, as dignified as their fathers. They don't chuck them under the chin, or make 'sacrifices' for them. They simply aim in the most natural way in the world to let children and adults live as happy and balanced lives as possible. One finds this philosophy of happiness in all the islands of the three archipelagos: the Marquesas, Tuamotu and Society Islands.

We are beginning our stay in the Marquesas with a month's holiday with childhood friends. Josée, a blue-eyed Bretonne, was at school with my sister. She is head of the kindergarten at the Catholic Mission School, to which her parents devoted their lives, and has three adorable children. Her husband, Laurent Haïti, a tall, good-looking Marquisien, is a sculptor. He gets his inspiration from ethnological works lent by Mgr Tirelli, and aims to revive lost art forms. When the first Protestant missionaries reached these islands, they destroyed everything of a religious—and therefore artistic—nature they could lay their hands on. It took years of research to find any trace of the lost works. And this is why you sometimes find wooden or stone *tikis* buried in the ground, which have survived because they were hidden. But the missionaries couldn't destroy the great stone *tikis* two metres high, or the chiefs' tombs, cut in the rock above 20- or 30-metre-high precipices, which you can see in the valley where Laurent's family lives, at Hakaui.

Christian is building a dinghy for us, with Laurent, and fishes for langoustines at night in the river, and goes goat hunting. Laurence takes her first steps, and has her first birthday—we blow out one candle on the boat. The time passes so quickly; already a month's gone and my sister wrote to me a year ago saying she was going to fly from Tahiti to Paris on 31 October 1968. I would like to see her so much if only for an hour. So on Sunday 20 October we set sail for the Tuamotu Archipelago and Tahiti. We have a week's tricky sailing to begin with. Luckily we're fit and rested after our month in the Marquesas Islands. Tahiti doesn't seem to want us and is giving us the cold shoulder. This blasted adverse wind. Laurence doesn't seem to notice the bad weather. She goes on playing happily. And I begin to feel more and more that I shan't see my sister before 31 October. When will I see her again? If she travels as much as I do it will be several years before we meet.

On the 27th, it says in capital letters in the log book: 'DRIFTING WRECK SAILS IN TATTERS.' What a night. This morning the boat is in chaos and we look ghastly. The wind, still in our teeth, got much stronger last night and it was so dark you couldn't see more than twenty metres ahead. Added to which, there was the fear of the atolls all round us, which kept us awake in spite of all our recent sleepless nights. We took turns on watch all night, but in fact we were both constantly awake, our ears pricked, and our eyes straining in vain to see through the darkness. The angry waves submerged the boat and then lifted us up to amazing heights.

Towards midnight, when Christian had been on watch for four hours, a tear several metres long appeared in the jib. It took him an hour, lying flat on his front and ceaselessly inundated by the waves, to lower it and put in its place the five-square-metre storm-jib.

The atolls are probably quite near; there are possibly some right in front of us. But it's impossible to see breakers or hear them thundering on a reef because the wind and sea are making too much noise. If we see one, at the last minute, it will probably be too late to do anything. We are strained and tense, not knowing where it's going to hit us next. Luckily a watch like that keeps all your senses alert and leaves no time for fear or reflection.

The mainsail is flapping horribly. At about 5 am Christian decides to take in another reef. While he's winding the reefing handle of the revolving boom, and with difficulty preventing himself from falling, a two-metre tear appears in the sail. We lower it and replace it with the five-square-metre white storm-jib. The sea is still raging and keeps washing over us. There's no question of stopping at the Tuamotu Islands. At dawn, the sun comes up, but the sea is still angry.

Our noon position places us to the south of the two last Tuamotu Islands, Matahivva and Tikehau. We must have passed between the two atolls last night, when the storm was at its height—without knowing or seeing anything. What saint was protecting us?

We are safe and sound, and there are no more atolls in the offing. The only annoying thing is that the wind is still against us and we only have ten square metres of sail to play with. We're unlikely to arrive in Tahiti before 31 October. How many days will it take us with our reduced canvas? When the wind's strong, we make some headway, but as soon as it drops, it feels as though we're going backwards. Christian is talking seriously about rationing our food and water, because we could drift for a month or two before we reach land.

Well, there's nothing for it but to struggle on. At worst, we'll hit Bora-Bora but we won't miss the islands. Miserably tossed to and fro, we are making some progress. We must be making some progress because Moorea is there, seven miles ahead of us. How good it is to reach this familiar island, opposite which I spent my childhood. I feel we've arrived already, that I can smell Papeete in my nostrils, the smell of the lagoon at six in the evening, when the tide is low. It doesn't go out very far, but the water's so calm then that there isn't a wrinkle on its surface. It was the time when we went in our canoe to the little island of Motu-Uta which has now been swallowed up by the causeway and the new harbour.

Moorea is there, but the wind drops more and more, preventing us from reaching land. We hoist our patched sails again, hoping there's life in them yet. We skim along for an hour, and begin to hope that we'll be there in a few hours. But after an hour the mainsail tears across. We reef it. It tears again. Christian starts the engine. We're making no headway. There's probably a rope round the propeller. We both have a bad throat and are not at all keen to get into the water. It's maddening to be becalmed, or as good as becalmed, so near our goal. The worst of it is that it could go on like this for several days, just long enough to miss my sister.

Laurence can do more and more on her own, finding herself bananas and biscuits and lying down fully dressed, as we do, when she's tired.

In spite of his sore throat and temperature of 39 degrees, Christian dives in at 4 am to clear the propeller. Then, as he can't sleep, he goes on with the repairs, dismantling the fuel filter, which is encrusted with dirty fuel from the Galapagos, which we had in fact filtered once. Then he starts the engine. There's just enough juice to get us to Tahiti.

At daybreak we're on a level with Moorea at last. Christian sleeps for an hour and I take the tiller as Tahiti approaches.

At last at 9 am, we drop anchor in Papeete harbour, alongside Paul Smet's *Tiare*.

We are in Tahiti. Exhausted. But we're in Tahiti.

Now we're here, we immediately feel less tired. I rush to find my sister, who hugs Laurence delightedly and says that she's not going to France after all.

We are in Tahiti.

Pierre and Catherine Deshumeurs, who saw us arrive from the *Vencia*, come aboard: 'Mmm, it smells good on your boat, you can tell you've just arrived.' Other yachts appear, or leave, and we make new friends every day. Christian does tourist trips on the *Alpha* with her tattered sails.

Laurence has found a friend: Elodie, a little fair-haired three-year-old on the *Ophélie*. When the two little girls both try to go along the plank leading from one boat to the other at the same time, they sometimes tumble in the water.

Also here is Julio Villar, the only Spanish solo-navigator, who speaks French perfectly. He's an ex-alpine climber. He was on the most advanced climbs when a frightful accident converted him overnight to sailing, which he had never done before. He did a little trial trip, on a Super Mistral, just to see how he got on, and found himself in the West Indies, having crossed the Atlantic—and eventually sailed right round the world. His dinghy is so small it will only take one person, and if you move at all you're liable to capsize: he made it from half a sheet of plywood.

Klaus is here, the German who built himself a marvellous flush-deck sloop of about seven metres in the West Indies. He copied the hull of an old fishing boat abandoned on the beach, and achieved a remarkably solid build with wood which he fetched himself from the mountainside. Inside, there's just a big floorspace on which you can sleep or cook on all fours. Ten or twelve people can be fitted in and it's great fun. Papeete harbour is full of every kind of boat from April to September, especially large American racing yachts, which are sailing round the world and call in at Tahiti before setting out for the Indian Ocean.

Then there's Bernard Moitessier who, like us, is here for some time. We all congregate every evening on the few blades of grass which Bernard Moitessier proudly calls our lawn and which we carefully water so that it will last as long as possible, or until the quay is rebuilt. We share some raw fish *à la Tahitienne*, salad and fruit, and chat—exchanging memories:

a desert island, a forgotten or lost beach, a dangerous reef, a recipe for preserving food. We talk of Cape Horn, Patagonia, the Galapagos or the Indian Ocean, as people in Paris talk of their country houses. We try to learn all we can about the Torres Strait, Indonesia, the Chagos archipelago, so that we will be able to avoid the worst dangers. And we dream. The little girls watch and listen, and ask their first questions.

Meanwhile a new boat is taking shape, the fruit of all our experience, our dreams. We sell the *Alpha* in Tahiti and move back to France, to Equihen. We've got an old second-hand Peugeot 203, and are going to le Marquentaire to see Monsieur Knocker, the creator of Bernard's *Joshua*. That's the boat we want.

XIII

'Pygmalion'

5 NOVEMBER 1970. The bare, rusty hull, with no deck and with nothing except a Yanmar 20 hp diesel engine, is coming down the Rhône to the Mediterranean through icy mist and cold, with the help of two friends of ours.

Then there's the horrible winter of the great building operation. We couldn't have chosen better. The Lyon–Marseille motorway blocked by snow, and 4,000 stranded motorists awaiting Christmas among the freezing ice-floes. Christian is building the *Pygmalion* single-handed, in Marseille, in the biting wind which never lets up. He sleeps and eats on board. Although he's hardly ever wielded a hammer and saw, he's doing it all himself. It's a miracle he isn't ill. On the coldest night of the winter it's minus five degrees in the boat, in spite of having two heaters on all day. One day, after painting the interior, while he was sleeping at the house of some friends, thieves went off with the welding gear, and the tools he'd been lent: spray-gun, electric drill, radio.

At last, in May, the *Pygmalion* is launched. I've been signing people up for sailing lessons, because that's how we hope to make our living this summer. Our main mast is an EDF post; the sails are best terylene, made by Loiseau. Rigging and guard-rails are galvanized. It's not luxurious but the *Pygmalion* is an excellent boat, as we prove. In June, she sets out for Greece, and returns via Malta, Tunisia, Sardinia, Corsica. We have numerous 'crew' for our sailing school and it's far from restful. It's very hard, in fact, being the skipper's wife. Because if he's alone on board everyone helps him as a matter of course, with the shopping, cooking, washing-up. But if his wife is there, no one bothers to do anything. She's expected to do the shopping for ten, to wash up for ten; no one pumps out the heads or washes down the deck, and they seem almost surprised that the poor unfortunate woman doesn't do everyone's washing as well—by hand of course.

It's nearly winter, and the Mediterranean is becoming more and more chancy. We are leaving Marseille for the Tropics, for the sun. One has to be prepared for frequent squalls at this time of year, and Christian and I both feel secretly apprehensive, as if we somehow felt we shouldn't tempt the devil, as if a voice were telling us that we should be satisfied with our first voyage from France to Tahiti with a baby on a tiny yacht. I dread this crossing as far as Gibraltar, and am glad Roger and Jean-Baptiste are with us: they are excellent divers and fish in the Mediterranean even in the middle of winter. They've never done any sailing, but they're big strong men and very co-operative.

Laurence is just four. Although she's always been used to sailing, she's still very young and has to be looked after all the time. I have no desire to share my watches with her if it's rough—especially as children are more prone to seasickness as they get older.

Monday 8 November. Roger comes on board the *Pygmalion* at about eight, bringing some fresh salad, farm eggs, and delicious home-made jam. At nine Jacques Linski and René Plouton arrive with their cine-cameras. The sky is very blue and a barely perceptible breeze is blowing from the east, with the sun. Jean-Baptiste arrives at 9.45. While Huguette does last minute shopping for us, Jacques Linski tries to tell Laurence that she should like Tahiti best, and the sea and the white sand. But she replies with all the assurance of her four years that she prefers Marseille, Jacques' motorbike and the roundabouts.

I look at my galley with its rows of lovely new labelled tins: flour, sugar, rice, pasta. Our *Pygmalion* is all new and shining, freshly painted and in perfect shape. A whole van-load of stores have disappeared into the lockers. And at 11.30, we're off—under the engine as there really isn't enough wind for the sails, which seem to hesitate in the light breeze. A yacht and a launch accompany us, with some of our friends. The sun is very hot and we put on our bathing things and Laurence wears a grass-skirt. We're all busy framing each other in our camera lenses and using up a lot of film. Addresses are hurriedly exchanged in the frenzy of departure and visitors' books signed.

By one o'clock we're alone at last, that is Christian, Laurence and I, with Roger and Jean-Baptiste.

Our first lunch at sea. In our bathing things on deck, in November. Marvellous. I'm wallowing in luxury: I've got rubber gloves for washing-up, and running hot water—the water for cooling the engine. I think of all the good things I'm going to cook in the days to come, because I intend to cook hot meals every day. I'm beginning to feel blasé. Now I've got a good Primus on gimbals, I only need a steady stomach to see me through.

At 8 pm France-Inter forecasts wind veering to the south-west in the Mediterranean, which wouldn't really suit us as we're making for the Balearics. But for the moment there's no wind from the south-west. A light north-easterly breeze gets up as it gets dark, as we're having the second, and last, meal of our four-day voyage—only we didn't know that then.

Christian is on watch until midnight: the wind's gradually getting up. I watch the speedometer from my bunk. We're carrying our usual area of sail, that is 100 square metres. At midnight Jean-Baptiste takes his turn. The wind's still increasing and a swell is beginning to get up. It must be the mistral. Christian goes on deck and decides to bear away from the wind. We keep all the sails set. The tiller is increasingly hard to handle—we haven't a wheel. During the whole of Jean-Baptiste's watch the wind continues to increase and the seas to build up.

Christian notes:

At 3 am I lower the mainsail. My two fellow crewmates for the week have never been on a boat before and can only stand and watch. 40 square metres is quite a handful in this gale. And in the pitch darkness it is even worse if the halyard catches half-way down the mast, because there's nothing worse than a sail half down and flapping itself to pieces. Shouting to the helmsman to keep downwind— to make it easier for me—I begin my perilous climb, hand over hand up the mast, with the help of the halyards and shrouds. By an incredible effort I reach the jammed rope. I try desperately to free it, but it won't budge and I have to shout to Jean-Baptiste, who had supported me terri-

fied at the beginning of my climb, to bring me the knife I'd
left in my oilskin. But while he's looking for it I manage to
heave myself up another metre and free the halyard with
my toe. And all this while the boat rocks to and fro with me
hanging by my arms to the smooth, slippery mast. I slither
down to the deck ten metres below, trembling from my
exertions, and tackle the difficult job of furling the sail.

4 am Tuesday 9 November. Roger takes his turn on deck. He
has more and more difficulty controlling the tiller. Christian
goes up and decides to lower the jib: 'The jib isn't much easier.
No net under the two-metre bowsprit jutting over the sea, and
sometimes completely submerged in the waves. I cling on so as
not to be torn off by the water and manage to take advantage
of a brief respite to furl the sail and lash it securely. What a
business.'

The skipper takes down the mizzen as well. By morning
there's only the storm-jib, which is suffering badly. The wind's
still rising and we're flying along, at eight or ten knots, and the
speedometer, which doesn't go beyond ten knots, keeps
sticking. We must be doing easily twelve knots with just the
storm-jib. *Pygmalion* is riding out the storm well and not
bumping at all. At about 8 am, Jean-Baptiste and Christian
lower the storm-jib. We're running at at least six knots under
bare poles, and at times at ten knots or more, with the speedometer sticking.

The patent log is squeaking horribly. The swell is still building up, with white crests. The waves are short, very steep, with
troughs of eight to ten metres. We are beginning to roll in all
directions. Roger, on deck, exhausted, has been submerged
several times. He's only prevented himself from being dragged
overboard by holding on to the tiller, with great difficulty.
We're all wearing a harness and go on deck as little as possible.

Seasickness strikes below. We've each got a little blue bucket.
Even Laurence is sick several times. She's very brave and
doesn't cry or complain, but she's only bringing up bile, and we
all know how painful it is retching like that. I'm sick too, for the
third time since I was seven. The waves continually wash over
the deck and the water is beginning to come in more and more.
We've got to shut the hatch. The water is icy, it's freezing cold,

and the helmsman is drenched through in spite of his oilskin, with his fingers red and swollen with cold, and the salt water stinging his eyes. Wouldn't it be wonderful if one could steer from below. But you'd still have to keep your head out: in this weather you wouldn't see a thing through a plexiglass bull's eye.

When I read Bernard Moitessier's *Cape Horn: the Logical Route*, I was horrified to see that the *Joshua* did six or ten knots under bare poles. I thought this kind of thing only happened in high latitudes. I would never have imagined that the same thing could happen to us in the Gulf of Lions. The wind and sea are making such a din you can't hear yourself speak outside. You have to yell. The helmsman has to use immense concentration to see he's not taken unawares, and to keep the *Pygmalion* heading into the waves. This is made more difficult because they are very choppy, and also coming from all directions, as if the wind were veering from port to starboard all the time.

10.30. Next watch. Jean-Baptiste takes the tiller. Roger comes below and crawls shivering into his sleeping-bag on the floor by my bunk. Christian, in the same state, is stretched out against the galley partition. We are all on the side the boat's listing, except Laurence who's asleep on the bunk opposite mine. We're all being sick. The breakers must be ten metres high now. They crash down on the helmsman, on the stern and on the starboard bows, thundering down on the deck with a great roar. Laurence opens one eye and says smiling: 'Mummy, I've seen some huge waves through the portholes.'

Craaack!

Christian leaps on deck. The mizzen boom has broken in two. A wave smacked it violently into the shrouds. Jean-Baptiste only just had time to duck down or his skull would have been fractured. The sky is pitchy dark and the white raging sea running in all directions.

We're beginning to be at the end of our strength [Christian dictated]. With incredible effort I manage to drop the sea anchor over the bows, at the end of a good strong rope of 22 mm nylon. The pull is terrific, but the boat refuses to head into the wind and waves. And it is hit so savagely on the beam that I have to cut the rope quickly, fearing the worst. Seeing that it would soon be impossible for anyone to hold the tiller, I make a sea anchor with some canvas to try from the stern—again with the hope of getting the boat headed into the waves. No good. I haven't the strength to set the five-square-metre storm-jib, or to send a message on my automatic transmitter. I'm afraid my safety harness will break, and have to keep throwing myself at the mast when a great wall of water sweeps over us. I go on deck several times, although I'm exhausted, to lower the sails one by one as the wind rises. Finally I attach any ropes I can find, with weights on the end, as drag lines, to try to slow down the boat.

At about 1 pm Jean-Baptiste sees a monstrous wave approaching from the quarter, much larger than the others and piling up with an ear-splitting roar. He pushes the tiller over as hard as he can, but he's already completely submerged. Both the *Pygmalion*'s masts are under water and her keel's in the air. Jean-Baptiste tries desperately not to breathe and the seconds drag as he waits for the boat to right herself. Then he clings to the starboard stay, on the side away from the list, thinking that he won't be submerged there, and not realizing that the boat's done a complete somersault. But immediately a second gigantic wave breaks over her, driving both masts under and lifting the keel in the air, smacking the boat into the water and crashing down on the keel with incredible force again and again. Jean-Baptiste takes the tiller at once and rights the boat, stern-on to the waves. A moment later, he says:

'I found myself at the bottom of the sea before I knew what was happening. I had to tell myself to keep calm. I said: "You're at the bottom of the sea, old lad: you'd better not get drowned." Luckily my harness held, or I would definitely have had it. It's a great keel, but when you see it like that it looks pretty strange. It gave me a terrible fright. My legs were like jelly. I stayed on deck for seven hours in that weather, thinking "they're all right down there, it's better if they don't see this".'

But meanwhile, below—— Tins are busting out of the lockers which we use as benches round the table in the saloon and raining down on us. I get up and clear some of them away. We merely think we're listing a bit more than usual—and I go back to bed.

The wind's howling and I keep thinking that the forehatch will be washed away. Then what will we do? Before we can put it back we'll have shipped a good bit of water, and a steel boat sinks rapidly when it's full of water. Lost in my worries, I'm taken by surprise and suddenly find myself in complete darkness. Pinioned under a heavy mass of planks, with splinters of glass all over my face. I can't see anything, or breathe. I push frantically to try to free myself—but it's no good. I realize we've turned completely over with the masts in the water. I have time to think that if the ballast comes away we've had it. Even if it were possible to get out of the boat in a sea like this—which is most improbable—it would be quite impossible to reach the life raft. And we wouldn't last long in the icy water, with those waves.

I can only see one thing: Laurence's face.

I gradually see a crack of light appearing—we're righting ourselves. Where is my daughter? I can't hear anyone and the planks pressing on me are stopping me breathing. I shout: 'I'm suffocating! Quick! Where's Laurence?'

'She's all right,' Roger shouts. 'I'm coming.'

He has to move several planks and then leans against the hull and pushes as hard as he can. My bunk has overturned and I'm covered with tins. But I'm unhurt except for some cuts on my hands and a splinter of glass eight millimetres long in my right eye. It's agonizing, and doesn't come out until 24 hours later.

Roger had seen all the floor planks, the carpet, metal fittings, tools, pots of paint, oil, varnish, etc. come tumbling down on our bunks. And Laurence had been catapulted over it all in her bunk which had done a complete revolution of 180 degrees, which meant she must have made an incredibly dangerous flight through the air. Fifty kilos of tins and goodness knows how many ropes had fallen with her on top of me. Some jars crashed on the ceiling which had dents made by the tins on it and a twenty-centimetre split. The eggs broke on the portholes.

Christian is upright, with his left leg caught under my bunk. Roger and I heave with all our might to free him. Then there's a brief respite. Roger holds Laurence in his arms amidst the planks trying to reassure her and keep her warm. We can't put anything back until we reach land. We each sit in the corner we've chosen, anywhere, surrounded by paint, débris, anything. Christian is the first to remember that Jean-Baptiste is still on deck. We realize with shame that we hadn't even given him a thought. I burst into tears.

All the starboard lockers have burst open and come adrift. The air cylinder has torn away the table leg to which it was fixed and has been hurled into the galley, where there is complete chaos. It is completely denuded of everything, including the two-burner Primus which is hidden under a mountain of tins, broken eggs, chocolate.

In the main saloon there is an awful smell from the pots of paint, and toxic fumes. In the forecastle a full cylinder of gas, which had come with the refrigerator Roger gave us, has broken loose with a snapped pipe and the gas was escaping for at least half an hour before we noticed anything. What can we do? We can't keep the forehatch open because the water's flooding in. But it might be safer. We can't possibly light a match down here. Roger insists on staying in the saloon, saying there's only very little gas.

I'm perched on the companion ladder with Laurence, with jets of water hitting me full in the face. I try going down but immediately feel as if my head's in a vice. I tell Roger to come out—he's beginning to feel dizzy. We leave the hatchway open. In the cockpit, the helmsman—still poor Jean-Baptiste—smells a strong smell of escaping gas from below. It's so bad outside that we have to urinate in the hold.

Luckily Laurence isn't making any fuss, but I'm very worried about her. The paint fumes are getting right into our chests and lungs.

'Shut the hatch,' Jean-Baptiste yells.

But Christian says drowning is better than being gassed. Laurence is completely submerged for a minute, inundated on the quarter-berth; she's drenched right through. She's only dressed from the waist up. She has to stay wet like that all night long, sleeping beside me in a blanket which is equally sodden, and never complaining or crying although she's had nothing to eat for over 24 hours. Brave little thing.

The automatic pilot has disappeared. Our life raft has slipped

a metre. The tender over it is held against the cabin-top by the
boom, and is luckily tightly wedged. The skipper makes sure
with a strong bit of line. You never know in weather like this.
No one has mentioned being shipwrecked, but these things
do happen, even to the best people. And if it gets worse, with
the sea like this it would be impossible to get aboard any boat
that came to our rescue. If we had to use our life raft, how would
we even launch it in this raging sea? How it roars.

Jean-Baptiste, Christian, Laurence and I are all huddled in
what remains of the quarter-berth. The hatch is open and
we're getting drenched. Laurence doesn't even take any notice
now when the icy water hits her. She's not asleep but pressing
up against me to keep warm. I'll hold her until we get to
Barcelona, because she's had a nasty fright. And she's so wet it's
the only way to keep her warm.

By some miracle, in the midst of all this chaos, her toys and
clothes are safe. And ironically, although some fine books on
navigation are trailing in the paint, and the crockery is broken,
and all the contents of the fridge and fresh food are uneatable,
a few ridiculous things like my rubber gloves are still hanging
there, untouched, as if nothing had happened.

Roger is at the helm. The tiller bar is beginning to bend,
although it was guaranteed not to, and it becomes more and
more difficult to steer. At about 9 pm Christian relieves Roger.
The breakers are a little less high. The wind doesn't seem to
have eased off at all but the swell has diminished: we are just
leaving the middle of the Gulf of Lions. Christian comes down
with the bar of the tiller in his hand.

'The tiller's broken. There are only two or three centimetres
left. There's nothing I can do. We'll try to mend it tomorrow
morning. We'll just have to drift tonight.'

The boat's still sound which is the main thing.

It's too much. A steel tiller broken.

All five of us are on the quarter-berth. We keep getting
tangled up in other people's hands and feet and heads. One or
other of the men keeps getting up to see if there isn't a boat on
the horizon which might come to our rescue. Half asleep, I tell
myself that anyone's boat would be in exactly the same state in
the circumstances. For a start, we turned right over twice. And
the second wave bore down on us several times with the weight

of several tons. And yet the essential parts of the *Pygmalion* are still sound: masts, rigging, hull, portholes, are absolutely intact. Our only major mistake was the gas cylinder, which we were intending to keep on deck during the voyage. You can't afford to make mistakes at sea, even for a second.

We're doing at least five knots, still under bare poles, and with no one at the helm. And the *Pygmalion* is keeping a disconcertingly steady course to the west.

Wednesday 10 November. Roger finds a hacksaw among the débris and tries to cut off the squashed end of the tiller bar to make it usable. He goes very carefully so as not to break the blade: we'd never find another in this mess. The stump of the tiller has mushroomed out, so Roger pushes the bar into the metal just above the stump and drives it in with a hammer. He reinforces it with a metal bar, bound with strong rope.

Christian and Jean-Baptiste hoist the sails and the wind drops more and more, preventing us from reaching land, which is still in sight by nightfall. Of course, as there is no sun, or stars, and no visibility, we have no idea where we are. We only know we're heading towards the north of Spain.

During the day Jean-Baptiste and Christian bale out the bilges as best they can. The quick-drying paint has completely blocked up our pump, and only a pathetic trickle of water comes out. In fact we haven't shipped much water, which brings home to us the advantages of having only two small openings in the deck—the forehatch which is always shut at sea, and the companion hatch which is only 50 centimetres across.

During the night of Wednesday/Thursday we see a light ahead, slightly to starboard. Is it Barcelona, or the Balearic Islands? At about 4 am we identify the Barcelona light.

On Thursday morning, we sail into the harbour, under canvas alone. The engine compartment is full of water. It takes us four hours to cross the harbour and moor with difficulty between two yachts. As soon as we reach the quay, my first impulse is to jump ashore and greet the *Drenec*, a lovely thirteen-metre steel ketch: 'If you've never seen a boat after it's turned right over twice, now's your chance. You won't see it often.'

And so Alfred Larcade is introduced to the *Pygmalion* and invites us aboard the *Drenec* while we clean up the boat. He tells us one boat is still drifting in the Gulf of Lions, her crew having abandoned her on Tuesday at the height of the storm. They sent out a distress signal and were rescued. And here is little Laurence drawing away beside me and giving lessons to her furry dog. It makes you think.

XIV

Shipwrecked On The Banks Of The Ebro

WE WERE ALL stricken with 'flu—luckily at two-day intervals, so that we could look after each other. Laurence was the last to get it. Yesterday she still had a temperature of 40 degrees. We are all coughing, and still very low. But we're leaving Barcelona. Jean-Baptiste wants to get to Aguilas, to the south of Murcia, as quickly as possible. It was a question of whether it would be better to leave now, ill as we are, with our crewmate, since it is already the end of November, or to follow on alone when we were better, but in mid-December, when it would be colder and far more likely to be stormy. Our recent experience in the Gulf of Lions decided us to leave at once. Jean-Baptiste will take the tiller as much as he can. Also, we bought a sixteen mm cine-camera in Marseille, with the last of our money, and a friend is bringing it to Aguilas for us.

I feel chilled right through and I'm worried about Laurence getting complications after her 'flu. We try to keep each other warm, but she complains about not being able to turn over. She likes watching the Barcelona–Valencia trains disappearing into the tunnels and coming out again, all the way down the coast. For the first time in all the years we've been sailing Christian has decided to keep within about five miles of the shore, on the advice of the fishermen, because at this time of year the wind is mostly off the land, and if you want to sail in relatively calm waters you shouldn't go too far from the coast. We are making good speed and are glad to be sailing south, in spite of our 'flu.

'Mummy,' Laurence says, 'when we get to the beach, and the sea's warm, I'll swim with you.'

When. When we get to the beach. I start worrying again about the kind of life we are giving Laurence. I think of the de Roys in the Galapagos, and am forced to the conclusion that these émigrés in the islands haven't really succeeded, mainly because of their children's education.

'Tui is fourteen,' Jacqueline de Roy told me, 'and she reads and writes like a child of seven or eight. With the education I've given her she finds it impossible to concentrate on studying anything. Now it's too late. If I send her to Belgium, as my family suggest, she won't study and as she has had no moral training, and knows nothing of the pitfalls of city life, she'll be led astray by the first person she meets.'

That's why I think isolation is so bad, the kind of isolation which I myself experienced, to a lesser degree, in an idyllic island and brought up by parents who wanted to keep us from anything that might be harmful. Children like that are utterly unprepared for life, and I think it is a crime to bring them up in that way.

That is why I think a boat is a better arrangement: it doesn't cut a child off completely. After a spell on a desert island one can rediscover the joys of city life, films, theatres, new books, new fashions in shop windows, all the many reflections of the 'spirit' of the times, and the crowds—the crowds made up of thousands of individuals who each have their own history, their own story.

The child who lives on a boat has the advantage of life in the open air: a healthy, energetic, realistic existence, aware of life and death, survival, the law of the jungle—you have to kill to eat—and also of civilization in all its stages—primitive, village life, city life. He will learn to integrate naturally into each. This is the true apprenticeship for our kind of happiness at sea. Besides the basic correspondence courses which his parents give him, he can also attend lessons for children of his own age for a month or so, to see how he measures up to them, and gain experience of group discipline, group activities, games and art. Moreover, mixing with all sorts of different societies and social classes, he will learn the relative merits of customs and habits. He will see how each person earns his daily bread and compare the various ways in different countries. Unlike the isolated child in the Galapagos, he will be constantly observing very different ways of life.

I believe that the greatest proof of one's love which one can give a child is to teach him to be perfectly independent from the very beginning. To make him feel, practically from birth, that his happiness will come from his own efforts, the labours of his own hands. Which means, from the parents' point of view, that they must understand once and for all that the child is not theirs, is not their thing, their property. I don't find this very easy, and often have to reason with myself.

It begins as soon as the baby is born. A baby which is put to lie on his back or side is absolutely dependent on his mother, and all his happiness comes from her. The same baby lying on his front sees the world quite differently. The first things which give him pleasure, which he can achieve for himself, are to lift his head and cheek to one side or the other. He very quickly learns to crawl and then to climb on all fours—satisfactions which are quite independent of his mother. From the very first weeks he will know how to amuse himself, will become aware that it is he who chooses to amuse himself.

I won't repeat the advice given by the child-care books, which recommend letting the child eat if he wants to—even if it's in his fingers, or if he makes everything dirty. Letting a one-year-old or a child of eighteen months dress himself, even if it takes ages, and he puts on everything back to front. Letting a child of twenty months wash himself, even if it isn't done as well as when Mummy does it. With a little patience you can easily teach a child to be absolutely independent by three years old. And what a joy it was to see Laurence, at that age, put on a pretty dress when we arrived in port, jump ashore and run to meet new friends. Or packing her little case to go and stay with friends for a week, who would be delighted to have a little thing of three who didn't wet her bed, could dress and wash herself, and who didn't make any extra work.

A self-sufficient child isn't the slave of his surroundings or his mother. You can work together on positive projects, because he's very mature. Not 'old', but conscious of, and responsible for, his actions, like the little Polynesians who go off fishing at three years old, taking it very seriously. They aren't made stupid by being shouted at, or praised extravagantly for the slightest thing. They are respected, as is their right, and they are very conscious of it.

It is this feeling of independence in the widest sense that I particularly like about Laurence's correspondence school—

Pédagogie moderne. It teaches the child, from the age of three, to do things on his own. It educates the parents through their child—teaching them about happiness. There are endless good things from the child's point of view: practical projects and fun tests, the chance of receiving a regular photocopy of work done by other children of the same age, and the pleasure of being corrected, criticized by someone other than Mummy. The child learns from the age of three to enjoy studying by himself. From the sixth form up, he has the chance of benefiting from programmed education, which is particularly important in subjects such as maths or physics, in which parents are not always very well up.

It's seven o'clock and we're listing more and more. I'm too tired to get any dinner. We each snatch something for ourselves, except Laurence, who is fast asleep. I put a little snack in her clown pyjama-case, so she can get it if she wakes up hungry, and hang a gourd of lemonade beside it, then go back to sleep beside her, in the starboard bunk in the saloon.

At eight Jean-Baptiste goes on deck again. He says he's willing to do an eight-hour watch so that we get there more quickly. Christian and he consult the chart and the lights: to sail down the coast all you have to do is keep to the seaward side of all the beacons. The list of lights, which is new, with corrections inserted, is spread on the table. The English chart is a year old—it's the most up-to-date of our 200 kilos of charts.

Jean-Baptiste is at the helm, and the wind is getting more and more violent; but the *Pygmalion* is riding smoothly. Passing the lights of Tarragona towards 1 am, we are very tempted to go into the harbour to spend the rest of the night in peace. We think of all the people there, safe and sound in the warm. No. It would be silly not to take advantage of this wind. We've already lingered too long in the Mediterranean. Tomorrow we'll be making for Alicante and it'll be hot. Our friend who has been waiting for us for a fortnight at Aguilas with the camera will be getting impatient. We sail on, leaving Tarragona behind.

2 am. Christian takes the helm. He is coughing a lot and comes below now and then to warm himself up for a few

minutes. From about three he stays on deck permanently. There's no moon. The sky is black, starless. The skipper stands farther out to sea. I'm always very scared at night in the Mediterranean because of all the boats. But it's even worse close to the shore. It's impossible to judge distances correctly. It was only the shock of capsizing, the 'flu and the advice from the fishermen that made Christian take the risk. As if I had a presentiment, I say to Christian: 'Luck doesn't last for ever, you know.'

At the end of Christian's watch, we can see a flashing light every two and a half seconds—Cape Tortosa, at the mouth of the Ebro. Christian goes back to bed, worn out and feverish, coughing more and more. Jean-Baptiste, at the tiller, keeps to the course set by Christian, out to sea. But the seas are building up and are coming from that direction. The boat is bucketing more and more and becoming uncomfortable. And our recent experience in the Gulf of Lions has made Jean-Baptiste wary. He's afraid of overturning again and steers closer to the wind in order to hug the coast more closely. It immediately becomes more comfortable. Christian, exhausted by his fever, falls asleep like me, in spite of the howling of the wind in the rigging and the thundering of the waves. The *Pygmalion* runs, runs, flies along—Jean-Baptiste isn't worried. As he can see the beacon, a tiny light way off over there, quite clearly, there's no problem about going closer. Christian went too far out to sea during his watch and that was why we were buffeted about—it's more comfortable now.

And Christian recounts:

I had only been in bed half an hour when there was a jolt, not very bad, but quickly followed by others. We must be on a shoal. I rush out, yelling at Jean-Baptiste to leave the tiller and lower the jib—which he has never done before. He only does so now at my command, letting the halyards fly while I throw myself at the anchor, cut it free and heave it overboard. What else could I do in the darkness? I know land is a hundred metres off. France, terrified, with Laurence in her arms, wants to send out an SOS rocket, launch the life raft. But I calm her. We wait below for the dawn.

Jean-Baptiste explains:

'We must be on a shoal, probably sand displaced by the Ebro, because the light's still a long way off. When we touched, the first time, I thought it was just a little shoal and that we'd get off again. With this wind and going at the pace we were. So I kept the tiller in the same position. When the first waves hit us from astern, I realized we weren't moving. So I banged the tiller over, but Christian was already on deck.'

I peer through all the portholes, but can see nothing but darkness all round us, and over there, a long way off, the blinking of the light. Laurence is still in my arms, and says: 'What a naughty sea, isn't it?' Poor little thing, all 'fluey, tired and only just recovered from capsizing twice and now shipwrecked in the Ebro, in the middle of the night. Frightening experiences for a little girl of four.

The waves hit us with terrible force, lifting up our fifteen tons of steel and crashing us down with incredible violence. Both we and the hull tremble. We are all huddled in a ball on the floor of the saloon, clinging on to each other as hard as we can and trying in vain not to be hurtled about. Each blow bruises us more and threatens to break the masts. But they're still holding.

Each time we're hit, we all strain our ears, waiting for the slow shuddering of the mast to stop. Not this time. And then it begins again. The 50-kilo anchor is torn from its place and is wreaking havoc as it shifts about. In spite of his agonizing throat and the cold Christian goes up to secure it. The close-reefed mizzen he set hasn't succeeded in turning us stern on to the wind. He takes it down. What can we do now? The shore is 100 metres off, bare, deserted, a sandy bog. What boat will come to our aid here, if we can't get off alone?

'The only thing to do,' Christian says, 'is to drop an anchor well to one side to make the boat heel over with the help of the main mast, so it will float in a little water. Then, drop another anchor, and haul us off with a pulley.'

A grey dawn is breaking. The wind is still howling in the rigging. The rudder begins to bang loudly, being lifted on its hinges and crashed down again. The tiller is completely twisted. And we had it welded in Barcelona.

As it grows light the sea redoubles in violence and the east wind increases. It's the worst possible wind for Cape Tortosa. We ought to wait till it dies down—but we have to try to get away from here. By eight, it's broad daylight, and in spite of the overcast sky we can see that it's not an isolated sandbank in front of us, but quite simply the land which stretches several kilometres beyond the light. Christian and Jean-Baptiste try every possible manœuvre with the two anchors, but the wind and waves always drive us violently back towards the shore, lifting up the *Pygmalion* and dumping her down closer inshore. We are stuck a few dozen metres from the dead trees which lift their bleached branches skywards.

The waves crash down on the roof, *Pygmalion* shudders; we have hermetically sealed the hatches but we lack air and are suffering from migraines. As soon as one of us opens the hatch a wave washes over us and inundates the stern.

It's very painful to know that one's boat, one's home, one's means of existence, everything one possesses is stupidly stuck in the sand because a light is no longer where it was. But what a comfort the steel hull is.

'We're testing out the Joshua hull,' Christian says laughing.

The interior is completely dry. But in spite of an incredible number of sweaters, trousers, tights, socks, jackets and oilskins we're cold in our sleeping-bags and blankets. We are still waiting for the sea to grow calmer, so that we can try some other way of getting off.

'I'm hungry, Mummy,' Laurence says. 'What a naughty boat, going on the sand like that.'

I get up painfully to heat some water. Standing in front of the stove, I automatically glance across to the beach opposite us.

'There's a man coming towards us, and two others behind him.'

Jean-Baptiste leaps up and goes to meet them, struggling against the waves which submerge him and the current which is threatening to carry him away.

They are fishermen. The boats from Ametlla de Mar caught sight of us early this morning. One of them apparently sailed over—some distance off, probably, because we didn't see or hear anything—but they couldn't see anyone. The fishermen in the Ebro also saw the *Pygmalion* at about seven o'clock. They came over at once. Seeing no one on board they thought the boat had been abandoned. They reported it to the coastguards and the maritime authorities. They are now coming to make sure no one needs help.

Jean-Baptiste is the only one of us who speaks Spanish. The fishermen are very impressed to learn Laurence is on board. They insist that Jean-Baptiste should persuade us to leave the boat before nightfall, because the wind and seas will get up again. The boat will be safe, they say, because of the sand. At the village we can get blankets, food, warmth, everything we need.

In spite of Jean-Baptiste's enthusiastic report, we refuse to leave the boat. We don't want to leave our *Pygmalion*. She is not, and must never be, a wreck. She's holding up well, we're dry inside and there's enough to eat and drink. And Laurence had a temperature of 40 degrees the day before yesterday and is still coughing; I certainly don't want to take her out in the icy wind. I don't want to catch cold again either. We'd have to walk 150 metres through the water, be drenched by the waves, and then do several kilometres on foot. We might just as well wait for better weather on board. Seeing that we're quite decided, the fishermen leave. Jean-Baptiste says that he'll spend the night ashore if we haven't got her off by then.

By noon, the boat is broadside on to the sea. We are getting the full force of the waves and the *Pygmalion* rises and falls on her keel with a great roaring sound which makes everything tremble. The situation is becoming impossible, at least for Laurence and myself. Each time the boat is thrown from one side to the other, we cling together but are shot across the saloon. I finally decide to pack a small bag of warm clothes for the two of us: we'll go and spend the night in a fisherman's cottage. I put on my isolon wet suit and get Laurence ready.

At 3.30 the little band of fishermen, accompanied by the coastguards and the commanding officer of the navy in Tortosa, come to advise us most strongly to leave the boat for the night. Christian still refuses. But we insist, saying that nothing will happen to the *Pygmalion*—except that it will be lifted nearer the shore. Worn out by his fever, sick and tired, he finally agrees to leave his boat.

Jean-Baptiste takes a rope across to the beach, where the men hold it taut to make a lifeline for us. Laurence goes first, warmly dressed and wrapped up in her anorak with her inflated arm-bands, a life jacket round her waist and a security harness attached to Jean-Baptiste. As she's lowered towards the water she lets out a great howl, but then clings to Jean-Baptiste's shoulders and stops crying, and doesn't make any more fuss.

Arrived at the beach, a fisherman—Pantorilla—immediately wraps our little girl in a warm blanket, and stays beside her, not leaving her till evening and helping us untiringly. Left on board, we each pack a bag: besides my few indispensable clothes, the ship's papers and our personal papers, I put in a packet of sweets, a green plush tortoise and my cine-camera. Jean-Baptiste takes a doll. He makes two journeys with the waterproof bags, while Christian continues to lash down anything that might get broken or spoilt. In the exodus-like atmosphere, we leave all our most precious things on board: navigation equipment, radio, tape-recorder, binoculars, photographs—all our treasures.

The naval commander tells us that since the beacon was moved, we are the fourth yacht in one year to go aground on the same spot for the same reason. Six months ago, an Italian cargo boat got into the same trouble, and all the cargo had to be unloaded before she could be moved.

It's disgraceful that the beacon should be so far inland and that there isn't a light. The sand, which is on a level with the water, is so difficult to distinguish, either in daylight or at night, because there is no vegetation, no houses, no lights. They could at least put a light buoy there.

The mouth of the Ebro has shifted from east to west, and the light was moved accordingly. One wonders what use it is to have a light at the mouth of the Ebro: the few boats that venture up it do so in very fine weather, when the water is clear and calm, because the channel is continually moving. The present beacon is a 21-metre pylon with a feeble light, which makes it seem even farther off at night. And the worst thing of all, which is really criminal, is that the great reinforced concrete base of the old beacon has been left off the Tortosa foreland. It sticks up about two metres, and a small boat can sail right round it. They tried to blow it up with dynamite, but didn't succeed. And no one seems to realize how terribly dangerous it is. If we had been a hundred metres nearer, we would have been dashed against it. It shouldn't be all that difficult to put a pylon and a light there. After us, in 1972, two other yachts and a Spanish cargo boat ran aground in the Ebro sand. A sad sight.

The skipper finally leaves his boat, after having made a last tour of the deck, shutting the hatch securely, and swallowing his disappointment. Perhaps he is remembering his Titanic labours building his dear fifteen-ton *Pygmalion* with her fifteen- and twenty-metre masts, alone, in Marseille, in the icy cold. He's completely crushed. He doesn't say anything, and one feels that for him to leave his *Pygmalion*, his handiwork, means the situation is very serious. We'll have to rest and think what to do. There won't be any miracle.

The fishermen don't talk much. They too are thoughtful. One of them merely says that one of the last yachtsmen to get stuck there had to wait for three days for the wind to go down, before he could get his boat off. Three days. It seems like an eternity to us. To have to wait here for three days. If we'd only known what was in store for us.

Pantorilla is carrying Laurence on his shoulders, and José puts another warm jacket round our little girl, who is wondering what is happening and hugging her doll tightly to her.

We are making for civilization—or at least that is what we thought then.

We walk for 40 long minutes across the wet sand, pitted with marram grass, across marshland where a herd of small black cows with long, sharp, curling horns are feeding. Sinister grey sand—absolutely deserted. Not a house, or a person in sight. Only the great trunks of dead trees washed down by the Ebro, over the whole stretch of land several kilometres in length, and on a level with the water. With here and there a few objects thrown up by the sea. A doll with no arms, a plastic arm and leg, cooking utensils, an old piece of clothing. Everything which is in the *Pygmalion* and which could easily end up on the beach, lost in the sand, carried away by the sea, if the hull cracks, tonight perhaps. A shipwreck, a real shipwreck.

A long, sad journey taking us farther and farther from the *Pygmalion*. Our feet sink in up to the ankles, and for most of the way we're walking in water. We turn round from time to time to look at the boat. She's still there. But we can't tell how she's doing now; we aren't there to come to her aid if something breaks. All we can do is come back helplessly to see what harm's been done, our hearts heavy at having left her to be battered to pieces alone.

We reach the mouth of the Ebro at last where there are two ruined houses. Pantorilla's motor-boat is tied to a decrepit landing-stage. We all get in and are across the Ebro in a few minutes. Jean-Baptiste has great difficulty in interpreting for us, because we are in a very isolated part of Spain, where they speak a barely comprehensible type of Catalan for 25 kilometres around. These kind men probably think we are rich tourists on holiday, who own a yacht. But it's long past the holidays, and no one would go on a cruise in this weather with winter coming on.

The naval commander suggests taking us to an inn, in the village, fifteen kilometres away. We'll be quite comfortable there until the weather improves. Then he'll ask in Ametlla port for volunteers to come and haul us off with their big fishing-boats. We can count on him, he'll take care of everything. An inn? But it's out of the question. We can hardly spend our last few sous now. Especially when it means going fifteen kilometres away, with no means of getting from the village to the boat.

The fishermen listen in silence. When I turn to look for Laurence, they point to a little fisherman's hut at the edge of the water, 50 metres from the foot of the beacon. Laurence is sitting in front of a lovely wood fire, eating some bread and a grilled fish.

'We don't like to offer you such a poor hut,' the fishermen say. 'But if it's any help you can stay there as long as you like. There is rice, fish, wine.'

It seems like a castle to us. It's just what we need and it is we who feel embarrassed at accepting so much kindness. The hut is four by five metres, built of white-washed brick and weather-beaten. There is a little chimney, and a large bed of planks covered with dried furze on the earth floor. Four stools, a table, two shelves and a tank for drinking water. The doorway opens on to the Ebro. Two little glazed windows look over the river and towards the boat; because you can see the *Pygmalion*—a tiny speck on the horizon. The commander leaves his binoculars so we can keep an eye on her. Pantorilla takes a list of what we need from the village for the night. A fisherman gives us some fish, which we grill over the cinders with some potato. We have all we need to complete our happiness. At 7.30 pm when Pantorilla comes back with his wife and José bringing some supplies, mattresses and a straw palliasse, we have finished eating. By eight, we're all asleep. Jean-Baptiste on the plank bed; Christian, Laurence and I on the mattresses on the floor.

Sunday 28 November 1971. At eight-thirty the *guardia civil* drag us out of bed, just to have a look at us I imagine. The sun is shining and the sky's blue, but the wind and waves are still squally. The *Pygmalion* is still shifting, being knocked from side to side. Christian is longing to go back to her, but no one wants to go with him: the current is very strong in the Ebro and one would need to cross with a powerful motor-boat. There are only rowing boats here today. Finally Jean-Baptiste and Christian decide to go to the village, La Cava, to telephone Georges, our friend with the camera in Aguilas.

Two of the *guardia* accompany Laurence and I to Tortosa where the commander welcomes us in a most fatherly way, giving Laurence a packet of caramels. Jean-Baptiste and Christian are there too, because we each in turn have to make a declaration about our running aground. The report takes three hours, during which we try to make them understand that we haven't abandoned the boat, that we never asked for help, especially as we weren't in danger. And that in any case we can't offer to hire a boat to tow us off. The boat is all we possess —our house, our means of work, and we're not insured.

General stupefaction. They're used to holidaymakers giving themselves out to be poor. But no insurance. Our home? The boat! Our place of work? The boat! The country where we usually reside? The planet Earth. Our family? Everywhere, in France and Tahiti for a start. The commander becomes more and more amazed. He promises some trawlers to tow us off when the weather gets better. They accompany us back to the little hut and the terrible hours of waiting begin, with our hopes continually dashed and the back-breaking work to try and haul *Pygmalion* off. Above all, with everyone around us helping as best he could, there was a great feeling of togetherness.

We're still very down, and sick, with no means of earning a

Pygmalion stranded. The water round the boat was only ankle deep

Despite capsizing and going aground, *Pygmalion,* built with such care, crossed the Atlantic in only eighteen days

sou. Laurence plunges into all the delights of the countryside.
A grey donkey is her great joy. Two sheepdogs her first loves:
she strokes them and presses her face against theirs. Then she
follows the movements of the herd of little black cows in the
neighbouring marsh.

In the evening we have a meagre meal, while the two guards
who seem to be bored to death come to take advantage of the
fire.

Tonight we're assessing the situation, while mice run over us
and the smoke from the fire makes our eyes water. When the
fire goes out, it's freezing. You can hear wild duck calling in the
darkness. The Ebro delta is a famous shooting-ground for wild-
fowl. And the next day we can't wait any longer; Christian and
I decide to go to the boat, leaving Laurence in the hut with
Jean-Baptiste. A fisherman lends us a boat which he uses to set
his nets. The current and wind carry us off course, and we have
to row hard. We tie the boat up on the opposite bank, and set
off on our way to the *Pygmalion* in our diving suits, Christian's
in thermoprene and mine in isolon. This island would be a
marvellous place for a holiday, with hunting and fishing—with
a good boat in a safe mooring. So much wildlife for our daughter
to enjoy. This morning she said: 'Mummy, we must buy this
house with all these animals round it.'

The boat hasn't moved much. She has dug herself a trough
in which she is still rocking. Round this hollow the water comes
half way up our calves. It will be very difficult getting her out
of there, and it's depressing when we know there's no tide here.
Nothing has moved inside. What a relief. We can't help
remembering that our daily life is here, that this is all we
possess. Feeling more and more like shipwrecked sailors, we
bundle up more warm clothes, blankets, sleeping-bags. We
bring the guitar, some games and school books for Laurence.

Going back across the Ebro, we have to struggle against the
current and the wind. We realize why the boats always have
two or three oarsmen. The oars are so heavy I can only use one
at a time.

The newspaper *La Vanguardia* has published a slightly fantastic account of our shipwreck, but it results in a welcome
surprise: in the evening, just before supper, the *guardia* arrive
with a message—a scrap of paper on which is scribbled:

'Llamar Ricardo Zendrera Tel 204.' It's Alfred's friend whom we met in Barcelona. How nice of him—we hardly know him. We are greatly cheered to know that there's someone we know in Spain, someone who knows where we are.

The next day we see all the trawlers from Ametlla go out about 20 kilometres beyond the *Pygmalion*—but there's still no word from the commander. The fishermen repeat that they are entirely at our disposal, that they are only waiting for the green light from the commander to act, that they'll all help us. Meanwhile they give us fish every day. Christian, who is longing to go to the village to telephone Ricardo, doesn't go, because he's waiting for the commander, who never turns up. Finally he goes to the village and telephones the commander himself: the trawlers will come tomorrow morning early. He also rings Ricardo, who says he'll come as soon as he can. There's no wind tonight, and the sea has gone down—if only it lasts. The sun has set. On the horizon we can see the boat, in the sand, then more sand which looks very black in this light, and the dark marshes, above which fly hundreds of gulls and wild duck in arrow formation. Then some ruined houses, more black sand and the island of Buda, a strip of land planted with poplars, which are darkly silhouetted against the sun, setting in a pinky orange streak across the horizon. On the other side the hazy blue *sierras* gradually melt into the darkness. The beacon—the wretched landlocked beacon—sends out its wrecker's rays.

The wind gets up in the night and blows more and more strongly. Damn! Yesterday we could have. . . . And today, of course, in this wind, there's no commander. To cheer us up, Ricardo arrives with his brother Pablo. They have done over 200 kilometres to come and help us. Ricardo is eighteen. Pablo is twenty, the eldest of a splendid family of eight children. They are both students. A new phase is beginning for us, which we couldn't appreciate at the time. It all sounds so simple. But our work was only just beginning.

Jean-Baptiste has decided to take a train to France tonight, as he feels sure the trawlers will soon get us off. At 6 pm we go to Tortosa to try to see the commander: we use the Zendreras' car as they speak Spanish—but all the offices are shut. We put Jean-Baptiste on the train, and come back with Ricardo and Pablo, who sleep in the hut with us.

We've been here five days already.

I do a few *Pédagogie moderne* kindergarten lessons with Laurence. They can be endlessly adapted. Yesterday she drew the stranded boat and everything she has collected on the beach. Most of the day is spent in games of observation. This morning she caught her first frog. 'Look, Mummy! It swims like a big girl, but only with its legs.' When she's played with the little creature for a while, I say:

'You must put it back in the water now. Otherwise its Daddy and Mummy will be worried.'

After a minute or two one of the fishermen comes up. 'Your little girl keeps asking us to catch the Daddy and Mummy frogs.' I should have thought of that.

Another discovery. Laurence arrives out of breath: 'Mummy, I've seen a bear. It didn't have any horns, it's got soft round ears and hair like a bear, not a cow.' It was a calf.

In the evening it starts to pelt with rain. I hurriedly gather some dry wood. The three boys are not back yet. They arrive when Laurence and I are in bed.

The Tortosa commander went with them to Ametlla to see the fishermen and lent them a walkie-talkie set so they could speak to the men from here. Then they went to Tarragona to buy some ropes and a steel cable for 100 dollars, as the fishermen are clearly not keen to risk breaking theirs. Tomorrow morning four trawlers are supposed to be coming to tow us out. We feel very nervous. I keep thinking that 100 dollars is almost all we have left. And two more days pass: too much wind and rain.

In the afternoon several people visit us, including Pantorilla and his wife, who bring us two loaves. This morning Felix gave us three ducks' eggs and some fruit jelly for Laurence. How kind they are. Laurence has a visit from her friend the dog, his fur dripping with water. The wind howls the whole day, and all through the night, and the rain pours down. It soaks our pillows, and part of the floor, and drowns the fire, which has already gone out. It's so cold we can't get to sleep again, and we feel 'fluey once more. Nothing dries out and Laurence is wearing sodden socks and tennis shoes.

Another day—the weather's no better and Pablo and Ricardo go back to Barcelona. The fishermen come very early this morning, clearly because the current flowing down the Ebro appears to have vanished. The waves are pushing upriver. The men have got their boats out, but they are swamped, as if the Ebro were suddenly twice as large as usual. The little jetty opposite the hut has disappeared under the water. As soon as we go outside the water comes up to our knees, and it's seeping into the hut everywhere. Going out to get some wood, which I have to drag out of the water, I get my last pair of socks wet. My feet are frozen. Some fishermen are vainly trying to haul up a net, which they put out in the river yesterday, because the branches which are being washed down are tearing the nets.

An Ebro fisherman's life is a hard one. They don't get much for their fish. Every day they spend the whole morning cleaning the net they put out the evening before, often for only one basket of fish. The only rewarding fishing is for *angulas*, young eels, only a few centimetres long and transparent. They are a great delicacy and very expensive. That is the only reason why our hut is there; they use very fine nets in the shape of a cage, which are anchored to the end of the little jetty which is now under water. A small paraffin lamp is installed on the jetty to attract the *angulas*, on moonless nights.

The wind is so strong that it's very difficult to open the door. The guard didn't come yesterday evening, or this morning. The beacon is in a lake, and the visibility is so poor that at eleven in the morning we can't see the boat even with the binoculars. As long as it's not working even closer to the shore. There's obviously no point in getting in touch with the fishermen in Ametlla. We'll have to wait till tomorrow. Provided the meteorological office is right and the weather improves. The wind is so violent that it feels as though the hut will be blown away. Laurence is busy drawing and colouring.

A group of fishermen and a shooting party from Barcelona arrive with the commander. He brings us some clothes, boots and biscuits for Laurence. One of the men from Barcelona gives us some money for Laurence and a jersey. Enrique and Luis, two of the fishermen, bring us a box of frozen sardines, some anchovies, a tin of Nestlé's milk, some cheese and oil. It's fantastic. We're absolutely overwhelmed. They are as tactful as they are kind, and disappear as rapidly as they came, ploughing through the water and wind in the blinding rain.

'*Frio, frio,*' says Laurence, practising her Spanish.

And we are indeed perishingly cold. She put on her boots at once, instead of her sopping shoes and socks.

More days pass, and it gets worse and worse. The boat is digging in more deeply and we are increasingly run down. We have got 'flu again and are suffering from the cold and deteriorating food supplies. It's most serious for Laurence, who is growing rapidly. I'm very worried, although she hasn't lacked for anything up till now. But what else can we do other than wait until we can get the boat off somehow or other? We'll do it if it kills us.

The oldest fisherman brings us some potatoes, rice, parsley and garlic. Two of them rowed over from the other bank, in spite of the rain, wind and cold. How generous they are. But we have never asked them for anything or bemoaned our lot. Both blessings and miseries seem to be raining down on us from heaven—it's very confusing.

The fire refuses to light, but Laurence is still very cheerful, playing all day long. It will soon be Christmas and we're making things in preparation, with the help of her little school. The educational adviser in her office in Paris would be very surprised to learn that one of her little four-year-old pupils is shipwrecked and getting ready to spend Christmas in a small fishing hut.

A sudden commotion: the mayor of La Cava, a very young, friendly, dynamic man, arrives in a Land Rover with a guard.

'Bring your things—I'm taking you to La Cava. When you are famous you will be able to tell everyone that there's a very nice little village in Spain.'

We leave some of our things in the hut, with the bedding, and just take a small bag. There's so much water everywhere that it's like driving through the sea. On the way to La Cava we see only rice fields on every side, with pink flamingoes and white herons who have come to feed.

In the village, the landlord of a café pension, the 21 Bar, gives us a drink. He tells us a room is all ready for us, and that we can have all our meals there. We can ask him for anything we need and we mustn't worry about anything: the mayor and he will take care of it all. As for the mayor, he disappeared so quickly that we didn't even have time to thank him.

And then a beautiful *paëlla* is laid before us, without our asking, with some soup for Laurence. A real house, with dry floors—we can't believe our eyes. Pablo and his other brother, Miguel, are there, delighted to see us safely in the warm. Laurence plays with a caged owl. It seems that there has never been weather like this within living memory: yesterday, in Benidorm, in the south, they rang the tocsin for the whole population to go and save the boats in the harbour. We couldn't have chosen a worse moment to run aground. It seems there is nothing we can do, and so it is pointless to worry about being a bit farther from the boat. We can gather our strength—we'll need it.

XV

Afloat Again

JOSÉ AND REGINA, the owners of the café, have a little boy of six, José. We are treated like members of the family. On the first evening I washed all over, including my hair, in five litres of warm but brackish water. And how well we slept that night between clean sheets.

After the last few days' gale, the *Pygmalion* has shifted over the bank of sand against which she was lying. She is more exposed than ever, with only a little water in the hole she's dug, and dry sand to walk on all round. The rope to the dead tree has disappeared and the tiller is completely broken. Apart from that there's not much damage. The boat is still sound; there are no dents and the masts and interior are in perfect shape.

Christian stows all the sails below. It's terrible to see *Pygmalion* lying all bare on the sand like that. It's getting damp inside, especially by Laurence's bunk. We fill two rucksacks with our most valuable possessions, and things we need urgently.

'We'd better not take too much,' I say. 'Perhaps she'll be off tomorrow.'

And Christian replies: 'You're being over-optimistic. Take anything that's precious. Then at least it will be safely ashore.'

Such mixed feelings of hope and despair.

I look sadly at all Laurence's toys and favourite things, everything she'd like to have. Decide to take the typewriter, our photographs. Despite this I can't help feeling that the boat will soon be afloat again. Christian, on the other hand, is thinking only of lightening the yacht as much as possible. We wonder if it would be best to unload all the ballast, to make the boat lighter?

And the days pass; we go on making plans. The weather is no better, with wind every day. None of the fishing boats would risk sailing closer even if the wind dropped a bit, even if there were only a few small waves, because they need a perfectly calm, clear sea—summer weather in fact. But it won't be summer for a long while yet.

This morning Ricardo has arrived with Antonio Beghetti, of Yate and Motonautica, and one of his friends, Ramon Barcels, president of the Barcelona Sailing Federation. We share a *paëlla*, and talk sitting round the table in the warm with a *carachillo*—coffee with cognac—each drawing plans in our various corners on bits of newspaper or table-napkins of how to haul off the poor *Pygmalion*, sinking farther and farther into the sand in the wind and rain.

We cover miles every day. Every person we meet is like a ray of hope in this nightmare of fifteen tons of steel stuck in the sand, rapidly sinking funds and mouldering possessions. Christian is ill, looks utterly pessimistic and his face contrasts sadly with the happy smiles at the café where everyone is sure the trawlers will soon have us off.

Waiting, waiting.

I am in bed with a temperature, aching from head to foot: I must have caught a new virus. But Laurence is completely happy. Her life is full of excitements. She plays in the café and is given cakes and sweets and chewing-gum—which she enjoys all the more because she knows we thoroughly disapprove. The only stable element in her life is the little school, which we persevere with whatever happens. It takes up about two hours every day, which we fit in when convenient according to what we're doing. In this way she feels that time is devoted to her, and isn't under our feet all day long.

She goes out with her friend José, and goes shopping with him, even at night. She's very independent and spends as little time with us as possible.

We'll never get off. The *Pygmalion* has been stranded on the sand for three weeks now, and, as in a nightmare, each move seems thwarted, doomed before it starts. We now know that the famous trawlers will need a whole day to tow us off; they can only come on a Sunday, so that they won't lose a day's work. Which is reasonable. If it's not fine on a Sunday, but on a week day, the sardine fishermen will come, because they work at night. But they have far less powerful engines. If it means hauling with a windlass, there's a big difference between theirs and the trawlers'. On the other hand they draw far less water and could get nearer the *Pygmalion*. Mundelli has promised to come with his very large black sardine boat. And in the café, as glasses are raised, they say: 'There'll be no problem, with Mundelli's boat.' Oh dear.

Mr and Mrs Zendrera come to see us. It does us so much good—impossible to say how much it helps us—especially as it is all done with so much tact and kindness.

'Anyway,' Mr Zendrera says, 'we won't desert you till the boat is off.'

And I think of all that means: missed time at the university, possible failure of exams, the cost of the car and petrol, doing hundreds of kilometres nearly every day, unstinting telephone calls, their keep at the 21 Bar for weeks on end. The bar has never had so many guests before in the winter.

We are in a very embarrassing position, because we're receiving help from all sides: the mayor of La Cava and the 21 Bar are keeping us, the Tortosa commander is doing all he can, and the fishermen. If it wasn't for them we would be sick and miserable, and would have to go back and live on the boat until our stores ran out, fishing every day and trying our utmost to rescue the *Pygmalion*.

The sardine boats have failed, even Mundelli's. They can't get close enough. So the trawlers wouldn't stand a chance, surely?

We were half expecting this to happen, but our hopes are dashed, none the less.

There's a great hubbub at the 21 Bar. Everyone is incredulously re-telling the events of the day: 'The sardine boats, even Mundelli's big one, didn't get the yacht off.'

Our haggard faces, thinness, are more noticeable than ever. I feel I've aged twenty years.

And Christmas is coming. Laurence and I are peacefully making preparations for it. We're making paper chains, and strings of paper figures; painting gold and silver stars and fir cones. We look at the toys and bright decorations and snow-balls in the shop windows in the village. Laurence is brimming with excitement, bless her little heart.

*8

I explain to her that with the boat stranded, it will be a very simple Christmas, with not many toys, but that all the same it will be very beautiful. And I think back to her first Christmas at sea, four years ago, on the *Alpha*.

How much would a tug cost? Because we must get the *Pygmalion* off even if we have to borrow the money. We can earn some later with the boat, to pay it off. But who can we borrow from? Our families are too poor, and no bank would consider it. But we could try. If by some miracle. . . . Pablo telephones an old friend of his father's, Commander Miguel Coll, to ask his advice.

'Go and see Mr Ortola, and ask him.'

So in the afternoon we set off for Tarragona, and get there that night. We find Mr Ortola, and his son, who is married to a French girl. We look at the chart of the Ebro, show him some enlarged photographs of the *Pygmalion* on the sand, and at first Mr Ortola says it's impossible for one of his tugs to tow us off.

'There's only one way,' he adds, 'which is to get the boat to slide towards the nearest bit of deep water with a heavy anchor and a winch, that is, about 80 metres, to the River Ebro itself.'

Then he thinks again, and a few minutes later has another idea:

'There is a way. Our tugs need a depth of six metres, because they draw four to four-and-a-half metres of water. If you can lay a cable from the boat to a spot where there's an overall depth of six metres, we'll do it for practically nothing, a token sum. You'll need a twenty-mm steel cable. You will appreciate that if we do it on this friendly basis, we can't risk losing our cables. Besides the most difficult part is getting the link between the yacht and the tug. Towing will be easy in comparison.'

As we know all too well—especially with cables the price they are. But why is Mr Ortola offering to come and tow us off for nothing if we do all the ground work? We hadn't asked him for any favours. It isn't Christmas yet. How marvellous—even if our problems are only just beginning. In principle it sounds very simple: all we've got to do is take soundings, lay the cable, and telephone for the tug. But in practice it's rather different.

The hunt for a cable begins. We can only find ones which are too small or too short. The commander in Tortosa telephones the commander in San Carlos de la Rapita to see if Shell could lend us a 22-mm steel cable 300 metres long. And the director of Shell goes to Castellon to see if there's a cable he could buy to lend us. It's fantastic.

Ricardo telephones us to say that Zodiac in Barcelona will lend us a Mark II with a 10 hp engine, to use for the soundings. God bless Zodiac. Pablo is there with the Mark II the same evening.

Christian spends his birthday, 17 December, taking soundings all day long, and the result is hardly conducive to a birthday mood: the water is six metres deep 600 metres from the boat. We go back to Tarragona the same evening to see Mr Ortola. It's not a very good start, to have to find 600 metres of cable. It would weigh about two tons, even if we could find it. Mr Ortola says he'll lend us 300 metres of nylon rope, which he'll bring on the tug. We must get 300 metres of steel cable, if possible in a single piece.

We feel hopeful again; things are looking up. The days fly past, all too quickly. I've written a long letter to Bernard Moitessier telling him that instead of giving all his royalties to the Pope—to whom I don't bear any ill will—he should have kept a small share for the shipwrecked Joshua crew.

We're still hunting for the cable. No one talks of anything but the towing—in the bar, among the fishermen, in our room, playing with Laurence. Ricardo telephones to say there's some cable we can have in Barcelona. He also says the French lycée would like to see some colour slides and hear an account of our voyages. And that his parents would like us all to go and spend Christmas with them, if we'd like to. If we'd like to!

How marvellous to be in a proper house—warm, comfortable, with a bath and as much fresh, hot water as we like. But the most restful thing about the house is the calm atmosphere there. Although there are never less than ten or twelve people around, mostly children, there is no fuss or rush. Everyone goes peacefully about his own affairs. Each child is treated as if he were the only one: his tastes and personality are respected. But at the same time there's a great family feeling in the little community, and they're immensely active and very welcoming towards outsiders.

The streets of Barcelona smell of Christmas. It would be nice to be able to give everyone presents.

The cables we can borrow are fine, but they're too short. They'll have to be joined with shackles.

What a comfort this house is, after a month of waiting, and uncertainties, and false starts. We are enjoying a family Christmas—yes, it may be wrong of me, but I feel as though I am with my family today.

It's Christmas Eve. A real Christmas Eve, with midnight mass in a tiny church. Lina showers us with presents, and Laurence sits up to eight o'clock dinner for the first time, at Tibidabo's.

26 December. Ricardo, Pablo and Miguel are supposed to be going to the Christmas week regatta south of Alicante. They've been thinking of nothing else for weeks, but give it up to stay and help us.

We leave Barcelona at ten in the morning in two cars to go to La Cava. The Seat 850 tows two cables and a van belonging to *Juventud*—Mr Zendrera is an editor—brings two more. We can't go very fast as the cables are terribly heavy.

Pablo and Christian bring the cables to within 60 metres of the boat, on the sand, with a boat lent by the fishermen, towed by the Zodiac. They also bring some bags of things from the boat, because everything is rapidly getting damp there. My job is to empty the bags, clean the things and wrap everything I can in plastic under our two beds, because there are no shelves or cupboards. I have to wash everything in briny water, used sparingly, in the restaurant kitchen sink, and spread it out to dry on the terrace amidst the trout drying in the sun, pegged out like washing.

La Gaceta wants a feature on us. I am typing out an article— it'll mean a few extra *pesetas* anyway. Pablo and Christian spend hours joining the cables, with enormous eyelets and shackles. It's terrible the amount of work these 300 or 400 metres of cable entail. And it's still got to be carried out to sea and the boat turned so that it is lying on its port side with the stem facing the open sea.

The three boys are in the icy water up to their necks all day, and lay the cable metre by metre with incredible effort. The boat, which was easily turned yesterday with the help of two anchors, has swivelled back during the night. It takes hours to get it right again. Then they struggle valiantly on, encircling the *Pygmalion*'s hull with a thick chain, and finish the day by joining more cable.

1 January 1972. Happy New Year! It should begin well, if we can get the *Pygmalion* off. Lovely sun all day, but terribly cold. Pablo, Ricardo and Christian, in the icy water, add 400 metres of nylon to the end of the cable in the water, and take it to the buoy placed 600 metres from the boat. At last everything's ready.

They get back as it's getting dark, tired but happy. For three weeks they've been promising us the tug: lay the cables the 600 metres and we'll come at once and tow you out for practically nothing. On Christmas Eve they said: 'Telephone any time day or night, when you're ready and the sea is calm and the tide high.'

For three weeks we've been working ceaselessly in all weathers to get everything ready for the tug. And tonight, the great moment has arrived; everything is ready and the sea is calm and high.

Music is blaring from the bar. We carefully shut the staircase door and move the telephone from the end of the corridor into Ricardo and Pablo's room. Sitting on the beds, none of us dares speak. Pablo picks up the receiver and asks the exchange for Mr Ortola's number in Tarragona—a solemn moment. We are all tense and full of hope, and the words he spoke would be indelibly engraved on our memories.

Disaster struck, and the ground fell away from under our feet. In a distant, neutral, impersonal and steady voice, Mr Ortola said, in tones which brooked no argument, that it was impossible, that the tug couldn't come, that they couldn't get closer than 2,000 metres, that it was too risky and that even if we paid the proper sum it couldn't be done. He would come and 'see', but it wasn't possible.

We are speechless—especially as it was meant to be a present. Why didn't he tell us earlier? Why did he let us go on working for weeks when it would have been so easy to pick up the telephone and tell us to stop, to think of something else? It's incredible. We feel as though we've fallen into a bottomless pit after scaling a high wall. We can't say or do anything.

It's easy to say 'no' at the end of a line when you can't see the faces of those whom you are letting down, suddenly and without any warning, without any indication that you might change your mind. We are completely stunned. What happened? It seems that time—these three weeks that have passed so quickly while we were struggling in the icy water, with sand blowing in our eyes and a biting wind—has worked against us. One must strike while the iron is hot, certainly, and the iron has obviously had time to cool. There's nothing we can do. Yet we achieved the impossible in being as quick as we were.

'At any rate,' Ricardo says, 'the boat's got to be got off. If necessary we'll get all our friends in Barcelona—30 or 40 of them—to come and haul. How did they build the pyramids? and cathedrals?'

'The first thing to do now,' Christian says, 'is to empty the boat completely.'

So we agree to empty it.

'If you can't get her off,' a very old fisherman says to us with a toothless grin, 'she will make a good fishing hut for us.'

He reminds me of someone in a Luis Buñuel film, one of the old men parodying the Last Supper. Although it was meant as a joke it's still hurtful.

Zodiac—*Pygmalion*. *Pygmalion*—Zodiac. Zodiac—*Pygmalion*. It's so stormy that we have to carry rucksacks, sail bags, plastic bags, all full to bursting, at least 500 metres from the boat in the icy wind and cold, with sand blowing everywhere, before we can load them on to the dinghy in a more sheltered corner. We've got most of the bedding, clothes, toys, books, tinned food and tools lying on the sand.

Laurence is happy to see all her treasured possessions again, which is why I've brought her in spite of the wind. Running about excitedly she says: 'Mummy, look how straight the boat is. We can live there and play on the beach. It's nice here.'

When everything's out of the boat, including the wood and metal fittings, we'll telephone the commander in Tortosa to ask him to lend us a trawler, now the cable's laid.

We've stayed at the 21 Bar too long, too. What will we do now? How much will it cost to stay somewhere? How can we make some money? At present, a few articles or lectures seem the only possible way. Our morale, which had lifted at the thought of the tug, is at a very low ebb.

There's a great mountain of things in our room. I am going through them, washing and mending. The poor old Seat 850 goes on carting our many hundreds of kilos of possessions, going over the grass and through the brackish water, and like the Zodiac eating up several litres of petrol every day.

The vultures are closing in. Two boys from Tarragona come to look at the boat and say, 'When you've given up hope we'll buy your boat for the price of the iron. We can get her off—we know an easy way.'

And they give us their visiting card. 'Underwater Operations. Tarragona.'

The endless stripping of the *Pygmalion* continues. The boys are now trying to break the cement covering the ballast, with chisels and sledge-hammers. As they are coming home in the evening there's a commotion in the street: the three kings from the East are riding down the main street of La Cava before going to the church to distribute toys to the children. In Spain it's the three kings who bring toys.

Laurence has made two coloured-paper crowns, and proudly sings a little song she has learnt: 'Melchior and Balthazar have left the ship, have left the ship.' Obviously, to her, 'ship' makes more sense than 'Egypt'. And instead of the kings our three workmen come in covered with black smears.

'We've broken nearly all the cement, which is ten centimetres thick,' Pablo explains. 'Then we got out about 300 kilos of ballast, which we put on sacks on the beach.'

When one remembers that the ballast is iron pellets soaked in damp pitch, that it's just sticky enough to be very difficult to get out, just soft enough to cling to everything and leave stains on the deck which will have to be rubbed down, and that there are 3.5 tons of it, it's quite a task.

And at the 21 Bar we continue to mull over possible ways of towing off the boat. We could dig a channel through the sand, about 80 metres long, from the boat to the Rio Ebro. With a dredger. But how would we get a dredger? And so on.

The boat is so much lighter that she's floating already in the hole she has dug. Then she moves on to the sand, towards the sea. She's out of the hole and in 40 centimetres of water—she's moving. It looks as though it would be easy to tow her off with the fishing boats now. But there's a bank of sand 150 metres farther on, before she gets to the sea. Can she get over it?

I'm still giving Laurence her lessons, especially as she's slipping back here. Everyone treats her as if she were a baby.

A sardine boat is coming to tow us off.

Today it's overcast. There's no wind. The sea is flat and calm. At 8 am Ricardo and his father arrive from Barcelona, having left at five. They bring our mail, an anchor and some pulleys. The boys fix two large double pulley-blocks in the *Pygmalion*'s stern fastened to the rudder and pointing towards the river. (All that the cable which it had taken us so much effort and weeks of work to lay out for the tug achieved was to lose our CQR anchor for us.) Then 200 metres of cable are laid towards the river, where the sardine boat will be. Pablo and his father, in the Zodiac, take soundings of the channel, and the river where the sardine boat will have to go. It's two metres deep everywhere.

After much manœuvring, the towing begins. The men are all in the icy water in their wet suits. After an hour the *Pygmalion* has moved a few centimetres, according to the guide marks. It's not much; she may have simply turned a bit. But at least she's moving, and our hopes revive. It's like seeing a person whom one is afraid may be dying move—it suddenly gives you renewed hope.

We're still there as it grows dark. We make a huge fire on the beach, while the sardine boat struggles to haul up its anchor. No one has had anything to eat. We go slowly back to the hut in the Zodiac, in the pitchy darkness, the only lights the blinking one-eyed beacon and the tiny paraffin lamp for the *angulas* on the jetty by the hut.

Our valiant rescuers, Paco, Tomas, Carlos and Ushi have a celebration dinner at the 21 Bar with us. They make a huge *carachillo*—flambéeing some cognac with thyme and rosemary in an earthenware bowl. Then you add a little cinnamon and drink it hot or mixed with boiling hot black coffee. The men are sleeping at the 21 Bar because tomorrow we're going to tow the *Pygmalion* again, but with some tractors from the island of Buda.

Ten o'clock. After several set-backs the tractors arrive. Unfortunately there's a north wind again and in spite of the sun it's arctic. The sea has built up and there's a current. We make our first attempt, with one tractor alone. The boat doesn't budge, although the pulleys get closer together. The *Pygmalion* only turns round a bit. It takes a good half hour to put the tackle back in place. The wind redoubles in strength and sand gets in everything, even in the plastic bags our sandwiches are in. Paco wants to stop and so does Tomas. Only Carlos, Pablo, Ricardo and Christian are left in the water—the latter hanging on desperately and repeating that it's a lovely day, that it's quite normal weather for this part of the world, that we're lucky to have some sun and that if one can't work under these conditions one will never be able to.

On the beach our nerves are stretched to breaking point. We're all exhausted and we thought it would be so easy, that the boat would continue to move. But no one dares leave while Christian is still determined to go on trying and not wait for a day when it's calmer. At two o'clock we make our second and final attempt. Without success. The tractors go off.

The agent on Buda Island lends them to us again two days later. At the first attempt the line to the tractor breaks. There's no wind. It's hot. Second attempt: the 200-kilo anchor gives. Third attempt: some sacks filled with sand have been hung on the mast to make the boat heel over as much as possible. And the boys hang on to the sacks, to give extra weight. The boat shifts five centimetres, but the 200-kilo anchor still comes away. So all the other anchors are added to it—with no success. The Tortosa commander will send his trawlers on Sunday. But on Sunday it's no good: it's raining, the sky is overcast and although there's no wind they would never dare come to the Ebro in this weather. All the gang go down to the boat. I'm exhausted, and as neither Laurence nor I have mackintoshes and it's raining harder and harder, I decide to stay at the hut with her.

At about eleven Carlos arrives with Ushi and some friends. He's distraught because the sea is quite calm, higher than he's ever seen it in seventeen years, and the trawlers aren't here. We can see what happens from the hut with binoculars, in spite of the rain, and watch as the *Pygmalion*, as the boys would later recount, visibly begins to float, and then as she moves several metres towards the Rio Ebro. Then she turns right round on herself—it's fantastic. It's one o'clock—the *Pygmalion* is in the river, floating free and rolling dreadfully because there's no ballast—SHE'S OFF THE SAND.

The heroes relate: 'We were all in the water pulling on the tackle. There was a great shout of "hurrah" each time we gained a few metres, which spurred us on. *Pygmalion* moved farther and farther, and was finally moving under her own steam. So well in fact that we had to stop her by dropping anchor.'

Miguel and Pablo set off for La Cava to look for Pantorilla, to come and tow us with his boat, as the trawlers aren't there. He was fishing all night and got in late this morning, and is in the middle of having breakfast before a well-earned rest. But as soon as he hears Pablo and Miguel's news he leaves his meal and starts off at once with his son. The *Pygmalion* is fifteen kilometres from La Cava. It takes over two hours to get her there, heeled right over so as not to touch the electric wires of the railway-line. A few months later a trimaran would go up the Ebro without taking this precaution, and three men were electrocuted.

We follow on in the car with Pablo. It's fantastic to see her floating again after two months on the sand, on a rainy day, when no other boat wanted to come—when the sea was higher than it had ever been before.

'I got her off "all by myself",' Christian was able to say, when he moored at La Cava at 6.15, near the ferry.

Delirious excitement at the 21 Bar. We all fall hungrily on a giant *paëlla*, and spend the evening at Carlos's house. Then our four Barcelona friends have to leave: 'See you on Sunday!'

And we telephone at once to Mr Zendrera: '*Pygmalion* is off the sand.'

After having been re-ballasted, scraped, repaired, painted and re-painted, the *Pygmalion* is our home again, and in May we set out to sea. We spend the summer in the Balearics, and Laurence's little sister, Mareva, is born on 28 October in

Barcelona. While she is being introduced to life amidst the smell of pine trees, rosemary, thyme and lavender, Christian sails solo across the Atlantic.

He has decided to sell the *Pygmalion* and build the perfect yacht, the yacht of his dreams.

XVI

Alone Across The Atlantic

> 'I am going towards the wind, people of
> Orphalex, but not towards the void.'

Arrecife, 23 November

YOU MUST BE thinking that I'm alone in the middle of the
Atlantic, but I'm not, because the splendid north-east wind
which brought me here has vanished and I'd rather wait in
harbour until it returns than wait at sea or use the engine,
while I'm alone.

. . .

I keep asking myself a thousand questions about the future.
Pygmalion has caused me so much trouble, and I had sworn not
to begin all over again. The years are flying past—the years
when we can walk naked along deserted beaches on sun-
drenched islands. I'm beginning to love my boat so much
(yesterday I spent six hours putting a net round the stays to
stop the flying-fish getting back to the water—today an hour
washing down the hull). I don't even know if anyone will sell
me a bare plastic hull, or how much it would cost. One needs a
lot of courage and optimism to think of starting all over again.

. . .

Las Palmas, 28 November.

. . . I envy you at heart, for being on dry land, on sweet
smelling earth. Especially as I'm going mad alone on board
without any social contacts. The crossing is assuming propor-
tions that it would never have done if you were with me. A
month alone at sea, in this great boat: the last crossing was
bad enough. But I haven't told you yet.

I was burning with impatience at Arrecife, waiting for the

wind, and suddenly left on the spur of the moment, on Sunday morning, without any provisions, telling myself that I could call in at Las Palmas on the way to get in some stores. I ran into a dead calm a few minutes after leaving, although I had set sail with a good wind. I started the engine and decided to call in at Lobos, a little island between Fuerteventura and Lanzarote.

Four boats moored alongside the *Pygmalion*; barbecue on the beach; back on board and off to bye-byes after my long day.

In the middle of the night the wind got up on the least protected side. The mooring became impossible, with the wind blowing harder and harder. I got dressed, hauled in the Zodiac, stowed everything away and started the engine preparatory to leaving. Day broke, grey and uninviting, the barometer very low, and we all decided to go to Las Palmas in the evening, in order to arrive by daylight, as it's 95 miles away.

And there was *Pygmalion* with her sails set, wind astern, waiting for the two others to start, and then flying along at nine knots like some fantastic horse, with the automatic pilot. We overtook the other two boats and lost them from sight. And one of them was doing twelve knots—a racing yacht which had won at several regattas.

Then it was night, pitch dark and with a strong breeze. The Coleman lamp lit up the boat beautifully but blinded me, so I couldn't even see ten metres ahead. What a marvellous night. The speed. By 2 am I could see Las Palmas. By five I was entering the harbour. 95 miles in twelve hours. And in spite of the wind, I would have had a good night's sleep if there had been no land ahead.

So—I got in stores and up and off. My heart in my boots at not having you with me to tackle the Atlantic. It will be a long month.

. . .

Pygmalion, 4 December.

I'm writing this letter in mid-Atlantic, having left Las Palmas four days ago, alone with *Pygmalion*. There was a strong breeze and the sky was grey, but I was longing to get on with it, to see you again. My friends in the boats moored all round sounded their sirens and wished me *bon voyage* as I set sail in spectacular style.

Four days. The barometer and winds are fine, but I'm not. It's sad being alone, especially when one knows that there are three marvellous little women waiting for one in Spain. The days and nights seem endless. I don't go on deck much—only for a few minutes every day. I've only taken one sight since I left to check my course, towards the south-west. I'm not particularly hungry or physically tired, but am not sleeping very well.

You don't realize in harbour how long a month can be. Luckily *Pygmalion*'s making good speed, 160 miles a day at least, on average (185 miles the first day) but I always have the same problem with the sails, sailing before the wind: the jibs are screened by the mizzen and mainsail. If I change tack and sail on a broad reach, I get off course, one way or the other. So I am taking it more slowly, without the jib, with mainsail and mizzen goosewinged.

I hope to arrive in Ametlla before this letter, but it does me good to write to you. If only we could spend Christmas together. But I'm not looking forward to being cold again; I'm just reaching the sun. I'm naked, believe it or not, and the sun gets hotter every day.

. . .

4 December.

A good night. Towards midnight the wind strengthened and veered to the east, so I'm sailing off the wind with all the sails set. The speedometer has stuck at nine and there are often spurts at ten or even eleven knots. But it can only be relied on up to ten, it must be a bit inaccurate after that. 620 miles in four days—not too bad. If I continue at this rate I'll be across in under twenty days.

So last night I put her on course again, and changed bunks because we're listing a bit now, and squeezed a lemon over my head. My hair was looking very sad—it did it good. Then I rinsed it in the dark in salt water, on deck. I'm longing for the sun to be hot enough to have a good wash on deck. Anyway I'm running at high speed towards the south, the Equator.

I'll have to take my bearings for the second time in four days because I said 620 miles, but that's by the log. With a one-and-a-half knot current I must have done much more. We'll see: but there's a swell, it may not be accurate.

Why aren't I a forester instead of a sailor? I could at least see my little Mareva feeding and smiling and sleeping in your arms. I'm a bit worried in case you leave her with Laurence, who might pick her up while you're out—accidents can happen so quickly.

I'm looking at the speedo dial as I write: we're doing ten knots practically all the time, with spurts of eleven and twelve. One needs a log-speedo graduated from one to fifteen. But the wind isn't all that strong because I've got all the sails set, and am writing below. It's force five or six. It's really terrific and I'd like it to stay like this all the way.

The refrigerator's not working. I got in a lot of fresh meat: a two-pound joint, a pound of fillet steak, ten slices of ham and a chicken. The joint was already smelling a bit yesterday when I put it in the pan.

What a pity I haven't got a cine-camera or camera with me. I keep thinking what a voyage like this means. A desert 6,000 kilometres wide, without an oasis; alone on a machine made of fifteen tons of steel driven by breeze, wind and tempest.

4.30. You've no idea how long the days seem. I can't stay lying down, it makes me feel queezy all over. But there's quite a swell and I ought to be tired. I listened to France-Inter this afternoon on my new transistor—that did me good. It was a programme about toys for handicapped children. Will we be together for Christmas? I hope so so much.

The pan's steaming away with all the meat in it, and some diced vegetables, unpeeled. I only give the Primus a run once a day: what a business.

While it's cooking I'm making an enormous salad which you wouldn't get ashore: apples, bananas, green salad, tomatoes, almonds, dried raisins, onions, peanut butter, olive oil, lemon, olives, peppers, oranges, etc.

I make a ritual of a few things which keep me sane, because it's enough to drive you dotty, you know, to be alone on a boat for so long. I haul up the line once a day (of course the spoon's gone and I had to put on a new one). While up there I saw my first flying-fish—but I spend so little time on deck.

Then I cook my hot meal. Then check our position. I went up a little too early for the latitude and had to wait half an hour until the sun started to get lower. My arm was aching and my legs giving way. What a chore. I have of course put a compass in the middle of the saloon and I have to get up from time to time to adjust our course a little, but it's not often. And you only have to give a pull to alter it five degrees. No manœuvring with the sails at the moment—hope it lasts like that. Of course all the seams of the mainsail have given where it rubs against the shroud but I'm leaving them like that until we get to the Antilles.

What writing. I'm having great difficulty keeping my hand steady.

4 am. Three fish on deck. At last. They couldn't escape because of the net I put up at Arrecife.

What a shame to be passing so close to the Cape Verde Islands without calling in there. I sometimes think I might just put this letter on a yacht, without dropping anchor or lowering the sails.

Las Palmas hasn't changed at all since we were last there, except that this time I didn't moor alongside all the other boats at the end of the harbour, but in the open water opposite the yacht club, and I also signed the visitors' book there. There were several other boats there and the water was clean. It was much more comfortable with the Zodiac. If I wanted to go to the market I just chugged across the harbour.

I'm dying to know which yard will sell me a fibreglass hull, decked over, and how much it will cost.

. . .

And I'm writing all this in mid-Atlantic. The miles flash past at nine or ten knots (but never quickly enough for me), and I've already done 760. If I do an average of 160 miles a day, I'll be across in eighteen or twenty days: not long enough for my beard to grow. Ah—these fast boats.

I notice I'm hardly touching my reserve of drinking water. I only need a little Coca-cola, a little fresh milk, or some fruit. The water in the neoprene tank hasn't got a nasty taste any more. It's on the deck and the pressure takes it down to the sink: you'd be delighted.

5 am. I'm going to sleep for a while. Good night my love.

8 am. I dreamt, so I must have been asleep. I had left you on board with Laurence while I went to get the mail, with the boat gently drifting along a river. When I got back the boat wasn't there. I found it at last; you were on land and I had great difficulty tacking against the current which had got stronger.

Three more flying-fish on the deck—one enormous one 30 centimetres long or more. But I'm not very hungry. However I'm going to cook them all today.

I'm afraid you've got an awful lot on your hands with Mareva needing to be fed and changed all the time, and Laurence's lessons, and all the meals, and shopping. You can't have much time left over for writing.

. . .

It's grey and gloomy, with a strong wind. When will I be able to wash myself in the boiling sun? I'm rather miserable at the moment, and low , like someone with an incurable illness teetering towards death.

I'm not even bothering to navigate; the boat's doing all the work. I just glance vaguely at the compass to see that we're going more or less towards the west, and pull a bit of rope from time to time.

5 pm, 5 December.
And also my fifth day at sea because I left at midday on the 30th. Well we're past the Cape Verde Islands. Oh, quite close, I could almost see them, 60 miles away on the port side, but it's still just as grey and windy, the barometer's low and in short it's all rather gloomy.

It's a great strain on the nerves. How did Moitessier stick it? Did he stick it? I really think it could make one insane.

. . .

I'm not very good at imagining all the things I think up in this floating box. Let's go and live on a farm. But I need a climate where one can go naked all year round. Which means Polynesia. But how old will we be before we get there again? Look what's become of my log book: a long letter to my little wife.

If you could see the interior of the *Pygmalion*—utter chaos. And what I look like. I'm going to have a blitz and clean and tidy everything. Only five days. I'll never get there. But the log says 840 miles, thank goodness. Tomorrow I'll have done a third of the voyage in six days. Hope it lasts. But I'm not particularly trying to go fast. I haven't the means. One would need two large booms and two genoa sails, or a spinnaker and a square gaff sail. Not a mizzen, in fact, which takes the wind from the mainsail as soon as one's on course (running before the wind) and a mainsail which takes it from the jibs.

But I've proved several times since Casablanca that the *Pygmalion* is going very fast, passing racing yachts of her own size.

5 pm. Same day. It's not bad seeing three kilos of meat (joint and steak) cooking away in the pan because they were beginning to go off. It's the second or third time they've been cooked. The first time, with no water, the joint was delicious—pink and tender. The next day I had to add the steak which was smelling a bit and make it all into a stew, also very good, but today it was a bit tough.

I'd like to do the whole voyage without opening any tins, but I haven't got enough vegetables and fruit. I'm sick of the cheeses, although they're very good—goat's, Dutch, roquefort, gruyère—and yoghourt, and usually plump for the meat. Tomorrow I'll have my hotted up stew again, and my first avocadoes (bought unripe). The bananas, peppers and pears are finished. Only the oranges would have lasted, but there are only twelve left. I've still got five kilos of onions, ten of potatoes—and I'll soon be on rice and corned beef. The peppers are rapidly withering, and the aubergines have had it.

. . .

6 pm. The day is passing very slowly: the mizzen is flapping, then the staysail is set badly, so I have regulated Gigi a bit. The trade wind seems much stronger than the one we had. I haven't seen any dorados, probably because I'm always down below. And the spoon on the fishing-line's no good: it twists and jumps out of the water and gets tangled up—and we're going too fast.

. . .

Meanwhile, my pen's given out and we're rolling, rolling,

under a pitchy sky, and the barometer's falling. Brrr. Now I really feel I'm battling with the Atlantic. Another 2,000 miles and we're there. I keep thinking about that book on the Sahara, Frizon Roche's *La piste oubliée* which I read just before leaving. A risky kind of trip, where you sometimes have to go on without knowing what lies ahead and without enough water to turn back, lose your camels, have to withstand sand-storms.

How I long to see my little Mareva. There are thousands of questions I want to ask and I do hope there'll be a long letter from you when I get to Barbados. And you will never have had such a long one as mine to you. I didn't make the crossing direct from Tangier, although the winds were favourable, because I couldn't resist the temptation of seeing Casablanca and the Canaries. So we will have been apart for two months. One begins to expect it, but I've had enough. When will we at last have a real married life? Time passes so quickly. New Zealand, then the instant photograph interlude, then our voyage on the *Alpha*, a year in Tahiti, aesthetic construction of the *Pygmalion*, sailing lessons in Greece, off again, shipwreck, winter in Spain, Mareva, separated again—what a life.

Oh well, only a few more days and I can look forward to seeing you again, as lovely as on the evening when you arrived in Palma this summer.

I've found a pen! and will leave you for a minute to go and eat a raw tomato with mayonnaise, with a cup of hibiscus tea with honey which I put in the thermos. God—it's really rolling now.

9 am, 6 December.

Good morning, madam. I've just got up. Pee—glance at the horizon; turn on deck; and now I've come to talk to you for a bit. Chaos reigns here, although I could soon tidy it up: all the Arabian cushions are spread on my two mattresses on the floor, with the radio, compass, some books and magazines that I always leave lying around, a bottle of Coca-cola, the amplifier, a packet of Cornflakes—that's all in the saloon. The kitchen is filthy.

Did I wake up in the night? Yes, feeling a bit sick. Where is that healthy third-day feeling? I felt better when I had got up. I ate an orange and drank a little concentrated milk in water, which did the trick. But my stomach is churning madly. I don't know if it's muscular, because of the movement of the boat, or because of my poor diet or all the worry recently, but it really hurts when we roll. I don't want to end up with one of those stomach ulcers they all get.

Often at night, almost every night, I have lovely dreams; I'm on land again, and suddenly I wake up and it takes me a few minutes to realize where I am. It's so disappointing to hear nothing but the waves, the water rushing past the hull, to be bucketing along in this tub, for weeks yet, when five days already seems like an eternity. But this morning I feel more hopeful because the log says 950 miles, which is a third of the way, and I can look forward to getting there. Hot baths, swimming, sun. Even if it's only for a day or two it will do me good. Best of all would be if you could join me with the girls; but it would be such a bore for you to have to pack everything up.

This block has 80 sheets, or 160 pages, and I expect they'll all be for you—a little parcel instead of an ordinary letter.

The wind has strengthened because the speedo reads nine knots: with only half the sails set that's pretty good. Not so good was a vicious wave which attacked the boat and drenched the after cabin. I had put the cheese and other food on the floor: all that plus the carpet got a bath.

Did I tell you about Morocco? Tangier first—you'd adore the Medina which is all sloping streets, with beautiful dresses, very cheap. I was longing to be there with you and buy everything. (Hey, we've just done some surfing at ten knots. It would make some good film shots, I can tell you.)

From Tangier I did an excursion to Moulay Bousslem; my parents' little house is still there, but completely abandoned. But if we cleaned it up a bit we could spend a holiday there one summer. It's got water and there are three rooms, looking over the sea. The Arab fishermen who live there recognized me at once and asked me news of everyone.

. . .

The Casa yacht club has many more boats, but it hasn't got the same friendly atmosphere as before.

6 December. Midday by my watch which is still on Greenwich

Mean Time. In fact it will be midday in two hours' time because we've already gone 30 degrees to the west, and it's one hour for fifteen degrees. So in two hours' time I'll go and take my noon sight. Meanwhile the fix I have just taken puts me too far to the south again. I can't seem to head for the West Indies. But I see why: twenty degrees magnetic variation, twenty degrees compass deviation from the steel deck. To steer west (270) I must steer 310 by the compass. One would have to steer 330 if one were sailing on the wind (drifting), almost due north by the compass to steer a true westerly course.

We'll see what tomorrow's sights will say about my corrections.

3 pm. I'm getting the upper hand. Average since we left: 160 miles a day, which means eighteen days for the crossing, so we'll be there in twelve days.

The wind's dropping, and the sky's getting bluer, and it's marvellous to feel the sun on one again.

What a lot I've done since I got up: I haven't lain down for an instant. Changed the fishing-line, long session taking bearings, a little tidying up, cooked and ate stew. Never mind about the flying-fish on deck. Listened to France-Inter and some good music on my mini-cassettes: Carol King, Cat Stevens, James Taylor.

It's crazy to make women sail and I wonder if you'll make any more long voyages.

5.30. The day's dragging a bit. The sun will soon be setting. I read some articles in my sailing magazines, and suddenly remembered the avocadoes: just ripe. It's a bore they all get ripe together because I'll soon be sick of them. My first one, which I ate just as the log came up to 1,000 miles (the log's an optimist!) was delicious. In fact I've only done 950 miles in a direct line. If I subtract the boat's 'deviations' and little excursions, there must still be an error of five per cent.

How quickly time flies. And I want so many things. My seventeen metres of fibreglass: Will I ever get it?

8.30. And the sun's set on my sixth day at sea. I stayed on deck quite a while and changed course: now I'm sailing towards the sun. The *Nautical Almanac* gives the bearing at sunset (263 degrees today). So if I go a little more 'to the right', I'll reach Barbados in a few days. It was good on deck. The wind's dropped a lot, the Spanish courtesy flag, which I haven't taken down, is flapping gently, but *Pygmalion's* still making good headway, and waves which look impressive to some people, but which I find exciting—I adore it in fact—send us surf riding.

So for two hours I thought about you and how cold you must be. If only you had the sheepskin coat I saw in Tangier. I expect Laurence loves her *djellaba*?

I keep telling myself *Pygmalion* is a stunning boat. The hull at any rate, and the rest—masts, deck, cockpit, interior, windlass, etc.—could be gradually replaced.

The Joshua I saw in Arrecife was two years old too and was in perfect condition.

Yesterday, listening to the Minister of Education, I thought that children of Laurence's age upwards should be taught to make a précis or repeat aloud the whole lesson they've just been taught. Then (a) you would know that they had understood it and (b) you would be training their memory and intelligence and (c) you would gain a lot of time by avoiding those hours of dreary repetition in class learning the same thing. But it has to be started at an early age, because how many people listen to a text or information and are then capable of repeating what was said, or discussing it? And it's the final aim of education to be able to converse, isn't it? So teach Laurence to repeat what you've taught her. But now I think of it you already do that with stories: good, continue and don't take no for an answer. Ouf! end of lesson. Have you any news from Tahiti?

The loneliness is enough to make one hysterical. For a start you forget how to talk, and find yourself yelling in order to hear yourself and break the silence, or looking quickly behind you to see if there's a giant octopus tentacle. But that isn't the real danger, I know. It's during the long nights asleep when the boat could run smack into a steel wreck which would pierce the waterline, and it would all be over in a few seconds. Perhaps not even time to launch the life raft. And what about water, clothes, tins of food? Then you'd drift for months, towards almost certain death. It makes me think of poor Didier, lost at sea, whose last moments must have been terrible. I blame myself for dragging him into this adventure.

7 December.

(In ten days time I shall be sadly spending my birthday alone at sea.) A fine calm night. Cloudy and more wind this morning, but not as much as the first few days. We're only doing seven knots. I cooked my first hot breakfast: hot chocolate and eggs and bacon. But I'm scared stiff of getting food poisoning from this flabby bacon from the 'warm fridge' although it doesn't smell bad.

Had a good laugh with France-Inter afterwards: it's so funny at this distance, hearing how a producer puts it during an interview. His film was being shown in two Paris cinemas, but he said: 'The manager of the second cinema took it off. He decided he'd rather show a pornographic film.'

Still no luck with the line. This time it's a plastic bottle on the hook. But I've got enough meat at present. And there are some flying-fish on the deck. And the eggs, which I haven't felt like for weeks, are still perfectly fresh as I discovered this morning. Did you drink the hibiscus tea I left you? I've just made myself a thermos full, sweetened with honey from Ametlla de Mar. It's delicious and reminds me of our holidays.

What an exciting little moment going down with the figures and sextant, and tracing a new cross on the chart (only 140 miles today, our worst day. If the *Alpha* could hear that). At last it's warm enough not to wear any clothes. The waves are much smaller so that sometimes when I'm lying in the saloon on my Moroccan cushions with a newspaper and music to drown the noises outside, the motion is so slight, although we're doing eight knots, that I wonder if I'm really alone on the *Pygmalion* in the middle of the Atlantic.

Seventh day gone then. Still averaging 160 miles a day, and maybe I'll be across in twenty.

6.30; still 7 December. That's it; I won't cook the meat up again. There's still a lot left. It's turned into a nice mush, still edible I admit, as I haven't much desire to eat the smoked brisket which would be so good in a *cassoulet* or *Quiche Lorraine*. Which leaves some dried sausage and the eggs which don't tempt me yet. In two days' time all the coloured vegetables will probably be gone and it'll be ten days on potatoes, onions, tins, rice. Luckily there are still some almonds, raisins, peanut butter, cakes, chocolate, etc. What a feast.

Baro still very low, stormy sky, but nothing much yet. Perhaps I'll find myself running at ten knots under bare poles again in a minute, but I can't count on it. I'd just like a force seven on the quarter.

This afternoon (my goodness how quickly the day has flown by) I devoured some copies of the *Nouvel Observateur* and *Express* and two copies of *Play Boy*, of which I've had my fill, and *History of the West Indies*, by the English Hydrographic Department (Nautical Instructions)—it's all I've got to read. If only I had *Le Petit Prince* or *Le Prophète*.

8 December.

An odd night. I thought a lot. These days alone make a good retreat. '9 am' France-Inter says. It's six here, and the sun's just rising. It's very grey. The barometer is low; and with you, too, the meteorological bulletin tells me—a force seven east wind in Spain. *Pygmalion*'s going like a real steamer: steady course, little movement, constant speed, and her only passenger, captain, cook, *maître d'hôtel*, radio officer, etc. is finding time passing very slowly. But as I get in better physical shape I'm beginning to get a lot out of this time alone and have no regrets.

. . .

I haven't yet shaken off the effect of the staggering story of Captain Scott's expedition to the South Pole: I've just heard it in the dark, on a tape recording. They all died, eleven miles from the camp, on the way back. They found his diary in the tent where they were waiting for the storm to pass before doing the last few miles. With only one day's provisions and a temperature of minus 40 degrees, they must have suffered terribly.

The desert, the polar ice, the ocean. Brrrrr! I wish the barometer would go up—but it's the needle of the speedometer which is touching nine; so it's blowing outside but the waves aren't too high and it's still quite comfortable below. How I wish I had a good heavy genoa and a long boom, a staysail etc. We'd do ten all the time.

I hope you're keeping snug in your little house and not having any doubts about the future, our future.

1.30. I'm at it again—dreaming about boats. My dreams get

more and more fantastic, and the Morgan hull haunts me—
even if it takes all my money. It would at least be a floating
roof. The rest would follow in due course. A mast, two sails, a
bit of wood. Providing they'll do it. And we'll build it at Russ's.
It would be really good in Florida too, because of the climate.
5 pm, still 8 December. What strange days. A few hours reading,
but it's too passive. It makes me ashamed to lie about reading
when a country like Vietnam is torn by war.

Eighth day at sea. Why am I being punished like this? and
I'm only a third of the way through, if all goes well. But I
needed this retreat in fact. I'd just like it to be a bit more
active because at the moment it's all armchair stuff and the
loneliness is getting on top of me. Yet I'm a born loner. I've
always done things by myself, and I enjoy it. And really I'm
enjoying this voyage a lot.

6 pm. Tired of reading, so I've come out to have a little chat with
the sunset which will tell me if I'm really going towards
America. Because you begin to have doubts about everything
in this (rather funny) boat, even the bearing of the setting sun.

What a fantastic adventure, really. 6,000 kilometres across
the sea at twelve kilometres an hour, alone, with no pollution,
no talking. You will know that I'm feeling much better. And I'd
like to be on top form when I arrive because my plans for the
future will need a lot of energy, to make up for lack of money.

I go on writing and writing but none of it is reaching you and
I wonder if you're bearing up all right. But it's good to write to
someone in whom one has total confidence, whom one loves and
to whom one wants to give everything; it's better than just
thinking about her, one feels closer writing and one makes a
little more effort.

Naturally I'd rather be making love on a sunny desert island
than scribbling these lines. Wouldn't you?

Impossible to sleep. It's midnight—woken by the motion of
the boat, perhaps, right in the middle of a dream: all my past
life. One bit which I can't remember properly now, but
Laurence was following me. Another with me climbing up a
slope with X, and myself flying again—followed by a giddy fall
into a forest. Luckily a great mattress of dry, loosely packed
pine needles at least 30 metres thick saved me. The only thing
was it was impossible to climb out. My feet couldn't get a hold,

and I wasn't going up or down and was in a fifteen-metre hole. Uncle Pierre de B and two other lads got me out of there.

1 am. I lit a lamp to read for a while, but the light shifts too much and it's tiring on the eyes. So I've put it out and think for a while staring into the darkness, and suddenly get up feeling lyrical as a sixteen-year-old.

Deep, powerful, sibilant breath; *Pygmalion* gallops along majestically. Soft, regular, musical movements; my steed forges on, eating up the miles, tirelessly. Along her flanks, the water rushes, sparkles, gleams in phosphorescent spray; her stem cuts through the dark night. *Pygmalion* glories in her speed and to make her pleasure last, crosses the vast ocean without haste.

Yes, well, spontaneity is a fine thing but writing is like swimming: you need to work hard before you get it right. It's a game, an art, this wielding of pen or words.

> Oh time! suspend your flight; and you, auspicious hours!
> Stay a while:
> Let us savour the fleeting delights
> Of these happiest of our days!

Tonight I'm happy to be alone in the middle of the Atlantic on this boat I built myself, which I know utterly, like my body, with all its faults and qualities; which resembles me; which I love.

I put the light out and lie down or rather dive into the cushions and under my sleeping-bag, howl into my pillow, try to hide myself and don't dare look at the small bright square in the ceiling, the hole of the hatch opening on to the outside world (it's dark inside). I can see the huge tentacle of a giant octopus coming in and slowly wavering towards me to seize me and squash me between its suckers and carry me off to the bottom of the ocean. I shut my eyes, pull myself together and don't think about it any more, but there are odd noises—is someone on board? How could he be? And yet. I don't dare get up. Hysterical fear, then a smothered cry of relief.

Now I've come to write these few words to you by the light of the torch, hurriedly, before going to sleep.

3 am. No, I'm still not asleep, so you can have the benefit of my lyricism again. Too many things have been running through my head during this hour in the dark. Of course, words in one's head are so much better than those at the tip of one's pen. For a start you forget everything. And yet it's all so interesting. But rather like dreams: you forget them. So much the better. To remember, and write, is to stop it being.

'You speak when you cease to be at peace with your thoughts; . . . Because thought is a bird of the air which in a cage can open its wings but cannot fly.'

I was thinking that man is basically good. In what connection? Telling myself that tomorrow I would make some pastry. No—I've hundreds of more important things to do to make myself feel good: wash myself all over, clean the boat.

Everyone dreams of being happy. If I don't do this or that, it's because I haven't the strength. Laziness is a sickness.

No drugs on board: no coffee, tea, tobacco, alcohol, medicines, nothing. How nice. And I think every orgasm, whether physical or intellectual, sublimated or not, which one attains with the help of these drugs puts back the threshold of the one one will have the next time without their aid. Drugs make people impotent—impotent people have need of drugs.

Blow, whistle, blow! From below I hear a rumbling: a wave comes, lifts the stern, *Pygmalion* goes up, up; it eddies, she rides on the surf; it's vertiginous, terrifying; she comes almost broadside on to slide down more slowly and then rests for two or three seconds. The wind takes over, fills the white canvas to bursting point; everything strains, trembles, we are taking wing, but *Pygmalion* likes swimming. A new mountain comes up behind us, high, swift but calm, lifts her gently, grows, up and up, faster and faster, then bursts, foaming with happiness.

Hullo there!

3.30. One can get excited without drinking coffee, you see. I stay on deck for a minute; it's so lovely—words would spoil it. Yet I'd rather come below to write to you than go on looking. What a marvellous night; the wind is tireless, cool, but good on my bare body. The stars have never seemed so close, so alive, their light so soft, like the ceiling of my vast palace. The pole star, very low, well to starboard, shows me I am going due west. The masts cut proudly through the night, a precisely fixed, softly resolute trajectory.

I say to the night: go more slowly; for dawn
Will scatter the darkness.

9 December.

I didn't get my sudden squall. I told myself: you'll see, it's
always when one stays up till four in the morning, just when one
has most need of rest, that it gets up and you have to go on deck.

But I didn't get up at eleven, either; far from it. I began and
completed a magnificent wash-up on deck, which gave me the
chance to wash my hands and legs a bit at the same time—all
because I wanted to make some pastry (I needed the pan and
the salad bowl).

No meat or fish yesterday. I began to feel in urgent need of
some. But it's all right now. While I was washing up a flying-
fish was cooking nicely and I've just tucked in—before writing
this.

And now I'm getting down to the cakes: one third butter,
one third flour, one third honey and into the pan, in little
mounds. We'll see what happens.

I've still got too many links with the outside world: one ought
to do this without books, radio, music, comforts. It would be a
hard but thrilling experience, a retreat from the world.
Although I'd miss reading.

'Mummy is America a long way off?'

'Be quiet and swim!'

'Mummy, why is the sea all white?'

Be quiet and behave yourself, and I really don't want to
swim all the way to America. Besides, there's something I forgot
to tell you: there's a line being towed along behind us since we
left, in case of accidents, because the waves aren't the same as
they were a moment ago; there are real monsters which thunder up on you like an express train. But you know all that.

The pastry's delicious! cooked very slowly and gently, on
both sides, until it's crisp as though it had been in an oven.

. . .

Only another ten days, or less, if the wind holds up, because
tomorrow I'll have done half the way in ten days. I've done
1,400 miles and there are 1,500 miles to do. Hurrah! With the
marvellous winds I've had I could have beaten records if I'd

had the right sails. But I'm sailing without a jib or storm-jib and the mainsail is often flapping.

We ought to organize an annual race of the Trade Winds Club from Las Palmas to Barbados. It would give a bit of life to the group and get it talked about in the sailing magazines, who seem never to have heard of it.

Today it's boiling hot at 'my home' too. Not long now before I have a lovely cold shower on deck. Meanwhile I play some music, dance about like a madman, laugh, feel good all over. I've just eaten an avocado (they are delicious) and a tomato with mayonnaise. I've spent quite a bit of time working out calculations, averages, miles done, still to do, course to take etc., forecasts. The beautiful Moroccan carpets, richly covered cushions, mirrors and particularly the large full-length one in the saloon, all give a feeling of delicious luxuriousness (I beg your pardon, luxury) to my floating palace.

7.30. A good day. I've read a lot—sitting because I'm tired of lying down. Cooked some potatoes, onions, peppers—steamed. My cooking probably lacks imagination, but it was a real feast, with lemon juice and olive oil.

I've taken a fix at sunset. I hadn't seen the sunset for a long time because of the bad weather.

I drew the bearing of the sun on the chart, and my course— that's it, I have to go a little to the right to get to Barbados.

Meanwhile the barometer is still low, the sea is a bit rough, the wind steady at five : roll on, arrival.

4 am. I've been awake for hours. I've devoured the *Express*, particularly the 'If I lie' columns by Françoise Giroud. I still distrust everything I read or hear, but one wants to believe this newspaper when one discovers that girl.

I had put on some good music, I was so engrossed, and found that for an hour I had forgotten that I was sailing in mid-Atlantic. I felt a bit like a passenger in a sleeping-car in the Paris–Marseille express—above all, in France, with her, at the heart of what she was writing about.

But to come back to earth. This life on board (at sea) is conducive to exercising one's intellectual faculties. You have to make a physical effort for 24 hours out of 24, and end up by being alert all the time, and fresh, with your mind clear, a bit like the Greeks who studied while walking. In fact it would do you the world of good to sail again. Once the first few days are over, which are a bit tough, if you get the upper hand, it is terrific and you get an extra bonus from it.

5 am. I have an idea that women are bearing much of the burden in the evolution of our society. It seems to me that, liberated, they will cleanse the social climate, which has been made rotten by the traditional male government (men also becoming less and less so themselves).

Tenth day. Hurrah! I've had my bath: fabulous. Scrubbing brush, scouring powder, washing-up mop, buckets of sea-water over my head, all on deck: absolutely gorgeous. What fun with it rolling like this. I've changed colour—am a sort of scarlet. The sun's burning and the water's warm. And then I've got the amplifier on deck with Carol King on.

I've changed my pillow-cases, and in doing so discovered a whole packet of sliced bread I had forgotten. I'd begun to miss bread. So you see I'm living in high style, and I'm well over half way now. In a little while I shall start having a big clean-up, inside and out.

Next, sunbath on deck: I can't wait.

What bliss, I did enjoy myself, alone on my steamer, my transatlantic clipper, on my mattress with a pillow. Then I checked with the sextant that we were where we thought and made a salad: tomatoes, cucumber, peppers, avocadoes, onion, garlic, potatoes. Yes—you'll see; I shan't touch the tins.

At last I've found a very comfortable perch on the tackle which holds the two back stays from the mainmast, near the mizzen-mast, and I stayed there listening to some music. From there everything looked different again. And, feeling on top of the world, I got down to make some adjustments to make us go faster: boomed out the jib to starboard, took the port runner and tackle for the main mast right off because it's so far back that it stops the main boom going far enough forward when we're sailing downwind. I changed the broken block of the mizzen-sheet—sweated, went red in the face. Ouf! It speeded us up most effectively. Oh! If only I had a heavy genoa sail.

I think I can understand Moitessier when he went on to Tahiti. It's so marvellous, the best drug. You see, on land to get the same degree of physical fitness you need a lot of willpower to make the effort, to persevere. Very few people achieve it. Here one is passive, as if under artificial stimulants, but it isn't artificial, and so it's much better.

8.30. Diet of steamed vegetables for a few days now. No rice or pasta yet. For days now: fruit, vegetables, grills—until we get there. I only miss one thing—mineral water. Mine is a bit flat.

Sick of cheese—mayonnaise—almonds—peanut butter—jam —butter—tins of course, even fresh milk.

A draught of good wine every day.

I've got to the 'only's' now (eight more days!).

To think that on form like this and with a spinnaker I could do Cape Verde Islands—Barbados in a week: what a record. 'THE ATLANTIC IN 7 DAYS, SOLO!'

As it is I've done 200 miles for two days running now. There'll be a full moon when I arrive: nice.

Although it doesn't sound like it, I think about my two little girls a lot, and miss them so much.

2 am. Impossible to sleep. I don't know how I manage not to be tired, sleeping so little. Problems with the jib tonight, rolling too much. Terrible desire to make love, too. 'Don't wash, I'm coming!' Bonaparte wrote to Joséphine, during the Italian Campaign. You can't imagine all the kisses I'm going to give you. Mmmm! I'm licking my lips in advance. If I had a spinnaker, I'd hoist it at once. Two, even! I'm so anxious to see you —relaxed, and happy.

. . .

3 am. Qué pasa? Rain, veering wind, almost no wind. It was too good to last. All that talk of sails.

. . .

> Love has filled me with delicious torpors
> Would that my keel would explode!

. . .

Oh how parched I am for love.

One week more at sea, if all goes well: no accidents, burns, fracture, food poisoning, falling overboard, squalls—dismasting —shipwreck or endless dead calms. I hope the contents of this letter will not be exclusively devoted to sex during this last week.

5 am. Still no shut-eye.

. . .

I have got to talk about love tonight, definitely; it does me good. It will be light in two hours time and I won't have slept all night.

. . .

5.30 am. Good night my love, my adorable, irreplaceable little wife. I would so love to be lying in your arms, to hold you and stroke you, kiss you all over, all over, from the tip of each toe to your hair, taking in on the way, armpits, legs, ears, neck, hair, tummy, buttocks, thighs, Achilles tendon, breasts, navel, mouth, eyes, nose, arms, hands, front, back, top, bottom.

An eternal night of love. Oh to go to sleep holding your hand tonight, thinking only of you and of everything I will be able to give you tomorrow morning. I want us to make our next baby like that, wanting it, with all our strength, in the sun. So goodnight, my love.

Still dark, I must have slept for a moment, but here I am again—with you. I'm restless. I go out, come back, go round in circles, linger outside, rush back.

. . .

Our minds are no longer on earth, we are like balls of fire, two complementary atoms, pressed—rolled—together, drunk, crazy, in the universe. The surface of our bodies trembles and no longer belongs to us, we are one supernatural whole. It is not just my own arms which press you so tightly to me. And your poem which is always close to me gives me your answer.

> and you,
>   do you know?
>
> what
> this soft sweetness
>   is

which floods
my whole being
to its
depths

what this
exuberance is
which explodes
overflows
compels me

what this
fountain is
clear as ice
sun leaping
and why
the sun
becomes my friend
the sea a dream
around me

why this air
I breathe
and all which touches
but does not keep me

why
all these
are so much part
of you?*

10.30, 11 December. Good morning, love. Slept well? I had hardly
opened my eyes—naturally I had already thought about the
night I had just spent with you, and smiled to myself—before I
had to go out and struggle with the jib (taken down in the
night, broken sheet, fallen halyard). It's all fixed now. We're
skimming along at eight knots towards Paradise, with 1,760
miles on the log. There'll be a lot of work to do when we arrive,
but I've decided to leave it and rejoin you straight away.

Only another 1,000 miles, at midday. If I keep up the 200
miles a day I'll be there in five days, on the 16th—2,900 miles
in sixteen days, which means an average of 187 miles a day. I

* Poem by France Guillain.

don't dare think about it. Half the time we took with the *Alpha*. My course is perfectly straight on the chart. How I wish you were here.

. . .

12.30. That's it. Rain! I've only had one day of really fine weather since I left, which was yesterday, as you know. Luckily the wind's not deserting me; far from it.

. . .

' . . . And lead us not into temptation . . . ' I thought I was succumbing . . . because of a very ripe avocado of which I ate half, creaming the other half over my body—which almost brought me there.

'Yes, pleasure is the song of freedom.

And I would willingly see you sing it with all your heart; but not losing your hearts in the singing of it.'

. . .

Big scrub-up on deck with brush and buckets of water, in spite of the bad weather. All at a steady nine or ten knots: flying along.

Read a lot again. Do you know Wilhelm Reich, a psychoanalyst contemporary with Freud?

. . .

6 am, 12 December. It will be dark for a few minutes yet. Suddenly there's an avalanche of water and the wind's roaring violently, incredibly violently. I'm taken by surprise and unable to act it all happens so quickly. An infernal din. I look at the compass: on course. The speedo: stuck at ten knots. I go out—we're flying. It's better, the wind's violent but the rain has stopped; I'm soaked but it doesn't matter because the air is warm. The sun's just about to rise, and on that side the sky is blue, red, pink, violet—and on the other, terrifyingly black. It's frightening to be alone under this great canvas, but at the same time it's incredibly exciting.

. . .

10 am. Well, I've had my little contretemps. A new squall hit me, with unheard of violence. Impossible to lower the sails with the wind astern and too frightened to luff up into the wind with all this canvas which would have flapped for an hour while I dealt with each sail. And as I watched the great boom of the mainsail simply broke, very slowly, under the terrific pressure of the wind in the 40 square metres of sail. I had to save the sail. I tried to gybe the mizzen during a short calm to take the wind out of the mainsail and lower it, but it was impossible. All this time the boat was yawing terribly and the jib cracking furiously, the boom threatening to break and pierce it with one of the splintered halves. I really had to fight, sweating in spite of the rain, sometimes hanging by one arm when a lurch took my footing from under me, with my other arm clutching my prize.

It was hard getting the jib down too, especially taking off the boom which with one end in the water was bending desperately.

So here I am at last with several hours work ahead of me: carpentry, sewing, painting etc., and still the same urgent desire which I have no wish to 'sublimate'. Without the mainsail the boat's still doing nine, ten, eleven knots (and so am I).

The funny thing is that the barometer, which has been down for so long, is rising—(it, too).

11 am. Fascinating, on a reach now: it's safer with this violent wind. Still with no mainsail, the needle of the speedo has just pointed to maximum, jammed on the zero, that is about fifteen knots.

. . .

Beautiful night. Orion directly ahead of me, the Great Bear and the Pole Star to starboard and the Southern Cross to port. The Evening Star and Venus behind us. There's a fairly strong breeze and that consoles me a little. I don't mind breaking everything if I get there sooner.

. . .

I finally reacted. A huge gust made me pull my socks up. I was really frightened. I imagined the mizzen mast breaking. Dismasted—bloody hell. I took the tiller, to steer us clear. Then I decided to lower the sails, but at the end of an hour of panic fear, I realized my body was badly in need of food. I took advantage of a slight lull to swallow something. Good, I'll keep all the sails set (except the mainsail of course). Then I put on a spurt of feverish activity below—reaction—as if we would be arriving in an hour although there are 700 miles to go. What torture. Pump the bilges—there's very little water—throw out the muck. Ouf! that's better. With or without masts, I'll get there.

14 December. Forced myself to take a long accurate fix. (Hadn't for four days.) During which I didn't go on deck. We were exactly where I thought. What torture this separation is.

. . .

Four more days. I'm maintaining an average of 160 miles a day, still without mainsail, which isn't bad.

So I'll arrive on 18 December and I'll cable you at once.

. . .

I'm going mad (no joking). I would never have imagined how testing it is. I fight against it, tell myself that others have done it, that it's only fourteen days (Moitessier was alone for ten months). Julio, whom I met the other day in Barcelona, told me one gets used to it. I see why people become sadists or commit suicide.

. . .

You don't know how low I am. I force myself to eat a bit, to survive. Completely psychological lack of appetite. I talk to myself in the glass, or talk to the sea, think up reasons to go on hoping: it's crazy. I've still got plenty of vegetables and fresh fruit, but have opened my first tin: *cassoulet* with two eggs. The last avocado. It's when your morale's low that accidents happen, illness, even death.

. . .

Barometer very low. I'm jittery about these squalls which hit us with violent gusts several times a day.

Last page of the block; I've no more paper.

> So, carried ever to new shores,
> Driven onwards through eternal night,
> May we not anchor for a single day
> In the vast ocean of time?

XVII

Call Of The Sea

THE VOYAGE CAME to an end at last, at Barbados, eighteen
days exactly after setting out. The best time done by this year's
flotilla. Las Palmas—Barbados has become a real motorway,
and it's more crowded every year.

But three-quarters of the navigators are newcomers to the
game, made optimistic by listening to the accounts of their
predecessors. They are still green on arrival—often with fear.
The size of the waves, strength of the wind, accidents and
breakages on board. True they tend more and more to use
standard boats with short keels, which yaw so much that it's
impossible to trust the steering to an automatic pilot. The latter,
moreover, breaks in the majority of cases, and they arrive
exhausted from taking watches, and disillusioned. Only about a
tenth want to go on to Panama. The others consider selling
their boat. The more courageous sail theirs back to Spain. So,
bravo, *Pygmalion*. With a 350-kilo mast, given by EDF, enormous EDF cables, and heavy EDF guardrails, iron ballast in
cement, and sails cut, fortunately, by the renowned Loiseau,
but finished by amateurs, you did very well.

Now, for a while, I'm dreaming wild dreams of my regatta
thoroughbred in fibreglass, for our solo family voyage, of having
the most beautiful hull possible—because our means will
certainly never enable us to buy a complete boat of that kind.
We walk in the countryside, near the little house where France
lived alone with Laurence and Mareva, and talk and talk. The
Pygmalion sold well; we must make another boat. The question
of fibreglass bothers us. Our dream racer, large enough to make
comfortable cruises in—or steel, a safe material which has
proved its worth to us?

Another Joshua, the Joshua of our dreams—light, with

aluminium masts, lead ballast, a flush hull. The very low
prices of the beautiful American fibreglass hulls tempt us—but
so does a new Joshua. For a month our wild enthusiasm see-
saws from one to the other, and we can't decide. We know
where we are with the Joshua. It's heavy. One would have to
reduce the scantling, bring it down to the size of the thousands
of Dutch steel boats which have sailed the seas for the last twenty
years. You would have to get rid of the great watertight com-
partments, the lockers, the superfluous steel tanks—not take,
like everyone else, a ton of fuel and a ton of water. We had quite
enough in the *Alpha* with 300 or 440 litres.

The Joshua heels over, so one would have to lessen the weight
of the topsides, lighten the masts and complex rigging, shorten
the mizzen mast and put lead ballast at the lowest point, right
in the middle. Sailing on the wind, the most usual way for us
navigators, the Joshua has the drawback of all ketches : the
wind is taken out of the mainsail by the mizzen. On the other
hand, as soon as there's any weather, even if you take down the
mainsail, the mizzen is still too big. So you'd have to turn her
into a yawl, that is give her a much smaller mast aft.

In the end the scales tipped in favour of the Joshua, and in
spite of the cost, we decided to go for this. We entered into
correspondence with our friends Fricant, at Tarare, while with
great skill Yves Constandriopoulos, a young architect in
Marseille, designed a very modern roof and cockpit for us,
worthy of the finest racing yacht, and giving a huge flush-deck.
But what will Meta do in our great plan? Will he find it too
expensive to realize? Will he help us a little—a lot?

While we waited for the hull and deck to be finished, we
went to build up our strength in Espalmador, a beautiful little
island in the Balearics, to make our third baby there, in the sun
on the white sands, as we had dreamed. Afterwards we went
back to the shipyard, and a new adventure began : sand-
blasting, melting lead, painting, etc. Two good months' work.

Those four months in Espalmador were a rest cure for us, a
haven of well-being and happiness. Carlos had lent us the
Désirée, half yacht, half motorboat, with a Norwegian hull in
varnished wood—but we hardly moved, remained faithful to
the sands of Espalmador.

This was our happiness at sea, this mirage which suddenly

became reality. We conceived our third boat and our third child consciously, with all our hearts. With all our strength, after ten years of uncertainty, quarrels, disappointed hopes, adventures gone awry. But there are magic words which it is better not to speak, for fear a bad fairy will hear them, and send you a malign fate.

This is what we thought, at least, when we almost lost life and limb in the *Désirée*, going back to France. There had been an excellent forecast when we left. As we sailed along the coast, about five miles off Port la Nouvelle, a sudden onslaught of the mistral transformed the flat water into a scenic railway in a few seconds. In the *Désirée* there was only one thing to do: get shelter at all costs. The *Désirée* under canvas is utterly useless: a Sunday plaything. It took us three hours, with the wind and rain in our teeth, the 65 hp diesel engine going full blast, and the manual bilge pump continually on the go, to reach Port la Nouvelle.

We understood for the first time, perhaps, that we were all going to die—all of us, even the children. The only dinghy—rubber—was deflated, and one of the tubes had a hole. Below, the beautiful woodwork was creaking all round us. The poor little girls—Laurence, five, and Mareva, ten months—were suffering terribly.

'We'll never get there,' Laurence said.

So I lied as hard as I could.

'Of course we will, darling, Christian promised me we'd get there.'

He had lied too.

When we reached Port la Nouvelle, the engine was submerged, there was only a litre of fuel in the tank and the oil had practically disappeared from the engine-casing. Everything was wet and dirty—but we were saved.

We will never, never again, set foot in an inadequate boat, especially a wooden one.

I need hardly say how impatient we were to see our Joshua, our floating fortress, which we called *Le Tonnant*, in memory of a boat of that name which Aubert Dupetit-Thouars commanded at the battle of Aboukir. Aubert, that ancestor of Christian who died gloriously, giving his last orders from a barrel filled with straw, because he had just lost both legs. His nephew Abel signed the act of cession of Tahiti to France with Queen Aïmata Pomaré.

I wanted to paint the large letters, identical to those on the warship, myself, in black on white.

Her builder, Meta, allowed us very generous terms. He wrote: 'We want to thank Christian Guillain most sincerely for the construction of his second Joshua, because it gave those less well-off the assurance that one can still sail as our grandfathers did, on simple seafaring boats, but ones on which everything has been thought out and considered carefully.' According to her architect, Mr Knocker, she's the lightest Joshua there is. She is also, without any doubt, the most streamlined, with her hull and roof. Christian eliminated all unnecessary superstructures: you can bicycle on deck.

The *Tonnant*, our pride. Nothing in the world would make us want any other boat. She is pure, and beautiful. Born of ten years of experience of the sea, and of our successful relationship as a couple. We are comfortable there: she's a home for us and our children, and we have taken advantage of the bigger area to give the children their own room, so that they have space to enjoy themselves. Enjoyment complemented by effort—manœuvring the sails, fishing.

Twenty days ago the *Tonnant* was skimming out to sea, all sails set, her canvas taut, sailing close to the wind with a fresh breeze. She is resting in a Spanish creek, champing with impatience to go to the isle of Espalmador where she was conceived.

And our little Aïmata, princess of Espalmador, was born with *Le Bonheur Sur La Mer*.

'Well—South America? Or the Indian Ocean via the Suez Canal, opened especially for you?'

'With Laurence, Mareva, and Aïmata?'

'Of course!'

'Oh, if I could only gather your houses in my hand, and like a sower scatter them through the forests and the fields!'